D1605218

ARCHITECTURE AS
A HOME FOR MAN

Lewis Mumford

Photo: Jill Krementz

LEWIS MUMFORD

ARCHITECTURE AS A HOME FOR MAN

ESSAYS FOR ARCHITECTURAL RECORD

edited by
JEANNE M. DAVERN

with a foreword by
LEWIS MUMFORD

ARCHITECTURAL RECORD BOOKS
New York
1975

The editors for this book were Hugh S. Donlan and Martin Filler

The designer was Elaine Gongora

The production supervisor was Susanne LanFranchi

The printer and binder were Halliday Lithographic Corporation

Published by Architectural Record,
A McGraw-Hill Publication,
1221 Avenue of the Americas,
New York, New York 10020

Library of Congress Cataloging in Publication Data

Mumford, Lewis, 1895–
    Lewis Mumford : architecture as a home for man.

    Twenty-one of the 24 essays included originally
appeared in Architectural record, 1930–1968; 3 appeared in Architecture, 1928.
    1. Architecture—Addresses, essays, lectures.
2. Cities and towns—Planning—Addresses, essays,
lectures. I. Title.
NA2560.M82   720′.8   75-21382
ISBN 0-07-015426-0

CONTENTS

LEWIS MUMFORD

ARCHITECTURE AS A HOME FOR MAN

ESSAYS FOR ARCHITECTURAL RECORD

FOREWORD

The period when I began writing for *Architectural Record* followed by a happy chance the studies of American architecture I had been making for the Guernsey Center Moore Lectures at Dartmouth College in 1929. These lectures on "The Arts in America from 1865 through 1895" came out in 1931 as *The Brown Decades.* Without knowing it, I was taking possession of the critical territory opened up by Montgomery Schuyler in a long series of discriminating studies, mostly in *Architectural Record,* capped in 1912, two years before his death, with his just appreciations of Louis Sullivan and Frank Lloyd Wright.

Though my active work in other fields kept me from enjoying the close and constant professional association that Schuyler had, I find satisfaction not only in having carried on his studies in contemporary building but in having had a hand in replenishing his critical reputation. In this sense, my contributions to *Architectural Record* have been bound by a double tie.

Fortunately for me, before *Architectural Record* opened its pages to me, I had come under the auspices of more than one able and sympathetic editor, beginning in 1919 with Charles Harris Whitaker, the editor of the *Journal of The American Institute of Architects.* But the first non-professional paper to accept my architectural criticisms was *The New Republic,* for as early as 1921 this weekly printed my essay on "Machinery and the Modern Style." By a curious chance, that journal had been founded in 1914 by Herbert Croly, who had left his own niche on *Architectural Record* to establish this "journal of opinion." Such editorial responsiveness is an incitement to both productivity and good work; all the more because timely editorial suggestions often unexpectedly stimulate fresh thought, as they did in the series of articles I wrote in 1962, at the suggestion of the then editor of the *Record,* the late Emerson Goble, on current conceptions of urban form.

The bulk and variety of my writings for the *Record* under a succession of editors gives testimony to the catholicity of their judgment and their readiness to accept contributions which, like those of Montgomery Schuyler and Frank Lloyd Wright before, me, were often out of

Montgomery Schuyler (1843–1914) was *Architectural Record*'s first architectural critic and undoubtedly its most prolific. From September 1891 ("The Romanesque Revival in New York") to the posthumous publication, February 1917 ("An Oasis in the Bronx"), the *Record* published 73 essays by Montgomery Schuyler.

harmony with the fashionable architectural, technological and urban trends. Not the least token of this catholicity was the *Record's* generosity in reprinting in 1964 an article of mine on "The Wavy Line versus The Cube" which had first been published in *Architecture* under Henry H. Saylor in December 1930.

Such a personal relationship with past editors of *Architectural Record* accounts for my special pleasure over the present editors' impulse to honor my eightieth birthday by bringing out this collection of papers. This is one of those rare birthday presents that the receiver would never have conceived of by himself.

Since this whole collection is, in more than one sense, "for the *Record,*" I have no temptation to weed out lesser articles or to revise any part of them by so much as one comma. I could only wish, I confess, that Montgomery Schuyler, toward the end of his life, had been similarly rewarded: so I accept the gift in his name.

Lewis Mumford

Amenia, New York
May 1975

PREFACE

Lewis Mumford is a philosopher with roots spread wide and deep through the rich earth of myriad resources of historic experience and human concern. Like the redoubtable George Perkins Marsh, he is a generalist without being a dilettante; a scholar without being a pedant; and an activist who insists on moral evaluation and discipline as essential components of all meaningful human effort.

As an architecture critic, he has been for more than fifty years the prophet of a new age of architecture we are still seeking to discover and establish. Through the long adolescence of "modern architecture," when architects were absorbed in exploring—and expressing—the potentials of the new technologies, he was persistently reminding them that architecture is for people, and must express the purposes and values of people, not machines.

"Those qualities that differentiate architecture from building," he said in a 1951 essay, "cannot be derived from the functional requirements of the structure; they spring from the character and purpose of the user, as these are interpreted and remolded by the architect."

For Mr. Mumford, there is no question that architecture matters in the lives of ordinary people—*all* people—*all* their needs, the aspirations of the human spirit as well as needs of body and mind. For him, the great issues in architecture have always been the human issues, and the central purpose of architecture has always been nothing less than the improvement of the human condition.

"Not the least part of my architectural education," he has written, "came from my walks through New York's Lower East Side, whose tenements, in their congestion, their darkness, their foul interiors, fully equalled, if they did not surpass, those of Juvenal's Rome. The absence of space, order, intelligent design, even sunlight and fresh air—the sense of all the human qualities that were missing—taught me, by contrast, what to demand in every work of humane architecture."

"In the end," he tells us, "I have come to recognize only one supreme art—the art of becoming human, the art of expressing and intensifying one's own conscious humanity by appropriate acts, fantasies, thoughts and works. So closely are esthetic form, moral character, and practical function united in my philosophy, that the absence of any one or the other of these qualities in any work of architecture turns it for me into a hollow shell, a mere piece of scene-painting or technological exhibitionism . . . not a fully-dimensioned building that does justice to all the varied demands of life."

Architects might learn to communicate more effectively with the users of their buildings, and more people might learn to know and love architecture, if there were more architecture critics like Lewis Mumford—or if more attention were paid today to what Mr. Mumford has been saying since the 1920's.

Architecture, unlike literature, music, the drama, and, now, the dance, has not been rich in authoritative and widely published criticism. Mr. Mumford himself has been quoted as describing Montgomery Schuyler, who wrote seventy-three pieces for *Architectural Record* between 1891 and his death in 1914, as "the only real architecture critic America has produced."

If Mr. Mumford is the most distinguished contradiction to his own dictum, there have by now been others, though none at any commensurate level of scholarship and eloquence. Apart from his Sky Lines in the *New Yorker* from 1931 to 1963, most knowledgeable periodical criticism was confined to the architectural press, with the notable exceptions of the occasional pieces by Edward A. Weeks in *The Atlantic,* Russell Lynes in *Harper's,* and George McCue in the *St. Louis Post-Dispatch.* It is only twelve years since Ada Louise Huxtable became the first architecture critic ever appointed by *The New York Times,* and thirteen years since Wolf Von Eckardt was named to the staff of the *Washington Post,* for which he acts as, without the formal title of, architecture critic. These appointments were milestones in the history of architectural criticism, as recognition by major daily newspapers of a continuing public need to know about architecture. Some notable earlier efforts by individuals, like those of Frederick Gutheim on the *New York Herald Tribune* in the Forties, were not encouraged by their publishers.

Mr. Mumford has been, in spite of his dedicated involvement as a pioneering scholar and author of many books in a half dozen other fields, the only architecture critic to write consistently, and over a period of many years (nearly fifty), for both architectural and general circulation periodicals. Beginning with *Sticks and Stones,* his nine books on buildings and cities have left their mark on succeeding generations both in the Americas and in Europe. And, *because* of his scholarly involvement in such diverse fields as American architecture since 1835, American literature, the history of technology, contemporary urban and regional development, and the origins and historic development of cities, Mr. Mumford's architectural criticisms have drawn on an incomparable foundation of humane learning and well-digested experience.

In the architectural press, his continuing association has been with *Architectural Record;* and out of that association there has developed a unique body of architectural criticism. Unlike the standard critiques of particular buildings and their failures or successes, it is architectural criticism at the level of philosophy: analysis and evaluation of architectural principles and concepts, related to human—and moral—goals and responsibilities. It deals not only with issues in architecture but—more importantly—with issues of the human condition and with how architecture could contribute to elevating the human prospect.

For Mr. Mumford has never doubted that architects not only should but *could* do something about improving the human condition; and the essays he has contributed to the *Record* did more than point out where architecture was going astray, they suggested directions yet to be realized for development of the real potential of modern architecture. They dealt with the issues at every scale of architectural practice and human concern, from the scale of individual buildings and neighborhoods to the scale of cities and regions. An they anticipated the human consequences of any architectural failure to recognize the fullest responsibility for responding to social and psychological as well as physical needs of human beings.

When these essays were written, they expressed new insights which were most often far out of phase with then current fashion; and so, for the generations of architects who read them in the pages of the *Record,* they opened windows on new horizons for architecture. What the architectural criticisms of Lewis Mumford consistently intimated was the possibility of a new age of architecture—a *whole* architecture for the *whole* man.

In his 1951 essay "Function and Expression in Architecture," Mr. Mumford analyzed the failure of modern architecture to communicate symbolically with the users of buildings. He ascribed this failure to overreliance on a machine esthetic based on a narrow view of the much-cited doctrine that "form follows function."

"Thanks to advances in biology, sociology and psychology," he wrote, "we begin to understand the whole man; and it is high time for the architect to demonstrate that understanding in other terms than economy, efficiency and abstract mechanical form.

"In the multi-dimensional world of modern man, subjective interests and values, emotions and feelings, play as large a part as the objective environment: The nurture of life becomes more important than the multiplication of power and standardized goods, considered as ends in themselves. The Machine can no more adequately symbolize our culture than can a Greek temple or a Renaissance palace . . .

"All this is not to say that the doctrine that form follows function was a misleading one. What was false and meretricious were the narrow applications that were made of the formula. Actually, functionalism is subject to two main modifications. The first is that we must not take function solely in a mechanical sense, as applying only to physical functions of buildings. Certainly, new technical facilities and mechanical functions required new forms; but so, likewise, did new social purposes and new psychological insights. There are many elements in a building, besides its physical elements, that affect the health, comfort and pleasure of the user. When the whole personality is taken into account, expression or symbolism becomes one of the dominant concerns of architecture; and the more complex the functions to be served, the more varied and subtle will the form be. In other words—and this is the second modification— expression itself is one of the primary functions of architecture."

In the Fifties, the problems of an aging population came strongly to the forefront of the national con-sciousness; and "housing for the elderly" began to develop as a new building type, sparked not only by the concern of various religious and charitable institutions but also by a considerable investment of labor union pension funds in "retirement villages" for their aging members.

There was a good deal of debate even then about the social consequences of such enclaves, quite a lot of it stirred up by *Architectural Record,* but it was Lewis Mumford who most vividly evoked the human dilemma:

"The worst possible attitude toward old age is to regard the aged as a segregated group, who are to be removed, at a fixed point in their life course, from the presence of their families, their neighbors, and their friends, from their normal interests and responsibilities, to live in desolate idleness, relieved only by the presence of others in a similar plight. Let us ask rather by what means we can restore to the aged the love and respect that they once enjoyed in the three-generation family at its best."

On the great issue of industrialization of building, and its applicability to housing, Mr. Mumford was, in 1930, writing in terms that would serve the nation well today if only they were heeded by policy-makers. In two articles, he analyzed the limits of mechanization (potential construction savings on the individual house too small to count compared with the cost of land, financing and taxes) and the role of community planning: "Mass production which utilizes all the resources of community planning is capable of far greater and more numerous economies than mass production which only extends a little farther our current factory techniques."

Thirty years later, the nation spent millions of dollars on yet another experiment in stimulating the production of low-cost housing through mass production techniques, "Operation Breakthrough," which ended in failure. And this year's session of the Congress failed once again to pass legislation which would have equipped the states to encourage effective land-use planning, not only at state but at community level.

Most of us may be on the barricades now to block any further pollution of our landscape or air through further proliferation of highways in the wrong places; but as a nation we were not ready to listen in 1958, when our vast Interstate Highway System construction program was about to get under way, and in an address to a National Conference on Transportation Mumford warned:

"If we want to make the most of our new highway program, we must keep most of the proposed expressways in abeyance until we have done two things. We must replan the inner city for pedestrian circulation, and we must rebuild and extend our public forms of mass transportation."

But we may today be reaching the level of consciousness Mr. Mumford predicted in the same essay might ultimately shake the faith of Americans in "the religion of the motor car"—"clear demonstration of the fact that their highway program will, eventually, wipe out the very area of freedom that the private motor car promised to retain for them." If so, it would not be too late to ponder the kind of advice now more universally urged upon us by planners and most eloquently expressed by Mr. Mumford in the 1958 essay:

"The fatal mistake we have been making is to sacrifice every other form of transportation to the private motor car—and to offer as the only long-distance alternative the airplane. But the fact is that each type of transportation has its special use; and a good transportation policy must seek to improve each type and make the most of it. This cannot be achieved by aiming at high speed or continuous flow alone. If you wish casual opportunities for meeting your neighbors, and for profiting by chance contacts with acquaintances and colleagues, a stroll at two miles an hour in a relatively concentrated area, free from vehicles, will alone meet your need. But if you wish to rush a surgeon to a patient a thousand miles away, the fastest motorway is too slow. And again, if you wish to be sure to keep a lecture engagement in winter, railroad transportation offers surer speed and better insurance against being held up than the airplane. There is no one ideal mode or speed: human purpose should govern the choice of the means of transportation. That is why we need a better transportation *system,* not just more highways."

When he challenged architects to deal with issues on a larger scale, Mr. Mumford found frequent occasion to caution against oversimplification of complex problems:

"Most of our housing and city planning has been handicapped," he observed in 1937, "because those who have undertaken the work have no clear notion of the social functions of a city. They sought to derive these functions from a cursory survey of the activities and interests of the contemporary urban scene. And they did not, apparently, suspect that there might be gross deficiencies, misdirected efforts, mistaken expenditures here that would not be set straight by merely building sanitary tenements or straightening out and widening irregular streets."

By the early Sixties, when the nation's urban renewal program began to appear as a social disaster, many observers were ready to reach conclusions almost identical to that Mumford observation of some twenty-five years earlier.

And in 1962–63, in the five-part series "The Future of the City," Mr. Mumford defined the challenge of urban design in all its true complexity. "The key to a fresh architectural image of the city as a whole," he wrote, "lies in working toward an organic unit of urban order which will hold together its component parts through successive changes in function and purpose from generation to generation. While such an archetypal image can never be fully realized, this concept of a city as a whole, restated in contemporary terms, will help to define the character of each institutional structure."

To read the architectural criticisms of Lewis Mumford is to be reminded of all that is most promising in the history of human community. Today, these essays are both history and prophesy: an eloquent and moving chronicle of architectural thought and aspiration during the first two-thirds of the twentieth century, and a testament to the limitless architectural possibilities still to be invoked in the service of humanity.

It was no accident that the pages of *Architectural Record* were open wide to such architectural criticisms as Lewis Mumford's, for the *Record* has a tradition of hospitality to scholarly debate on the great philosophical issues in architecture that goes back to its very beginnings (and continues to this day).

Not only the great Montgomery Schuyler but such contemporaries as Russell Sturgis and Herbert Croly were writing criticism for the *Record* from the start (1891); and before many years had passed, the early greats of modern architecture, Louis Sullivan and Frank Lloyd Wright among them, were beginning to contribute criticism to its pages.

In the *Record* tradition of criticism, the significant debates are always about principles and concepts, not about projects or personalities. Whenever the winds of change are stirring architects to question the responsible future course of architecture, the need for critical comment intensifies, and the editors are searching for responsible and creative criticism.

A number of the Mumford essays in this collection, notably the series on "The Life, the Teaching and the Architecture of Matthew Nowicki" and "The Future of the City," first appeared in the *Record*'s pages out of the dedicated effort of the late editor of the *Record*, Emerson Goble, to respond to such critical urgencies of the Fifties and Sixties.

Those were years when, as Lewis Mumford himself put it in a 1962 essay, "the order and consensus that modern architecture seemed ready to establish in the Thirties" were "still far to seek." In fact, Mr. Mumford wrote, "In so far as modern architecture has succeeded in expressing modern life, it has done better in calling attention to its lapses, its rigidities, its failures, than in bringing out, with the aid of the architect's creative imagination, its immense latent potentialities. The modern architect has not yet come to grips with the multi-dimensional realities of the actual world. He has made himself at home with mechanical processes, which favor rapid commercial exploitation, with anonymous repetitive bureaucratic forms, like the high-rise apartment or office building, which lend themselves with mathematical simplicity to financial manipulation. But he has no philosophy that does justice to organic functions or human purposes, and that attempts to build a more comprehensive order in which the machine, instead of dominating our life and demanding ever heavier sacrifices in the present fashion, will become a supple instrument for human design, to be used, modified, or on option rejected at will."

The critical crusade for the *Record* during those years, then, under Emerson Goble's leadership, was to call the modern architect to the cause of a more humane architecture, the cause which Lewis Mumford has so illuminated during all his years as an architecture critic. Mr. Mumford was joined in the *Record* pages in that cause, by such distinguished architects and commentators as Frank Lloyd Wright, Walter Gropius, Pietro Belluschi, William Wilson Wurster, Albert Mayer and Clarence Stein, John Ely Burchard, Joseph Hudnut, Henry-Russell Hitchcock, Osbert Lancaster, Edward A. Weeks and Russell Lynes—and many others.

The crusade for a more humane architecture continues, and gathers more adherents year by year. Hopefully, this book will help to spur it on, by bringing the Mumford essays for the *Record* to a new generation of architects, and to a public which did not have access to them in the *Record* pages. The promise of the new architecture was never more eloquently expressed than in the passage from a 1968 Mumford essay which gives this collection its title:

"This, then, is the task for today and tomorrow: to restore and eventually to elevate even higher than ever before the organic and human components that are now missing in our compulsively dynamic and over-mechanized culture. The time has come for architecture to come back to earth and make a new home for man."

Jeanne M. Davern

New York City
July 1975

JEANNE M. DAVERN, former managing editor of *Architectural Record,* and now editor of the twice-monthly newsletter *Legal Briefs for Architects, Engineers and Contractors,* was on the staff of the *Record* from 1948 to 1969. A freelance architectural journalist since 1970, Miss Davern has worked as a consultant, editor or writer on a variety of assignments, from architectural reporting and special publications to editing books. A graduate of Wellesley College, she is an honorary member of The American Institute of Architects, an associate member of its New York Chapter, and a member of the Architectural League of New York.

BOOK ONE

American Architecture Today

1928

"The energies that worked below the ground so long are now erupting in a hundred unexpected places; and once more the American architect has begun to attack the problems of design with the audacity and exuberance of a Root, a Sullivan, a Wright."

These essays were first published in the periodical *Architecture*, which was combined with *Architectural Record* in 1937.

American Architecture To-day

I
The Search for "Something More"

FOR a whole generation, from 1890 to 1920, the energies of American architecture worked under the surface. When one looked about the scene, it seemed that the American architect, like the child of the colonial settler described by Thomas Hardy, had been born old. Here and there the active energies of architecture broke volcanically through some fissure: the train-hall of the Pennsylvania Station or the concourse of the Grand Central lived by its own naïve virtues, in spite of every effort of the architect to ignore or belittle these qualities; but the mask of American architecture was frozen: the face was dead. The very skyscrapers were born old. "If," I wrote in 1924, "there has been any unique efflorescence of style about the entrance or the elevator doors, I have been unable to discover it."

In five years, the entire picture has changed. The energies that worked below the ground so long are now erupting in a hundred unsuspected places; and once more the American architect has begun to attack the problems of design with the audacity and exuberance of a Root, a Sullivan, a Wright. In a sense, we have at last caught up with 1890; but in another sense we have passed far beyond these early pioneers, for the steel cage is no longer an experimental form; the processes of reinforcing and casting concrete are no longer a mystery; and, during the years when, on the surface, little was being accomplished in design, the plans for specific types of building—the loft, the office, the theatre—were being worked out and refined. The economical width of bays, the minimum cubage per floor for light and ventilation, the whole arrangement of a house, a hospital, or a hotel as a working plant—all these things were progressively mastered. I do not say that there is not much more to learn; on the contrary, a good part of our knowledge consists in tricks to meet very specific conditions, like Mr. Andrew Thomas's plans for apartment-houses, which are admirable to the last degree provided one must respect lot lines and provided one does not change the depth of the block.

But the point is that the major technical difficulties are, for the moment, mastered. The proof of this is that the architect has become tired of his Corinthian columns, his acanthuses, or his ogives, of all the clichés that once served instead of the sterling mark on American architecture; and though the elder men, who worked through this period of "refinement," "taste," rectitude, may not be as ready to work out of it as was the late Mr. Goodhue, there is no doubt that the able young men who are following on their heels are in revolt. They are nauseated by acanthus leaves, and they know that if they pull down the stone columns the modern building, unlike the temple of the Philistines that Samson destroyed, will remain standing. One sees this spirit even more clearly in the good architectural schools. In the class in design at Michigan I saw strong designs and weak designs, but I saw no stale designs: the feeling was clear, frank, confident. No one thought that an airplane terminus was a place for displaying archæological knowledge.

What has been gained during the last five years? What general characteristics emerge in this new American architecture? What have we learned about the treatment of materials, the use of site, the handling of the structural forms? In abandoning the battle of the styles, have we solved the problem of decoration, or must we now face a more genuine issue and experimentally work to a conclusion? Finally: what are our weak points and where do we lag? I have posed these questions in the abstract; but I do not pretend I can give satisfactory answer to them; rather, I shall attempt to show the concrete forms in which the solutions present themselves.

II

The four great components of design are site, materials, technical construction, and feeling. All of these have been modified by the conditions of modern life; but they have been altered in different ways: if the architect has gained freedom in construction, he has, in our big cities, lost a great deal in the treatment of site. Let us see how these elements tend to work out.

In the rectangular plan of the usual American city, the site has become a passive factor: the vast majority of sites are blind sites, without sufficient direct approach, without the possibility of constructing a four-sided building, and without any opportunity to register the façade as a whole. This fact has affected the de-

Storage warehouse for the Detroit Evening News, Detroit, Mich.   Albert Kahn, Inc., Architect

ture as a setting for our great buildings; indeed, before we can have any tolerable modern ornament, we must first learn to erase every distracting vestige of earlier forms. The earlier skyscrapers in Chicago did this: they were as stark as the Pyramids: and our present efforts here mean, I think, that we are again at a hopeful point of departure.

In the dropping of the cornice and the improvement of the silhouette of our bigger buildings, the zoning and setback restrictions have been given a good deal of credit: but the current advance in architecture owes less to these legal aids than many people have supposed. As a matter of fact, between the "zoning envelope" as defined by law, and the best æsthetic treatment of a building on any particular site, there is no essential relation. The notion that any setback

sign of the great mass of buildings in the crowded parts of our cities: both the façade and the cubical mass have become negligible. I am aware that there are exceptions to this generalization: Chicago's lake front is an unrivalled approach, and there are similar points about squares or parks in New York: but within the central district of any city, even a small one like Grand Rapids or Providence, the architect cannot take advantage of his site. This is a genuine misfortune, but not all the results of it have been disastrous, for it has made the architect more ready to scrape off ornamental forms which have no relation to either the structure or the feeling of a modern building. During the last five years the clean façade, devoid of columns, pediments, balconies, cornices, has come back into architecture: the fronts of our better buildings are now as direct and simple as the backs; and sardonic observers of the American scene, like Mr. Erich Mendelsohn, need no longer confine their photographic studies of our tall buildings to the rear views.

This gain is indeed a negative one: the absence of a spurious note, the stripping down of design to elemental relationships, and the casting overboard of vestigial ornaments that do not register; but one has only to compare the unbroken planes of the Barclay-Vesey Building with the fussiness, the exaggeration of the vertical, the contemporary ornamental tricks of the older skyscrapers like the Woolworth Tower or the Singer Tower to see the advantage in design. In this negative gain, a great many buildings have shared: the Bronx tenement, the Park Avenue apartment-house, the Seventh Avenue loft building, have this common quality. This seems to me a real advance. Buildings should be distinguished, if possible, by their site, and by their expression of function and purpose: that a building should express the aims of the client or the personality of the designer is inevitable; but these things should never be the aim of architecture. We need a direct, simple, inevitable vernacular architec-

The Allerton 57th Street House, New York City. Arthur Loomis Harmon, Architect

building is better than any cubical one is absurd: when the architect is handicapped by a narrow lot and by the demand of the owner to enclose every possible cubic foot, the setback restrictions frequently create curious deformities. When people think of the architectural triumphs of zoning they think of Mr. Hugh Ferriss's ideal cities, or of one or two great buildings that have been produced on sites sufficiently large to build up into a great mass. This does credit, perhaps, to their hopes and their imaginations; but it has no actual relation to the buildings in our cities. Except for what little light and air the setbacks have introduced—and it is still precious little—it makes absolutely no æsthetic difference whether the great mass of crowded buildings are above ground or below, set up or set back. The architect

© Amemiya.

Houses at Sunnyside, Long Island City, N. Y. Clarence S. Stein, Architect; Henry Wright, Associate

No. 1 Fifth Avenue, from Washington Square, New York City. Helmle, Corbett and Harrison, Architects

realizes this quite well: he knows where the shoe pinches. As a result, since 1924, he has gone in for decoration in the few visible parts that remain; and my dictum that there has been no efflorescence of design about the entrance or the elevators no longer holds in 1928. It is precisely in this department that a revolution is going on; and before it is over it will influence many other things besides the vestibules of skyscrapers. Here there have been a dozen brave attempts at fresh designs: the Barclay-Vesey Building, the Radiator Building, the Alabama Power Company's Building, the Fur Capitol, the Graybar Building; and out of a great welter of fine effort, at least one almost complete success: Mr. Ely Kahn's entrance and corridor in the Park Avenue Building.

III

In considering the advances made in our commercial and industrial buildings we may leave out site, and put to one side materials: for the necessities of fireproof construction leave us with steel, concrete, brick, and terra-cotta, with glass still too dubious under sudden changes in temperature to play a big part, except in its conventional form. It is by utilizing new methods of construction and embodying a new feeling that our modern architecture lives: but the feeling and the construction are not always in harmony. In Europe modern architects, like Gropius and Le Corbusier, have faced this situation with inexorable logic: they have modified or curbed their feelings so as to fit the construction! To them, ornament is a snare; color is a smear. Does a dynamo need ornament? Does a Diesel engine need color? Our world is essentially a world fit for dynamos, Diesel engines, steamships, a thing of black, gray, white, conscientiously utilitarian.

Now, this is an extreme position; but it emphasizes a reality. One part of the modern feeling for form, the thing that distinguishes us from the Baroque or the Gothic, is a positive pleasure that we take in the elemental structure of an object. We do not paint pansies on our typewriters or griffons on our automobiles, nor are our office files covered with decorative plaster; and if we conceived the rest of our environment as freshly as we have conceived these new additions to it, we should strip it similarly to its last essential. To realize form-in-function, by its clear, lucid expression, is what constitutes the modern feeling: it is what unites the Brooklyn Bridge, the paintings of Cézanne, the sculpture of a Brancusi, a Despiau, an Eric Gill, the structure of a grain elevator, or a piece of clean engineering like the ventilator buildings of the Hudson Tubes. That feeling must exist in our architecture: Le Corbusier is right; *at least that much must be there*. But we are still human beings, not dynamos or Diesel engines; and there must be something more.

It is over the question of what this "something more" must consist of that the new battle of the styles will be fought. Let us admit as a foundation that an office-building, a factory, a garage, a church, a school, a home will, in any tolerable modern conception, begin at the same point: they will use similar materials and similar methods of construction—what we may now loosely call the vernacular of the machine. Their primary feeling—the tone and attitude produced in the spectator—will be the same: a factory like the Sloane linoleum plant near Trenton, a hotel like the Allerton House at 57th Street, a warehouse like the *Detroit Evening News* Building, garages and houses like those at Sunnyside Gardens, though they were designed by different architects for different places and purposes, all have a common signature. They are the direct, economical expression of material and plan. If any large part of our buildings approached this simplicity and directness, the outlook for our architecture would be a happy one: such a foundation could not be shaken by archaism, stylicism, or the fake picturesque derived from the latest foreign sketches and snapshots added to the architect's files. The demand for "something more" can only be met by those who have had the courage to go as far as this.

The Barclay-Vesey Building, New York City, from the waterfront.
McKenzie, Voorhees & Gmelin, Architects

14

How shall the final expression take place, once we have simple and direct forms to work with? The two opposing answers to this question are typified in the work of Messrs. Ralph Walker and Ely Kahn. In the Barclay-Vesey Building Mr. Walker, like Mr. Rogers in the Medical Centre Building, permits the mass itself to be cold, hard; the building as a whole has a feeling of dark strength; but in the stonework of the lower stories and in the interior the designer introduces a delicate, naturalistic carving, heightened within by the use of gold. When one enters the main hall, one almost forgets its purpose: it is as gaily lighted and decorated as a village street in a strawberry festival. Mr. Walker, in other words, accepts the contrast between structure and feeling: he does not attempt to reconcile them. One remains clear and logical, inflexibly committed to its programme; the other is warm and intimate and a little confused. In Mr. Walker's design decoration is an audacious compensation for the rigor and mechanical fidelity of the rest of the building; like jazz, it interrupts and relieves the tedium of too strenuous mechanical activity.

Mr. Kahn's decoration is the exact opposite of this. In the building that strikes the boldest and clearest note among all our recent achievements in skyscraper architecture, the Park Avenue Building, he has kept the exterior and the interior in unity: the first has become more warm, the second has become more rigorous and geometrical— and handsome. With a warm buff brick as a foundation, the Park Avenue Building works up into bands of sunny terra-cotta, broken and accentuated with red, green, bright sky-blue. The pattern is abstract; and every part, down to the lighting fixtures, has the same finish, rigor, swiftness, perfection. In this building, structure and feeling are at last one: the directness and sim-

plicity of the first have not been forfeited in the decoration; the warmth and human satisfaction of the decorative forms have not been overpowered in the structure itself, for they are expressed there, too. This building seems to me an answer both to the Europeans who, despairing of synthesis, have sought to enjoy the grimness and inflexibility of modern forms by sitting

The Park Avenue Building, Park Avenue at 32d Street, New York City.
Buchman & Kahn, Architects

Detail of upper stories, Park Avenue Building, New York City.
Buchman & Kahn, Architects

Detail of upper stories, Barclay-Vesey Building, New York City.
McKenzie, Voorhees & Gmelin, Architects

16

Lobby, Park Avenue Building, New York City.
Buchman & Kahn, Architects

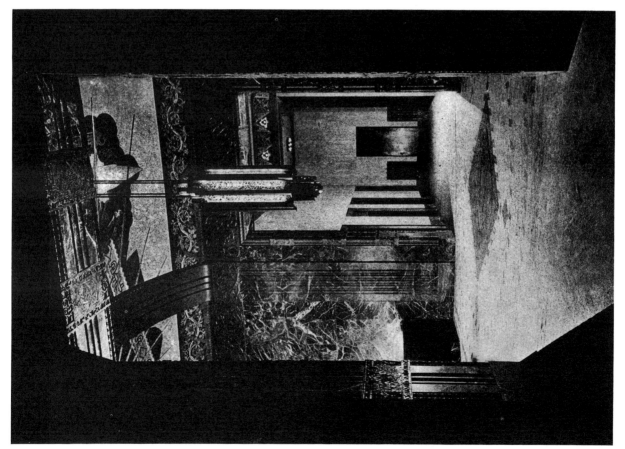

Lobby, Barclay-Vesey Building, New York City.
McKenzie, Voorhees & Gmelin, Architects

hard on their organic feelings, and to those who, equally despairing of synthesis, have permitted the human, sensuous note to break out irrelevantly—either in stale archæology, in fussy handicraft, or in unrelated bursts of modern decoration.

One swallow may not make a summer; but one building like this, which faces the entire problem of design, and has a clean, unflinching answer for each question, may well serve to crystallize all the fumbling and uncertain elements in present-day architecture. The success of the Park Avenue Building is not due to the fact that it is a tall tower or that it is a setback building. It is not a tower and the setback is

trifling. Its success is due to its unique synthesis of the constructive and the feeling elements: its method is as applicable to a two-story building as to one of twenty stories: it is in the line of that rule Louis Sullivan was seeking—which would admit of no exceptions. The Park Avenue Building shows the limit of the architect's skill, to date, under urban conditions, where the programme is inflexibly laid down by the business man and the engineer, and where the site is too costly to be played with. With the part of American architecture that has been favored by more sufficient sites, a more flexible programme, and a broader schedule of resources, I shall deal in another article.

Detail of upper stories, Park Avenue Building, New York City. Buchman & Kahn, Architects

Lobby detail in bright bronze, Park Avenue Building. Buchman & Kahn, Architects

American Architecture To-day

II
Domestic Architecture

THE architect would like freedom. He would like a site that is adapted to its purpose; he would like a purpose that is not indifferent to beauty; he would like large means and a certain margin to play around in. This sort of freedom is not often to be found in commercial and industrial building; but there is one province of American architecture where it still exists: the dwelling-house. What has the modern architect done with this opportunity? What new expression has he achieved?

The conditions here are all that the architect could ask. He has a site of five acres—or five hundred—in which to plant his house; he can utilize the landscape gardener to give his house a setting; he need not be troubled by the extravagances or disfigurements of neighboring houses; materials and fixtures are his to command. This seems like an ideal opportunity; yet the result is that to-day we are in precisely the same condition and state of mind that our best architects were in forty years ago. With every favoring circumstance, our designs for houses still lag behind every other type: they are mainly efforts to achieve the picturesque.

In our domestic architecture, the plans have of course improved a little: the utilities and services are more elaborate. So much one may grant, but the designs of our best country-house architects—men like Mr. Gilchrist or Mr. Meigs or Mr. Gregory—show little to-day that was not already in the designs of Mr. Halsey Wood or Mr. H. H. Richardson or young Mr. Stanford White more than a generation back. Such gain as one may record is a certain sureness in using the materials: the architect works *in* the stone

A cottage in East Orange, N. J., designed a generation ago by Halsey Wood

or the wood and uses it appropriately. If we have fewer Lorraine Chateaux, however, we have more Norman manor-houses; if we do not build Italian palaces quite so often we make up for our discretion by taking over the mode of the Cotswolds; and I am not sure that the net gain is very large. If one has to choose between various archaic modes one may legitimately take the more direct and simple; but one must remember that this is the end, and not the beginning, of an appropriate architecture. Such advances are not fundamental; they do not imply further growth and development.

The picturesque is the *ignis fatus* of architecture; and it is unfortunate that our country and suburban architecture should still be so hot in quest of it. When a sophisticated age attempts to reproduce the forms of a simple one, when a period of hasty acquisitions and attainments attempts to imitate the mosses, the genial weather-beaten tones, or the sag of a roof line which time alone has produced, the result is bound to be ephemeral for all its show of dignity and durability. These new country-houses are not bad of their kind; the point is that their kind is irrelevant. Every function that is performed in the house has been altered by modern knowledge and habits: babies are born to-day not without premeditation on the part of their parents; they are fed on a diet that would have seemed preposterous twenty years ago; they are treated to sunlight and fresh air in hitherto unheard-of quantities; and as they grow up they find themselves in a world so complicated that every aspect of life must be simplified to the last degree. In short, the requirements for a good dwelling-house have altered as the life it embraces has altered—in as

Apartments and service-station, Mariemont, Ohio, designed by Edmund B. Gilchrist

great a degree as the requirements for a fire-proof loft-building. But one could hardly guess from the aspect of our fine country-houses that these requirements had changed: on the contrary, there is an almost complete lack of relation between feeling, function, and design.

How often does one see a new colonial house in some perfect New England village marred by the addition of a sleeping-porch! How often does one feel, on going into a French hunting-lodge, that either the house should look different or the people should be

A housing group at Mariemont, Ohio, in which simple and inexpensive materials have been used with great directness by Edmund B. Gilchrist

different people and the place a different place! In how many Cotswold cottages could one arrange a screened but open second-story porch for sun-bathing without forfeiting the quaintness the architect has sought in every touch! I have no abstract bias against natural materials, against handicraft, against a simplification of mechanical utilities: quite the contrary, I enjoy these things and envy those who possess a firescreen by Mr. Samuel Yellin or a vase by Mr. Varnum Poore. That a country-house should be part of its landscape, that the architect can gain much through

modernist, because both in design and in methods of construction he has worked out new forms, instead of following the line of least resistance. His work must also be recognized—by us if not by his European admirers—as deeply regional in feeling: they are "home" and not merely an abstract expression of the machine age. Mr. Wright's prairie houses in brick and tile and concrete, his northern house at Taliesin mainly in stone, his Tahoe wooden cabins designed for a primeval mountain environment, and the Inness House, of textile block slab, conceived in terms

The Arthur E. Newbold, Jr., house, Laverock, Pa., by Mellor, Meigs & Howe

using local building materials, that a more organic rather than a mechanical feeling should pervade country architecture—all these things seem to me essentially true and fitting. But one must accomplish these ends to-day not as William Morris accomplished them in the Red House but as Morris would have used them had he been born in our own generation and had profited by our many advances. The most adequate examples of regional architecture in America that I know of are also the freshest and most original: the wooden cottages that Richardson built in the eighties, the concrete houses of Mr. Irving Gill in California, or the varied expressions of locality embodied in Mr. Frank Lloyd Wright's country-houses. Mr. Wright is usually looked upon as our most distinguished

of mountain and desert, have done as much to advance an appropriate regional architecture as our revivals have done to delay it. A hundred years from now this sort of architecture will seem mellow and traditional; while that part of our architecture which sought mellowness and warmth at the expense of health, convenience, and fresh design will serve as a reminder of the pretentiousness and trickery of early twentieth-century architecture, precisely as the jigsaw architecture of the seventies reminds us to-day of the barbarism of the Gilded Age.

II

If picturesque architecture is unsound even when it stands by itself, in the midst of trees and gardens,

Part of the government housing development at Bridgeport, Conn.

Part of the work at Sunnyside Gardens, Long Island City, erected by the City Housing Corporation of New York

which conceal and shelter its ineptitudes, its total inadequacy for modern design appears emphatically in any suburban street. I do not propose to dwell on the absurdities of Spanish, French, English, Colonial, Federal, Italian houses, all a little simplified and adapted to middle-class purposes and tastes, that greet us in Highland Park and Guilford and Squirrel Hill and Floral Heights. It is enough to say that if we had an architecture in any of our great regions, we should not have so many nondescript architectures.

What is just as bad as the concrete embodiment of this Wonderland of styles is the debauching effect such scenery has upon the mind and the æsthetic sense

cheaper branches of building, in substitutes that are even more futile than the original natural material, such as the fireproof imitation of half-timber on the upper stories of apartment-houses—an addition which again and again spoils an otherwise direct and rational design.

In short, the application of the picturesque mars and belittles the real achievements that have been made in American domestic architecture during the last ten years. These achievements have occurred in two capital departments. The first department is the manufactured parts of the modern house, the bathroom and kitchen fixtures, kitchen ranges, bathtubs,

Reginald D. Johnson's own home at Pasadena, Calif.

The Inness house, of textile block slab, by Frank Lloyd Wright

of the community. For most educated people to-day, certainly for most women, tutored by women's magazines and courses in historic appreciation, architecture *is* the picturesque and the personal; and strong, vigorous, rational designs, akin to those which dignify every great vernacular expression, are looked upon as ugly and mean. The tawdry emphasis of the picturesque spreads over all our commonplace residential building; there is scarcely a place that is free from it. It results in bad upper-story plans with many uncomfortable gabled rooms and dormer windows—every bumped head a tribute to the deity of the picturesque. It results in the conversion of decent concrete and stucco and plaster into unmentnioable smears and spatters and muds—textures which grit against the skin or the clothes, catch dirt, and encourage the manufacture of appropriately Italian furniture. It results, in the

cabinets, ice-boxes. The kitchen and the bathroom, as I have repeatedly said elsewhere, are the two parts of the modern American house that are entirely fresh and adequate in design—color, fitness for function, a nice disposition of parts, in short, all the elementary ingredients of form are embodied with great surety and finish; and one will look long for these characteristics in any other part of the modern house. There is still room for much improvement here: our locksmiths, our doormakers, our manufacturers of lighting fixtures and furniture have a considerable distance to go before they will catch up with the procession; but even here there are signs of a slow, if not so steady, advance, and the chief danger that threatens us is a relapse in those details where we are now triumphant —a relapse into "period plumbing," or into kitchen cabinets with a Tudor finish. Here we face the same

The living-room of Taliesin, Frank Lloyd Wright's own home in Wisconsin

24

Taliesin and its setting—one of the four courts, by Frank Lloyd Wright

paradox that confronted us in commercial buildings: our attempts at art result in bastard art, but our attempts to create thoroughly competent and finished utilities result in something that more and more approaches, in machine technic, what handicraft achieved in its own province.

The other direction in which advance has taken place is in site-planning. Our numerous achievements in war housing, both on paper and in construction, showed what could be done with simple housing units when they were intelligently related to a community plan, and when the house itself, instead of standing alone, gained further interest by its juxtaposition to other houses, to gardens and trees, and to remoter houses as background. Messrs. Stein and Wright and Ackerman have shown in Sunnyside Gardens how, with standardized plans and a few simple types of building, a whole may be built up which is more sound and.æsthetically satisfying than any amount of stylistic individuality and fake picturesqueness. No one of their houses has any remarkable individuality; the "style" is just the simplest possible treatment of common brick, with windows of standard size; but every section of a block, grouped around a common garden, has a distinct individuality and the total result is something that has genuine style.

Obviously, this is the same order of vernacular de-

sign that produced the fine gardens and squares of Bloomsbury and Belgravia, which are equally severe and rational in their elements; and the recent achievement of this kind of design in America is one of the few promises I can find in American domestic architecture. Here is an answer to those who believe that uniformity is another name for monotony, that standardization is a synonym for baseness, and that mechanical methods, scaled down to the very lowest costs, are altogether inimical to good architecture. The truth of the matter seems to be this: When these operations proceed automatically they produce very hideous designs indeed, as every new city extension in Philadelphia, Detroit, Brooklyn, or Boston unfortunately shows. On the other hand, when they are used with intelligence and imagination, when the architect as community-planner can produce a coherent whole, they may exhibit in the individuality of the whole what is lost through standardization of the part. The Committee on Community Planning of the A. I. A. has dwelt on this possibility in a series of comprehensive reports; and its findings now have the support of many concrete demonstrations. Hitherto we have sought to achieve by individual design—by "style," "period," "picturesqueness," "personality"—what can only be attained through collective effort. In modern architecture no individual can stand alone: in back of his effort stands

A modern bathroom; in this, having no precedent, we must create new forms

A modern kitchen in which practical considerations alone are allowed to govern, with a not unpleasing result

the work of a hundred crafts and manufactures, which will make or mar his own efforts; and in back of the crafts and manufactures stands the community itself—with its general level of taste, culture, and income. There is no escape from this condition. An architect of originality can further the collective advance; but unless there is continual improvement all along the line, improvement in manufacture, improvement in the methods of social finance for housing, improvement in community-planning, there is little prospect, certainly in domestic architecture, for a new and authentic architecture.

The Coonley House, Riverside, Ill.—One of the best known of Frank Lloyd Wright's prairie houses

American Architecture To-day

III
Monumental Architecture

WE live in an age that has still to create or recreate its symbols. Here lies the great difficulty for our monumental architecture; and this is why our utilitarian buildings are fresh and vigorous, expressing with confidence their own functions, whilst our churches and our colleges and our museums and statehouses are, for the greater part, subordinated to stale symbols which no longer work significantly on the beholder.

There is, it is true, one universal and accepted symbol of our period in America: the skyscraper. It came to us as a practical expedient: it has remained as a monument. When a small city wishes to show that it has an active Chamber of Commerce and a well-stocked Rotary Club it builds a skyscraper: when a university wishes to show that it stands for progress and big donations, it proposes to build a skyscraper: when a business man wants to express the pride of success or to advertise his product he builds a skyscraper: when, finally, a church wants to proclaim to the world that God and Mammon have, after all, a good deal in common, and that the man nobody knows was really a go-getter and a super-salesman, it builds a skyscraper.

There is no doubt that the skyscraper is a genuine symbol, that it fulfils our deep religious awe at size, power, bulk, and that each additional story has the effect of adding an extra zero on a million dollars. Unfortunately, this great religious symbol is not without a defect or two: for one thing, it is an ambiguous symbol, and because it is used for every purpose it cannot express adequately any particular one: which, for example, is the religious building, the Chicago Tribune Tower or the Methodist Book Concern—and how does Pittsburgh's proposed temple of learning differ from either of these as symbol? Again, the buildings which have a special imaginative function to perform, like schools, churches, synagogues, theatres, libraries, cannot always be wedded to a vast building project: they are often small in size and poor in resources or in prospective income; so that they simply cannot express their purpose by ostentatious size and height. Finally, not every one believes in the religion of the skyscraper; here and there one may still find a congregation that wants a church which is not buried under an income-producing apartment-house, or a college president who had rather support scholarship and science more adequately than squander his funds upon a super-fireproof tower with its expensive upkeep of elevators and heating service.

In short, the symbolism of the skyscraper is inadequate; its appropriate use is admirable; but there are still a large number of purposes for which it is not appropriate. If our success at monumental building depended upon the skyscraper alone, the prospects would not be very bright; but happily some of the best architecture that has been produced in America during the last fifteen years has been modest in scale and unpretentious in achievement. The pioneer in this new monumental architecture, as in so many other departments, was Louis Sullivan, with his little country banks and his mausoleums; and during the last decade this work has gone on under many different guises—without the factitious aid of ancient symbols carried over from the past, or of the one new symbol we have created in America out of the automatic operations of land increment and credit.

II

In treating monumental architecture, I must isolate and limit the field. I purpose therefore to deal chiefly with the last buildings of Bertram Goodhue, with the churches of Mr. Barry Byrne, and with a group of buildings that have been produced by different architects for the campus of the University of Michigan. Each of these examples is vital; and their achievements are instructive not merely on the positive side, but likewise by reason of what they have missed or fallen short of. In one way or another, all the problems that arise out of monumental building—out of free architecture as opposed to engineering—are embodied in these buildings.

While it is hard to forgive the late Mr. Goodhue his long and leisurely preoccupation with Gothic forms, his last works, the Los Angeles Public Library and the Nebraska State Capitol, are perhaps in their outward materialization among the most satisfactory traditional buildings that have been done in America. It must have been hard for any one who loved subtle and complicated forms, as Mr. Goodhue did from his earliest days as a designer of bookplates, to strip off one by one all these delicate acquisitions and to begin with fresh surfaces and planes, boldly modelled around the plan itself. He was aided in this effort, no doubt, because he had found through collaboration with Mr. Lee Lawrie, that it was possible to rely for excellence of detail, not on precedent, but on the sympathetic and untrammel'ed collaboration of the contemporary sculptor.

In putting this reliance upon modern sculpture, Mr. Goodhue made a great leap. The architects of the nineties, in their revival of classicism, had called in the painter and the sculptor, too: the Congressional Library, the Boston Library, the New York Library, the Carnegie Museum in Pittsburgh are examples of this co-operation: but no one can pretend that the result was a very satisfactory one. Where the pictures themselves were adequate, as in Puvis de Chavannes's murals in Boston, the frame itself was a distraction: usually, however, the pictures were as stale in conception and as

academic in treatment as the architectural detail itself; so that even when the two great symbolic resources of architecture, sculpture and painting, were introduced, they accomplished nothing that a blank wall could not have accomplished with less effort. Mr. Goodhue had the courage to provide a modern frame for his decoration, and then to rely heavily upon the sculptor's own resources. So, in the Nebraska State Capitol, the functions of the building are symbolized by the tower, and by the gigantic figures of the lawgivers that leap solidly out of the walls: instead of urns and lions there are buffaloes: instead of meaningless moldings, there are well-placed inscriptions. Plainly, this type of design places a load upon the sculptor; and it is doubtful if there is a man in America who would be entirely equal to it; for our artists are either unused to working within an architectural frame, or, like Mr. John Storrs, their best work is done in abstract forms. When one admits that Mr. Lawrie's design lacks the final vigor of great sculpture, one says nothing invidious. Our architects have made so little demand upon the creative artists, and they have done so much to encourage the sculpture of the Atlantic City sand-artist and the painting of the insurance-calendar lithograph, that they have still to create an environment which will evoke great talents and bring them to bear upon the architectural problem. One honors Mr. Goodhue and Mr. Lawrie all the more for having the courage to explore together some of the possibilities of a modern symbolic architecture: without this adventurous search, such interesting designs as those of Zantzinger, Borie and Medary for the Insurance Building in Philadelphia, or of Messrs. John Bright and Harry Sternfeld for a swimming-pool at Green Hill Farm would scarcely have come so easily into existence.

While we are on Mr. Goodhue's buildings one must reluctantly add that the interior decorations have not the life and strength and confidence of the façade: they are for the most part mediocre. This brings us to an inherent weakness in American monumental art, a weakness which every exhibition of the Architectural League and almost every new mural confirms. A little while ago Mr. Thomas Craven pointed out that the only respectable modern murals that existed in America were the maps on the walls of the Pennsylvania Station; and when one remembers the ceilings in our new office buildings and the walls of our state capitols, one is fairly well tempted to agree with him.

For this weakness, the American architect is chiefly responsible: he regards painting as a thoroughly subordinate part of design, and, as if to emphasize this, he passes by modern painters of great distinction and originality, like Mr. Kenneth Hayes Miller and Mr. Thomas H. Benton, and gives his patronage and interest to men whose work is as safely mediocre as a Commencement Day address. It was not always so in America: H. H. Richardson had the taste to pick out the foremost artists of his time and place, William Morris Hunt and John LaFarge: but one seriously doubts if many successful architects have the faintest notion who the foremost American artists are, or would have the courage to employ them if they did. There are a few notable exceptions to this generalization: Mr. Ely Kahn has more than once employed

Fireplace in Arthur I. Meigs's apartment.   Seagull by Gaston Lachaise, Sculptor; ironwork by Samuel Yellin

men like Mr. Bertram Hartman and Mr. Gaston Lachaise. Mr. Arthur Meigs used the latter artist, with exquisite tact, to design a very fine fireplace, herewith illustrated: but for one such example of positive taste, one could mention a hundred failures and lapses. As a result, a virile series of historic American murals, already partly executed by Mr. Benton, goes a-begging for space, whilst the work of some anæmic advertising illustrator is pompously installed in a great building, as an authentic work of art.

In sum, in monumental art we are in the midst of a vicious circle: until the architect's taste improves one cannot cry very hopefully for painting and sculpture to be employed more frequently in modern buildings: but until painters and sculptors are employed more often, they will not learn to meet the specific problems that differentiate the easel from the mural picture, and an incorporated sculpture from that which exists in isolation in a gallery or museum. If there is to be improvement, one must pin one's faith upon the emergence of architects, young enough or well-grounded enough to know that cubism was not a piece of charlatanry, that

Bronze elevator door. Gaston Lachaise, Sculptor; Buchman & Kahn, Architects

Los Angeles Public Library.   *Bertram G. Goodhue, Architect; Carleton Monroe Winslow, Associate Architect; Lee Lawrie, Sculptor*

Picasso and Matisse and Marin are not ridiculous daubsters, and that the expression of contemporary life can no more be accomplished in terms of academic pictures that date from Bougeureau and Leighton (bad as they were in their day!) than it can be managed in terms of dentils, guttæ, and acanthus leaves.

III

Mr. Goodhue's signal success came in buildings like the Los Angeles Library and the Nebraska Capitol that are not hoary with tradition: when we turn to Mr. Barry Byrne's Roman Catholic Churches we face the problem of tradition in its most extreme form; for here we have an institution with an actual continuity that reaches back beyond any American past, an institution that prides itself on the firmness of its tradition, its clarity of dogma, its finality of faith. If new conditions and old traditions can be reconciled here, they can be reconciled anywhere. If a Roman Catholic Church can make use of the forces that are active in contemporary life, there is no need for Colonial dormitories, classic engineering laboratories, or Gothic libraries.

We have here a clear-cut issue between the school represented by Doctor Ralph Adams Cram and that of Mr. Barry Byrne. Doctor Cram, who singles out a certain period in the church's history and desires to keep its architecture crystallized in the forms of this period, would seem to hold the historic position; but as a matter of fact, Mr. Byrne's practice seems to me the more deeply historic one. For the forms of church architecture change as everything else changes: a living institution keeps its shape, like a living organism, only by constantly modifying it and adapting it to outward circumstance and inward need. St. Peter's is not less a part of the living church than the Cathedral of Amiens: the Baroque of the Jesuit fathers is in the tradition quite as much as the architecture of the Romanesque. The symbols and dogmas remain relatively fixed; but their outward expression in a building is modified by all sorts of structural and social considerations that vary from age to age. The modern congregation does not stand, it sits: it does not merely chant and pray, it listens. Mr. Byrne accordingly builds his churches in the modern vernacular: he abandons the pillars, ogives, and vaults, and the stone or pseudo-stone construction: he carries his roof on steel trusses and creates a

Photograph by Mott Studios
Detail of the Los Angeles Public Library

wide, shallow, unbroken auditorium, with good acoustics, facing an altar. There is too much light in this auditorium: he narrows the windows. The walls remain bare and simple: but as a result of his economies in construction there is, even in the most modest churches, money available for fresh, original design in the altar, the font, the confessional box: instead of the usual tepid stockpieces, in the worst profane tradition, the designs of these elements in the ritual are the work of a collaborating sculptor and craftsman, Mr. Alfonso Ianelli. As in Mr. Goodhue's partnership with Mr. Lee Lawrie, the architect relies for art, not upon his draftsman and the historic sample-book of styles, but upon an artist whose work on detail is quite as important as the architect's general plan and design. The result is a building modern in construction, traditional in purpose and feeling, fresh in detail. In the best of Mr. Byrne's buildings, he has carried a very difficult problem nearer to its solution than any contemporary designer of churches I can name; more than that, he has established a valid principle and method for the architect who desires to respect tradition and historic associations without using the irrelevant structural forms and decorations of the past.

Church of St. Thomas the Apostle, Chicago.   Barry Byrne, Architect

Interior, St. Patrick's Church, Racine, Wis.   Barry Byrne, Architect; Alfonso Ianelli, Sculptor

Architectural Building, University of Michigan.
Emil Lorch, Architect

University of Michigan Union, Ann Arbor, Mich.
Pond & Pond, Architects

IV

No institution has been more lacking in fresh design than the church, except perhaps the college. The excuse for this staleness is that the college is an historic institution: the actual results would lead one to believe that it is also a dead one.

For this reason, a new group of buildings at Ann Arbor stands out with peculiar vividness. One of these, the Michigan Union, is by Mr. Irving Pond. On the outside, it is a building in variegated red brick and limestone, in the modern vernacular: the rhythm of the façade is established by the large, flat-arched windows: and save for the limestone trim, which seems to me to rob the design of some of its force, the wall and window and the low tower establish its character. The interior is done with remarkable freshness and fine feeling: the panelled walls of the dining-room and the lounge, the delicate use of color in the window-panes, and the quiet craftsmanship of detail, which extends to the drinking fountain in the hall, create a very genial whole. Is this a personal *tour de force*, or is it a living tradition? The new Architecture Building, designed by Professor Emil Lorch, is, I think, an answer to this question. Here is another interesting union of plan and elevation in which the relation of wall, window, and mass tells the whole story. These particular buildings represent a growth from a less rhythmic, but direct, vernacular that was established in some of the other buildings on the campus: none of them is perhaps quite so free from tags and solecisms as the interior of the Hill Auditorium, for that interior is one of the most poetic enclosures of space in America: but they are all obviously headed in the same direction. Put

these buildings alongside the Pennsylvania Freight Terminal in Chicago, or among some of the business structures I cited in my first article, and it is plain that they all "belong:" a common spirit and a common principle unite them.

The culmination of this particular development in monumental architecture has come, I think, in the new Medical Centre at 168th Street in New York City. Here the two prime elements of our new architecture are juxtaposed and united. The central wings consist of the severe unbroken masses of the skyscraper—masses which here have the unique advantage of a site that can be approached from four sides and seen equally well at a distance or near at hand. When these masses stood by themselves, one was conscious of a certain frigid lack of relation between the building and the site: they

Photograph by Manning Bros.

The Hill Auditorium, University of Michigan. Albert Kahn, Architect

The Columbia Presbyterian Medical Centre, New York City, under construction.   James Gamble Rogers, Architect

34

Another view of the Medical Centre

The Fidelity Mutual Life Insurance Company Building, Philadelphia.   Zantzinger, Borie & Medary, Architects

Detail of brickwork on the Medical Centre

might have stood at the North Pole—they might have been placed against blank paper—for all the help they got from the immediate environment. Now that the subordinate buildings have been put up—the receiving hall, the power-plant, and even the policeman's booth at the entrance—that which was merely a cold piece of rationalistic mathematics has become one of the most brilliant pieces of modern music that any modern architect has produced: on all but the south side the buildings are united with their site, and, in the full sunlight, the delicate abstract detail at the topmost parts counts like the sound of the first violins in an orchestra. By themselves the high unbroken monotonous masses were barely tolerable: set off by subordinate buildings, in which the elementary beat of window and wall in the main mass is modified by different accents of window and wall and chimney, and even by different tones of brick, one beholds a breath-taking monument.

The important point to realize is that the small buildings in this group are just as clean and modern as skyscrapers: in other words, what is fresh and positive in contemporary design is just as capable of expression in two stories as in two hundred. Our partial success with the skyscraper does not mean that we can achieve no great æsthetic effects without height and bulk:

it means that the lessons we have learned in skyscraper design are capable of far wider application. And one further lesson from the Medical Centre: a great building derives its beauty not from the impression it makes on a photographic plate, but from the impression that it makes on a living spectator: a building that lacks the advantages of site can never achieve the utmost effect of great architecture. From where does one best see the Barclay-Vesey Building? From the Hudson. Where does one get the finest impression of Number One Fifth Avenue? From Washington Square, with the old low buildings in the foreground. The great miracle of the Medical Centre is that there are a hundred points of vantage: one of the most exhilarating views is from the Drive below, with only a fragment showing. When the architect more often has these advantages at hand, and when he has the courage to make use of them, we will have an architecture that will nourish the spirit and stimulate the mind, not fitfully, partially, accidentally, as now, but as continuously as happens during the walk along High Street in Oxford. Æsthetically, we are on the road to this architecture: socially and economically, we have still a long, difficult way to go.

Photograph by Sigurd Fischer

Swimming-pool, Greenhill Farm, near Philadelphia
John Irwin Bright and Harry Sternfeld, Architects

VICTOR FREEMONT LAWSON TOWER, CHICAGO THEOLOGICAL SEMINARY, CHICAGO, ILL.
HERBERT HUGH RIDDLE, ARCHITECT

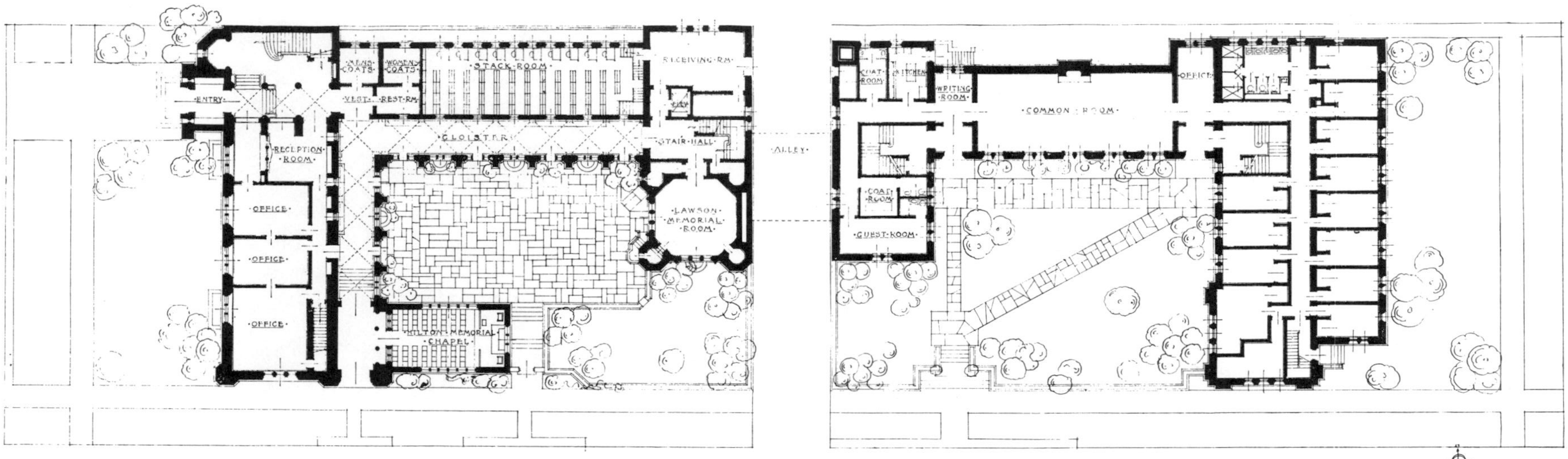

·FIRST·FLOOR·PLAN·

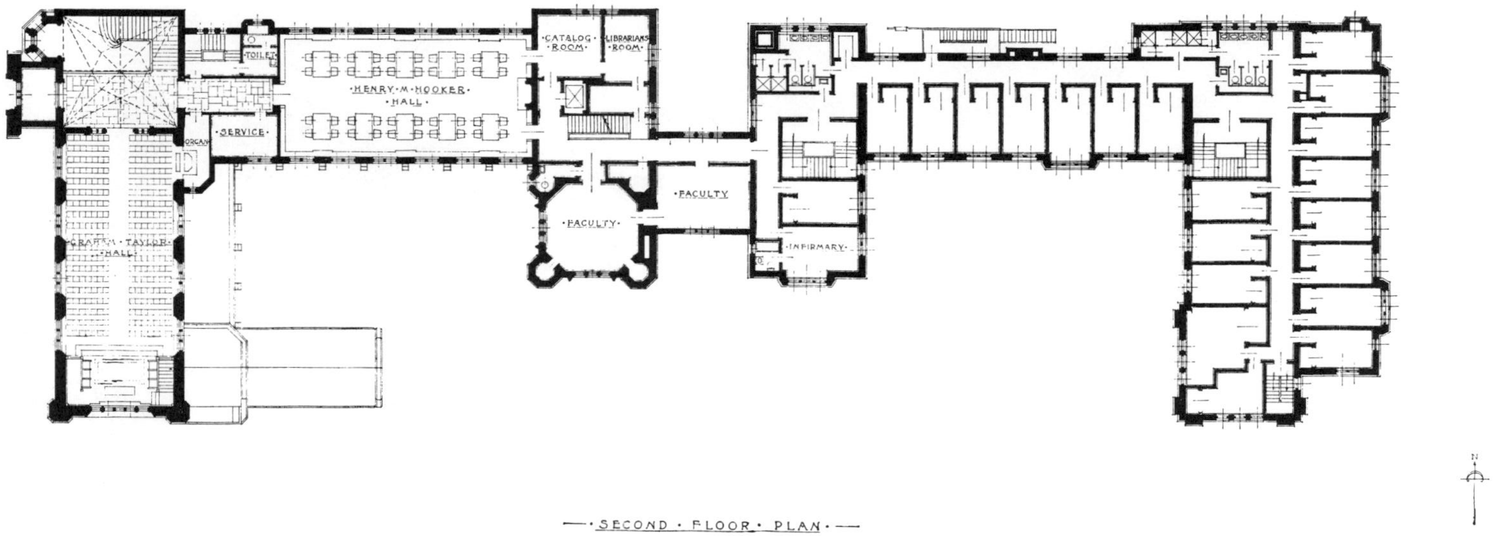

·OFFICE·

·COMMON·ROOM·

·WRITING·ROOM·

·COAT·KITCHEN·ROOM·

·COAT·ROOM·

·GUEST·ROOM·

·ALLEY·

·RECEIVING·RM·

·STAIR·HALL·

·LAWSON·MEMORIAL·ROOM·

·STACK·ROOM·

·CLOISTER·

·MAIN·REST·RM·

·WILLETT·MEMORIAL·CHAPEL·

·DAYS·COATS·

·RECEPTION·ROOM·

·OFFICE·

·OFFICE·

·OFFICE·

·ENTRY·

·SECOND·FLOOR·PLAN·

·CATALOG·ROOM·

·LIBRARIAN·ROOM·

·FACULTY·

·FACULTY·

·INFIRMARY·

·HENRY·M·HOOKER·HALL·

·TOILET·

·ORGAN·

·SERVICE·

·GRAFF·TAYLOR·HALL·

CHICAGO THEOLOGICAL SEMINARY

HERBERT HUGH RIDDLE, ARCHITECT

General view from university campus

General view from Woodlawn Avenue

CHICAGO THEOLOGICAL SEMINARY   HERBERT HUGH RIDDLE, ARCHITECT

The 58th Street entrance

Entrance on University Avenue

Main staircase

Corner of cloisters

CHICAGO THEOLOGICAL SEMINARY   HERBERT HUGH RIDDLE, ARCHITECT

Graham Taylor Hall, upper chapel

Chicago Theological Seminary   HERBERT HUGH RIDDLE, ARCHITECT

41

Hooker Memorial Library

Jessie Tree
window,
Graham
Taylor Hall

Nave window,
Graham
Taylor Hall

Glass work
designed and ex-
ecuted by
Willet Studios

CHICAGO THEOLOGICAL SEMINARY

HERBERT HUGH RIDDLE, ARCHITECT

42

BOOK TWO

Mass Production and the Modern House

1930

"Mass production which utilizes all the resources of community planning is capable of far greater and more numerous economies than mass production which only extends a little farther our current factory technique."

MASS-PRODUCTION AND THE MODERN HOUSE

I The Limits of Mechanization

DURING the last hundred and fifty years a great change has taken place in architecture. This change has nothing to do with the questions of superficial esthetics that agitated the architectural world: the quarrels between the classicists and the medievalists or between the traditionalists and the modernists are all meaningless in terms of it. I refer to the process whereby manufacture has step by step taken the place of the art of building, and all the minor processes of construction have shifted from the job itself to the factory.

How far this process has gone everyone is aware who has watched the composition of a building, and who knows how suddenly the whole work would stop if the architect were forced to design or specify with any completeness the hundred different parts, materials, and fixtures he draws from Sweet's Catalog. But what are the implications of this process? What results must it have on the status of the architect and the place of architecture in civilization? What further developments may we look forward to on the present paths: what alternatives suggest themselves?

Some of these questions can be answered: others will lead us to push beyond the current premises upon which the discussion of mass production and architecture is based.

II

By an ironic accident, the first use of fabricated parts in a building seems to have been ornamental: the plaster mouldings of the eighteenth century were introduced before the Franklin stove: but the age of invention ushered in a whole series of technical devices designed to increase the comfort or the efficiency of the dwelling house, and along with these improvements went a shift from handicraft to machine production. There are country districts in the United States where, until a few years ago, the kitchen sink would have been made of sheet zinc fitted over a box made by the carpenter, or where the ice-box might have been constructed in the same way. In the main, however, the shift was steady and inexorable: steam-heating, gas-lighting, electricity, baths, toilets, refrigerators, to say nothing of radio-connections and garages, have all led to the industrialization of architecture. Plaster, jig-saw, and cast-iron ornament, the first spontaneous gifts of industrialism, all happily diminished; but the technical improvements remained and multiplied.

In the great run of modern building, except in part the country homes of the rich, mass-manufacture has taken the place of local handicraft. The latter has remained in two places: the construction of the physical shell itself, and the assemblage of the individual parts

Now, this change was coincident with the withdrawal of the architect from the grand body of building during the early industrial period. The new factories and bridges and railroad stations were largely the work of engineers, while the great mass of private dwellings became the province of the speculative jerry-builder who, with a few stereotyped plans, created the dingy purlieus of all our large cities. The radical change that had taken place passed almost unnoticed, until during the last fifteen or twenty years the architect was called in to design small houses for industrial villages. He was then confronted with two brute facts: if he designed houses for industrial workers in the fashion that he did for the upper middle classes, it turned out that the costs were so high that only the middle classes could afford to live in them: that was the fate, for example, of Forest Hills, L. I. On the other hand, when he accepted the price limitations laid down by the industrial corporation, or, as in Europe, the municipal housing scheme, he suddenly discovered that he was no longer a free man.

ON THE WAY TOWARD STANDARDIZATION: A SECTOR OF BROOKLYN

The jerry-builder replacing the architect. Not only are stereotypes frequently repeated, but every house is largely an *assembly* of standard parts from the factory. Bathrooms have come; gardens have gone. Every house is but the visible shoot upon a great underground root mechanism, constituting "the land and its improvement."

Every variation he wished to introduce which departed from current practice was prohibitive in cost: his design was in fact little more than a composition of standardized patterns and manufactured articles. The elements were no longer under the architect's control; for the carpenter on the job could not construct a kitchen cabinet as well or as cheaply as the factory, nor had he spent so much time in finding out exactly what compartments and divisions the housewife preferred. As for windows, doors, bathroom equipment, the architect either had to accept them as they came from the factory, or he had to do without them altogether.

III

Needless to say, this revolutionary change had come about without any genuine renovation in design, and without any attempt to overcome the difficulties that the increase of manufactured articles brought with it. The chief of these difficulties, as Mr. Henry Wright was perhaps the first to point out, was that the building proper, without being cheaper in its own right, accounted for only forty-five to sixty per cent of the total cost, whereas a hundred years before it had represented, with its decoration and ornament, about ninety per cent of the total cost. Some accommodation to this condition was made; but the adjust-

Grosvenor Atterbury, Architect

THE ARCHITECT'S ATTEMPT TO INDIVIDUALIZE AN INDUSTRIAL VILLAGE: FOREST HILLS

An attempt that failed. The cost of spaciousness and individual design was too high for workers and the houses are now occupied by the middle classes. To the rear is seen the invasion of the jerry-building that must serve the poorer man who wishes to live in a "free-standing" house.

ment was a blind and fumbling one: now it came as jerry-building, a general cheapening of materials and workmanship, again it came as smaller rooms or fewer rooms per family, or finally, it came as an abandonment of handicraft on the remaining parts of the building, and the increase of ready-made equipment. Decoration had not so much vanished by itself, for lack of artistic talent, still less because of any doctrinaire prejudice against it: it had rather been absorbed, or at all events transformed into mechanical fixtures. The new costs of finance, mechanical fixtures, utilities, had to be met at some point in the design. Short of a proportional rise in the real income of wage-earners, there was no way of cementing the old requirements and the new in a single building.

In a word, building has shrunk, manufacture has expanded. One cannot suppose that this process will stop short at the shell. Apart from the fact that this has already been partly conquered—as yet, however, with no appreciable saving—in the mail-order wooden house, or in the sheet-iron garage, who doubts that the manufacturers of steel, aluminum or asbestos blocks, if not the large-scale motor manufacturers, looking for a new outlet for a market glutted with cars, will finally produce a light transportable shell, whose sections will be set up easily by unskilled labor? It would not be difficult to describe such a house: indeed, Mr. Buckminster Fuller in Chicago, and the Brothers Rasch in Germany have already gone a step beyond this. The chief differ-

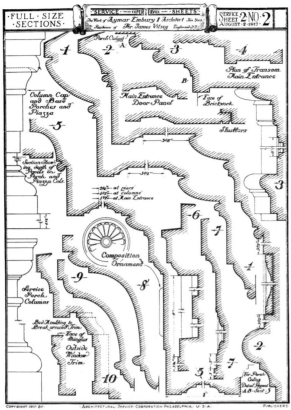

ALL THIS FOR A SINGLE CUSTOM-BUILT HOUSE

1917: The pride of the architect lay in giving every house, and every possible part of every house, its individual decorative treatment, specially full-sized and specially made. The effort was directed at what was very accurately named "enrichment." (House of Mr. James Wilsoy, Aymar Embury II, Architect.)

ence between the factory-manufactured house and the current product of the jerry-builder in Flatbush or West Philadelphia would be that in the first case the design would possibly bear some living relation to the elements out of which it is composed. The mass-house would probably be placed on a platform, if not on a pedestal, in order to provide garage space and avoid the expensive cellar; the plans would be standardized; the pipes and fittings and fixtures would be integral with the walls and ceilings, joined together by a turn of the wrench; and the use of light insulating materials would both facilitate transportation and permit the design of large windows which would otherwise, in cold weather, make a great drain on the heating system.

What would be the advantages of the completely manufactured house? There are many potential ones. First of all, the mass-house, like the motor car, will be able to call to its design and construction a corps of experts, sanitary engineers, heating engineers, hygienists, to say nothing of professors of domestic science, who will have their minds focussed, not upon solving indifferently an indeterminate number of problems, but upon getting a perfect solution for a fixed and limited problem. These research workers will have the opportunity to deal with fundamental mechanical and biological facts, without the distraction of attempting to compose these facts into a traditional frame, conceived when industry and family life were on an entirely different basis, and when the inventions of the last century were still but vague grandiose dreams in the minds of Utopians like Leonardo and Johann Andreae.

The introduction of this council of experts would undoubtedly hasten the rationalization of the modern house. A dozen standard plans, with all minor deviations ruled out, would probably take the place of the competitive chaos that provides our more traditional forms of monotony and squalor, or, as in the well-to-do suburb, of standardized "variety" and fake elegance. No one would be able to pretend that individuality and personality are achieved by meaningless departures on the drafting board from standard dimensions: once the mechanical requirements were granted, an equally mechanical solution would follow. The charm of good building, the charm due to the carpenter's or the mason's feeling for his material and site, would disappear; but as compensation there would be the austere clarity of good machinery; and since this charm is already a sentimental memory in most of our building, it is an illusion rather than a reality that would be destroyed. Undoubtedly the result would be "hard"; but such hardness is surely preferable to the spurious "softness" of imitation half-timbers, imitation slates, and imitation fires; and it would constitute a real improvement over the actual quarters in which a great part of the population now live.

There is no need to go here into the various technical improvements that may be possible in the mass-house. It is enough to assume that such matters as artificial cooling and heating, the removal of dust, and the utilization of sunlight would receive competent attention, and it is even possible that entirely untried methods, such as the heating of walls by electric grids, or complete insulation from outside air would be tested, if not incorporated in the mass-house. Such dwellings would represent a real advance from the standpoint of hygiene and constructive soundness; and since a good part of our population needs to be re-housed, its present quarters being unsanitary, crowded, vile, ugly, and entirely out of key with the best features in the modern environment, the mass-house holds out, on the surface, very attractive promises. Does the architect shrink from the prospect? He had better not. As a profession he has permitted something far worse than the scientifically designed mass-house, namely the unscientific one of the jerry-builder, to appear; and since he has shown as yet no capacity to face or master the real problem of housing, he cannot in all conscience turn away from this spectacle.

IV

Let us grant, then, the mechanical advantages of the mass-house; and along with this its practicability. We must now ask another question: to what extent would the mass-production of such houses be a solution of the housing problem, and how far would this form of manufacture meet all the needs that are involved in the dwelling house and its communal setting? Those who talk about the benefits of mass-production have been a little misled, I think, by the spectacular success of this method in creating cheap motor cars; and I believe they have not sufficiently taken into account some of its correlative defects. Let us consider a few of these.

First of all: the great attraction of the manufactured house is the promise not only of efficiency but of cheapness, due to the

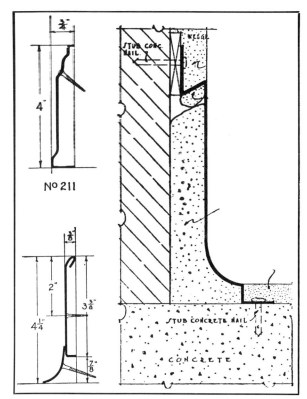

STANDARD PARTS FOR A THOUSAND BUILDINGS

1930: Showing the evolution of a metal baseboard from imitative decoration toward impeccable utility and clarity. Decoration has not vanished by itself because of prejudice against it: rather it has been absorbed or transformed into mechanical fixtures.

competitive production of houses in large quantities. It is doubtful if this will prove to be a great element in reducing the cost of housing. The reason is simple. The shell of the building is not the largest element in the cost; the cost of money, the rent of land, the cost of utilities, including streets, mains, sewers and sewage disposal plants, are among the major items on the bill. The two new spots where mass production would take the place of present methods, namely, in the shell itself, and in the assemblage of the parts, offer only a minor field for reductions. To cut the cost of the shell in half is to lower the cost of the house a bare ten per cent. The New York State Housing and Regional Planning Commission has shown that the lowering of the interest rate one per cent would effect as great a reduction; and the lowering of it to the level justified by the safety and dura-

MODEL OF THE "DYMAXION" HOUSE
BUCKMINSTER FULLER, DESIGNER*

bility of housing investments would reduce the costs far more drastically than the most ingenious cheese-paring on the structure.

Moreover, with respect to the other parts of the house, the fixtures, the mechanical apparatus, the finish, it remains true that while slight economies are possible through further standardization, a good part of these items is already produced by mass-methods —and most of the possible economies have been wrung out. Novelties in plan or design, such as those suggested in the Dymaxion house, should not obscure the fact that the great change in the shell is only a little change in the building as a whole. For lack of proper cost accounting our experimental architects have been butting their heads against this solid wall for years; but there is no reason why they should continue. Land, manufactured utilities, site-improvements, and finance call for a greater share of the cost than the "building" and labor. Mass production will not remedy this. To use cess-pools instead of sewers, artesian wells instead of a communal water system, and cheap farming land instead of

* Walls (no windows) of transparent casein; inflated duralumin floors; heat, light, refrigeration supplied to it individually, through central mast, by Diesel engine; water from well.

urban land, as some of the advocates of the manufactured house have suggested, is merely to camouflage the problem: and it is more than a little naive: for such expedients are temporary dodges, which may occasionally be favored by a sandy soil or inaccessibility to traffic, but they cannot count for two pins in any comprehensive and universal solution of the housing problem. There are many districts where an artesian well would cost as much as the house itself; and except in a communist society there are no spots on the earth where the Law of Rent is not operative—so that any large movement towards the open land, such as is now taking place fifty miles from New York, is immediately recorded in a conversion of farmland into building lots, with a swift rise in price. In short: the manufactured house cannot escape its proper site costs and its communal responsibilities.

The second hole in the program is the fact that mass-production brings with it the necessity for a continuous turnover. When mass-production is applied to objects that wear out rapidly, like shoes or rubber tires, the method may be socially valuable, although the late Thorstein Veblen has shown that some of these potential economies are nullified by the commercial habit of weakening the materials in order to hasten the pace of destruction. When, however, mass methods are applied to relatively durable goods like furniture or houses, there is great danger that once the original market is supplied, replacements will not have to be made with sufficient frequency to keep the original plant running. Our manufacturers of furniture and motors are driven desperately to invent new fashions in order to hasten the moment of obsolescence; beyond a certain point, technical improvements take second place and stylistic flourishes enter. It will be hard enough, in the depraved state of middle class taste, to keep our mass houses from being styled in some archaic fashion, pseudo-Spanish or pseudo-Colonial, as the fad of the day may be; and once mechanical improvements bring diminishing returns this danger will be a grave one.

MASS-PRODUCTION APARTMENT HOUSES HUNG ON MASTS
THE BROTHERS RASCH, GERMANY

Two rows of hollow masts with a set of passages between. The ground is clear. Masts hold one another in position by system of cables; anchored by cables; floors hung on cables. Proposed in 1928

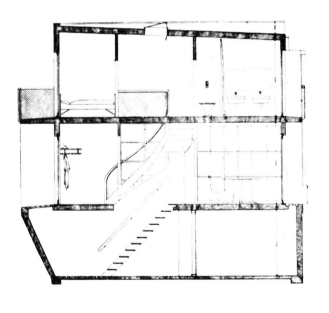
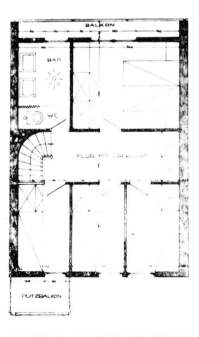

FROM ANOTHER CONTINUOUS ROW (STEEL HOUSES RESTING ON THE GROUND)
THE BROTHERS RASCH, GERMANY

There is still another defect in the manufactured house, just the opposite of the tendency to foist new style, in order to increase the turnover. One might call this the model T dilemma. Mass-production, just because it involves the utmost specialization in labor-saving machinery and the careful interlinkage of chain processes, suffers, as I have pointed out elsewhere, from rigidity, from premature standardization. When the cheapening of the cost is the main object, mass production tends to prolong the life of designs which should be refurbished. In the case of the dwelling house, the continuance of obsolete models would possibly be as serious as the rapid alterations of style; and it is hard to see how mass production can avoid either one or the other horn of this dilemma.

V

What, then, is the conclusion? So far as the manufactured house would base its claim upon its social value, that is, upon the possibility of lowering the cost of housing to the point where new and efficient dwellings could be afforded by the owners of Ford cars, its promises are highly dubious. Granting every possible efficiency in design or manufacture, the mass-house, without any site attachments, would still represent an expenditure of from six to ten times the amount invested in automobiles of similar grade; and this leaves us pretty much in our present dilemma. The new houses might well be better than the present ones—they could scarcely be worse. But, if better, they would not be radically cheaper, and since a new cost, a cost that is excessive in the motor industry, namely competitive salesmanship, would be introduced, the final results promise nothing for the solution of our real housing problem—the housing of the lower half of our income groups, and particularly, of our unskilled workers. The manufactured house no more faces this problem than the semi-manufactured house that we know today.

This does not mean that the processes of manufacture will not continue to invade the

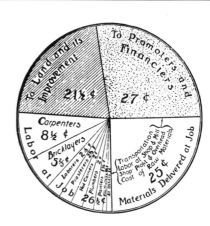

"A LARGE SAVING IN THE SHELL IS A SMALL SAVING IN THE FINAL HOUSE"

A little more than half of the building cost goes for construction itself. The shaded areas in this chart of the construction dollar represent factors of land and financing that mass production cannot very much affect

Chart from *Primer of Housing*, by Arthur C. Holden and others, Workers' Education Bureau Press

modern house; nor does it mean that the architect's present position in relation to the problem is a happy one. The question is whether he is able to devise an approach to the housing problem and to house design which will bring with it all the efficiencies promised by the Brothers Rasch or by Mr. Buckminster Fuller, and which will at the same time give scope to the particular art and technique of which he is master. Is there perhaps a more radical approach to the problem of housing than the engineer and the mechanically-minded architect have conceived? I think there is; for though Mr. Fuller for example believes that he has swept aside all traditional tags in dealing with the house, and has faced its design with inexorable rigor, he has kept, with charming unconsciousness, the most traditional and sentimental tag of all, namely, the free-standing individual house. If we are thorough enough in our thinking to throw that prejudice aside, too, we may, I suspect, still find a place for the architect in modern civilization. I shall deal with the alternative to the purely mechanical solution of our problem in a second article.

MASS PRODUCTION AND THE MODERN HOUSE

II The Role of Community Planning

IN modern architecture, I pointed out in my first article, the emphasis has shifted from building to manufacture. Since the parts of a building have been industrialized, it has naturally occurred to certain intelligent designers that the whole might eventually be treated in the same manner: hence various schemes for single family unit-houses, designed for greater mechanical efficiency. Those who approach the problem of the modern house from this angle suggest that the mass house may eventually be manufactured as cheaply and distributed as widely as the cheap motor car.

Although this development holds out promise for definite improvements in functional relationship and design, there is some reason to doubt, I pointed out, that costs could be cheapened as radically as the advocates of a purely mechanical improvement have supposed. A good part of the total cost of housing is represented by factors which, like the cost of money or land, are outside the province of factory production, or, like the numberless constituent parts of the house, are already cheapened by mass production. The mass house promises a better mechanical integration. That would constitute an advance; but not an overwhelming one; and the mere ability to purchase such houses easily and plant them anywhere would only add to the communal chaos that now threatens every semi-urban community.*

We have now to see whether there is not a different line of advance which rests upon a more thorough comprehension of all the social and economic as well as the technical elements involved. Without abandoning a single tangible gain in technique, there is, I think, a more promising road that, so far

* Mr. Buckminster Fuller already perceives this danger. "The Dymaxion Houses," he writes me, "cannot be thrown upon the world without a most adequate 'town plan,' really a universal community plan."

from eliminating the architect, will restore him to a position of importance.

II

Taking the individual house as a starting point, it is by now hopeless to attempt to restore it to a central position in domestic architecture. The individuality of such houses is already lost. Except for a bare ten or fifteen per cent of the population, such houses cannot be produced by individual architects, attempting to meet the unique wishes of a special client. The words Colonial, Cotswold, Tudor, in suburban architecture are mere attempts to cover by literary allusion the essential standardization that has taken place; and as soon as we approach the price level of the ordinary run of house dwellers, clerks, salesmen, skilled industrial workers, to say nothing of the more unskilled operations and the more poorly paid trades, the game is already lost; the manufactured shingle, the roughly turned colonial ornament, or the plaster "half-timber" show the strain on the purse.

Admirable as is the layout, the pervading conception, of our first American attempt at a "town for the Motor Age," for example, no candid critic can pretend that the individual one-family houses are particularly triumphant examples of modern architecture; and the reason is that even with large-scale organization and limited dividends, it is impossible to isolate such houses sufficiently and lavish upon them the attention that so graciously humanized the traditional house even as late as 1890. Architecturally, these studiously suburban types fall down badly beside the finer rows and quadrangles of Sunnyside, the work of the same architects; and if anyone thinks he can do better with the cheap free-standing house, let him try it.

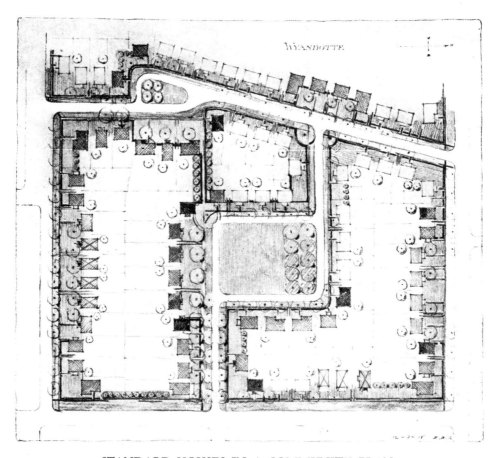

STANDARD HOUSES IN A COMMUNITY PLAN

A WAR-TIME DEVELOPMENT, WYANDOTTE, MICH., BY HENRY WRIGHT

These are still individual houses, but three main types suffice for both practical and picturesque requirements, because they are an integral part of a community plan

The isolated domestic unit cannot be made sound, beautiful, and efficient except at a prohibitive cost. If we wish to retain the single-family house, we shall have to accept it as a completely manufactured article; and in this event, we must throw overboard every sentimental demand. The advocates of the single-family house have never faced this dilemma: they dream of universalizing the work of Mr. Frank Foster or Mr. Julius Gregory; but the sort of domicile that their ideas actually effectuate for the majority of the population are the dreary rows of West Philadelphia and Astoria.

III

Now, a careful economic analysis shows that there are four possibilities from among which we must choose, if we are to have the renovated domestic architecture we so badly need, namely:

We may reduce the cost of housing from thirty to forty per cent by foregoing all the mechanical utilities we have introduced during the last hundred years. This would enable us to spend enough upon the structure and the materials to produce a fairly good looking traditional house. As a practical feat, this could be accomplished only in the country; and nobody would regard it as a serious remedy for the housing problem: so we may dismiss it.

Or, second: we may raise the wages of the entire industrial population to such an extent that they will be able to make a demand for houses of the same grade that the upper middle classes now create. This is not entirely outside the bounds of possibility; but it would necessitate an economic

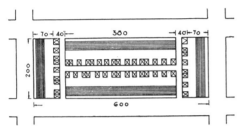

JERRY-BUILDING AND CLUTTER

There is no guarantee that this condition will be remedied by mass-production. The problems which most affect this community might be left untouched, or aggravated by the addition of more random contraptions.

But *community* planning at Sunnyside, Long Island, has so rearranged the same type of block that the building space regained permits economical removal of cluttering garages to another block; there is

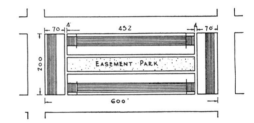

ARCHITECTURE AND OPEN SPACE

revolution, not alone in the distribution of incomes, but in a maintenance of the entire industrial plant up to the pitch of wartime productivity. Since we cannot create decent single houses for the relatively comfortable middle class today, it is doubtful if this could be accomplished even under an energetic and efficient communism. In order to make good housing practicable, the wages of the lower income groups will indeed have to be raised, either directly or under the disguise of a subsidy; but no rise will bring back the one-family house in an urban area that possesses a complete municipal and civic equipment, including waterworks and sewers and schools.

Or, third: we can preserve the individual isolated unit at the price of accepting all the limitations that now accompany it: lack of open spaces, scantiness of materials, lack of privacy, rapid deterioration of equipment, and lack of esthetic interest. Some of these evils would be mitigated or removed completely in the ideal manufactured house; but others, as I showed in my first article, would remain under our current system of commercial production.

Or, finally, we may seek to establish an integral architecture. This means that instead of beginning with one aspect of the architectural problem, we will begin with the community first, and treat the problems of economics, community planning, technics, and architecture as one, seeking a solution not in terms of the individual "cell" but in terms of the larger unit. This last scheme would derive the character of the house or apartment from the particular social whole of which it is a part; and the solution would not be a fixed quantity, but a variable, adapted to soil, climate, landscape, industrial conditions, racial groupings, and the whole remaining complex that makes up a human community. Instead of crabbing our solution by asking before anything else how shall the single-family house be preserved, we ask the broader question: how shall the fundamental requisites of domestic life be embodied in a modern community program—and that is a radically different matter!

The last course is the only one that really sweeps the board clear of preconceptions and inherited prejudices and faces the problem of the house as it comes before us in the Western World in the year 1930. Unfortunately, there is a considerable vested interest opposed to it: not merely the interest of the small builder, used to doing things in a small way, or the individual home-buyer who has been vainly dreaming of the twenty-thousand dollar house he will some day buy for a thousand dollars down and the balance in installments, but against it are such organized bodies as the "own-your-own-home" movement, to say nothing of a good many sincere and honest people who have concerned themselves with the evils of congested housing. We have all these groups, to say nothing of the standard Fourth-of-July orator, to thank for the notion that the free-standing individual house must be preserved at any cost, as if "home" and America were inconceivable without it.

Most of the arguments that support this sentiment are specious and fundamentally unsound; but they still carry an air of respectability. The individual free-standing house was as much a product of the Romantic movement as Byronic collars: it was the formal counterpart of the completely free and isolated "individual," and to look upon it as an immemorial expression of the "home" is to betray a pretty complete ignorance of human history—an ignorance that one can condone only because an adequate history of the dwelling house in all its transformations has still to be written. Spurred on by this romantic conception of the home, its partisans blindly cling to the poor mangled remnant of a free-standing house that remains in the outskirts of our great cities, rather than the fact that these dwellings are, in fact, sardonic betrayals of all the virtues they profess to admire, and possess scarcely a single tangible advantage. Under the cloak of individuality, personality, free expression, the partisans

A STANDARD HOUSE

One of the repeated units in the plan on page 111. Properly designed and placed, even the individual standard house need not be unattractive

of the free-standing house have accepted the utmost refinements of monotony and unintelligent standardization.

Unfortunately, intelligent planning and design on a community scale cannot proceed until this prejudice is knocked into a cocked hat. It is not until the architect has the courage to reject the detached house as an abstract ideal that he will have the opportunity to embody in his designs some of the advantages and beauties that are supposed to go with such a house. That is the paradox of modern architecture: we can achieve individuality only on a communal scale; and when we attempt to achieve individuality in isolated units, the result is a hideous monotony, uneconomic in practice and depressing in effect. We have sometimes succeeded in our synthetic buildings, the hospital, the office building, the apartment house and the domestic quadrangle: we fail, we will continue to fail, in the isolated house. In my first article I pointed out the economic and mechanical reasons for this failure; and I have now to suggest in concrete terms a more favorable program of work.

IV

The aim of an integral architecture, like the aim of the purely mechanical and constructivist architects, is to effect an economy which will raise and spread the standards of the modern house. Where is this economy to be effected, and how is it to be embodied in design? It is here that the difference in approach between the two methods comes out. Are we to attempt to incorporate in the individual house all the improvements made possible by a communal technology, duplicating every item as we now duplicate radio sets and vacuum cleaners, or shall the individual cell be simplified and the costs of all our new mechanical devices distributed through the whole group of cells, careful community planning being used to reduce the cost of equipment?

A concrete example will perhaps make the difference in approach a little clearer. Take a matter like the supply of fresh air. Apart from any human pleasure that may come from the gesture of throwing wide the window and taking in a breath of purer or cooler air, there is no doubt that the problem of pure air can be mechanically solved by means of an artificial ventilating system, which will clean, humidify, and warm at the same time. In certain places and under certain circumstances this system is highly desirable; but, however practicable it is, no one can doubt that its extension to the dwelling house would only add one further element of expense to that vexatious column of expenses which has been lengthening so rapidly during the last thirty years. Instead of working in this direction, an integral architecture, for the sake of economy, would endeavor to secure through site planning and site development, through orientation to sunlight and wind, a result that can otherwise be obtained only through an expensive mechanical contrivance. In a word: the mechanical system accepts all the factors in house production as fixed, except the mechanical ones: an integral architecture looks upon all the elements as variables and demands a measure of control over all of them.

This demand may seem to pass beyond the limits of pure architecture, and the architect may be reluctant to make it. No matter: he will be driven to it for the reason that the house itself has passed beyond the limits of mere building. The modern house functions as a house only in relation to a whole host of communal services and activities. The rate of interest, the wage-scale, the availability of water and electricity, the topography and the character of the soil, and the community plan itself, all have as great a control over the design as the type of building material or the method of construction. It is fantastic to think that adequate design is possible if all these other elements are determined by forces outside the governance of either the architect or the community. There are, accordingly, two critical places which the architect must capture and make his own if he is to solve the social and esthetic problem of the modern house: one of them is the manufacturing plant, and the other is the community itself. With the part that the architect has still to play in industrial design, I can not deal here; but something must be said further of the relation of modern architecture to the work of the community planner.

V

The unit, bear in mind, is no longer the individual house, but a whole neighborhood or community; and the place where collective economies are sought is not merely in factory production, but at every point in the layout or development. In Europe, where a serious attempt has been made, particularly during the last ten years, to cope with the housing of the industrial worker, such schemes are usually fostered by an existing municipality, as in Amsterdam and London, since there are no constitutional limitations upon the housing activities of cities in most European states: in America, apart from dubiously paternal attempts at better housing, undertaken by mill towns, the integration of architecture and community planning has been the work of the limited dividend corporation, such as the Russell Sage Foundation of the new City Housing Company, or the more far-sighted real estate developers, such as the founders of Roland Park in Baltimore.

The right political and economic form for modern community building is perhaps one of the most important social questions that architecture must face; all the more because there is no likelihood that private capital will enter the field whilst fabulous profits can be wrung out of less vital business enterprises. The instigation of such enterprises is not the private job of the architect; but it is a public matter where the weight of professional opinion may legitimately be thrown on the side of the public interest. Plainly, the architect cannot solve by any magical incantations the problem of supplying new houses to families whose income is not sufficient to cover the annual charges. There is no answer to that question except, as I said earlier, in the form of higher wages or state subsidy; although a wilful blindness to this fact is almost enough to establish a person as a housing authority in the United States. An integral type of architecture, seeking economies at every point in the process, is possible only when the necessary corporate housing organization has been erected.

Economy begins with the selection of the site itself, since the modern city, with its underground articulation, cannot be cheaply produced on a rocky or extremely irregular terrain. The next step is in the design of the street and road system. Here the differentiation of domestic neighborhoods from commercial or factory areas, and their permanent protections through easements, restrictions, and zoning of the land, not alone keeps the land-values low—since there is no speculative temptation through possible changes of use—but reduces the cost of paving and utilities connections. Mr. Raymond Unwin made a great advance in community planning over twenty years ago, when he proved that there is "Nothing Gained by Overcrowding" since the burden of multiple streets beyond a definite point more than counterbalances the apparent economy of more numerous lots; and Mr. Henry Wright has more than once demonstrated that there is enough wasted street space in the average American neighborhood to provide it with an adequate park—a demonstration which has now been effectively embodied in the plan of Radburn. The grouping of houses in rows and quadrangles, instead of their studied isolation, is a further factor in economy, not merely by making the party wall take the place of two exterior ones, but by reducing the length of all street utilities, including the paving of the street itself; and the result is a much bolder and more effective architectural unit than the individual house.

With control over these exterior developments, the problem of the interior economies is reduced and simplified; indeed, the two elements are co-ordinate in design, and if architects produced their work on the site instead of in the office, and did not habitually conceal the site costs from their clients —as "additional charges"—they would long ago have perceived this. Emerson said that one should save on the low levels and spend on the high ones; and one cannot improve upon this advice, either in living or in the design of houses. It is a mistake in esthetic theory to assume that the demands of vision and economy, of esthetic pleasure and bodily comfort, always coincide; and an important task of integral architecture is to balance one against the other. Where the means are limited, the architect must exercise a human choice between, say, an extra toilet and a second story balcony, between a tiled bathroom and a more attractive entrance.

This choice cannot be made on any summary abstract principle; it is determined by a multitude of local individual factors: the presence of mosquitos or the absence of large open spaces may, for example, decide the fate of the balcony. If the architect be limited in such local choices, he may have to spend riotously on mechanical equipment; if he have a free hand in community planning, he may let nature take the place of an extra heating unit, an awning, or what not. Again: if a family is forced to look out upon a blank wall, as so many rich people must do on Park Avenue or Fifth, expensive mouldings, draperies, fineries may be necessary to relieve the depression of the outlook: if on the other hand, sunlight and garden-vistas are available, a wide window may take the place of much footling architectural "charm."

In sum, mass production which utilizes all the resources of community planning is capable of far greater and more numerous economies than mass production which only extends a little farther our current factory technique. Such a program for the modern house holds out no spurious promises of a quick, ready-made solution for the difficulties that have been heaping up in every industrial community for the last hundred and fifty years. On the contrary, it isolates the problems of housing which are immediately soluble, from those that can be solved only through a drastic reorientation of our economic institutions; and it paves the way for necessary changes and adaptations in these institutions. If we are to modernize the dwelling house and create adequate quarters for our badly housed population—a far more important remedy for industrial depression than merely building roads—the architect must bring together all the specialized approaches to this problem, instead of merely trying to catch up with the latest specialty. The correct attack was initiated during the war in the governmental war housing program; it has been carried further during the last ten years, by architects and community planners such as Messrs. Stein, Wright, Ackerman, Kilham, Greeley, and Nolen; and although the designs of these men have so far kept close to traditional forms, their approach gives promise of a vital architecture which will in time surpass the work of the present pioneers as their own work surpasses that of the jerrybuilder.

BOOK THREE

The Life, the Teaching and the Architecture of Matthew Nowicki

1954

"Perhaps the life of no other architect so well reveals the dilemmas and choices that have presented themselves to the modern architect; or so sensitively indicates the direction that a more humane culture must take, if it is to save itself from the sterility and dehumanization that now threatens our civilization."

The Life, the Teaching and the Architecture of

MATTHEW NOWICKI

This, the first of four articles, deals with Nowicki's early background and education

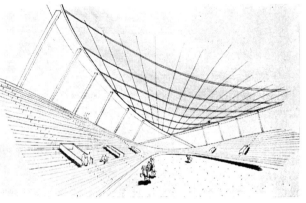

MATHEMATICIANS AND POETS often do their best work before they are thirty; but in the nature of things, the discipline of architecture requires a longer apprenticeship and it is a rare architect, like John Wellborn Root or Frank Lloyd Wright who gives the measure of his genius before he is forty. Matthew Nowicki * belongs in this special group. Though he left behind even fewer buildings than Root or Wright at the same age, he created at least one structure, the Arena at the State Fair in Raleigh, that establishes his place as definitively as the Monadnock Building establishes Root's. In addi-

Matthew Nowicki

tion, a wide variety of designs, culminating in his plans and sketches for Chandigarh, and a few succinct but brilliant papers on the nature of architecture all add to the impression he made upon those who knew him: that he had every prospect of becoming the outstanding architect of the coming generation.

The impression that Matthew Nowicki made as a man, his sensitiveness to his environment, his depth of feeling, his self-discipline and humility, raised even higher one's estimation of his potentialities as an architect. In him one felt that a new type of man had taken form: one capable of overcoming the barbarisms and automatisms of our time, one who would bring order and beauty, human purpose and the human scale back into daily life. At the time of the wanton plane accident that brought his life to an end, Nowicki was still growing. His Indian sketches, the work of a lonely summer in the foothills of the Himalayas, were already carving new channels through which the currents of his own creativity could flow. Long before, these currents had carried him beyond the well-explored territory of tradi-

Pronounced Novitski

tional forms; and now they promised to take him just as far beyond the fashionable stopping places of the contemporary mode.

Perhaps the life of no other architect so well reveals the dilemmas and choices that have presented themselves to the modern architect; or so sensitively indicates the direction that a more humane culture must take, if it is to save itself from the sterility and dehumanization that now threatens our civilization. Nowicki's work already showed greatness; but his potentialities go far beyond his visible accomplishment. To understand his life, to follow the process of his education, to evaluate his work, is to have a better grip on one of the great problems that every architectural school is now wrestling with. What are the essential elements in an architect's education? Though genius cannot be manufactured, it may be malformed by bad feeding and it can be nourished by a good diet. Hence Nowicki's reflections on education, which were brought to a focus when he became senior Professor of Design at the School of Design at the State College in Raleigh, N. C. are not the least of his contributions. Fortunately, on these matters, I have his prepared papers and lectures, as well as the testimony of his wife and co-worker, to supplement my own memories of numerous conversations.

1. The Background of a European Modern

Matthew Nowicki was born on June 26, 1910, into a Polish family that belonged, like so much of Poland itself, to an older day: a family with sufficient means to disregard extraneous economic pressures and sufficient social status to disdain any serious effort to seek wealth and power for their own sake. This is the group, now getting smaller in every country, from which the gifts of detachment, large-mindedness, devotion to public service and high causes, so often come. Though the Nowickis lived in Warsaw, they were attached to the country; and Matthew's father was for long the leader of the Agrarian Party, though in his earlier years he had served as legal expert or Consul in areas as far apart as Siberia, where Matthew happened to be born, and Chicago, where, happily, he spent a couple of formative years during his adolescence, acquiring his knowledge of the English language, and his love for the disarming friendliness and the free ways that characterized American life. When he entered the Warsaw Polytechnic in 1929, Nowicki's main aptitude seemed to be in drawing, rather than in architecture proper, and this school, though affiliated more to engineering than the fine arts, gave him plenty of scope for his talents. His professors in art distinguished here between the needs of the

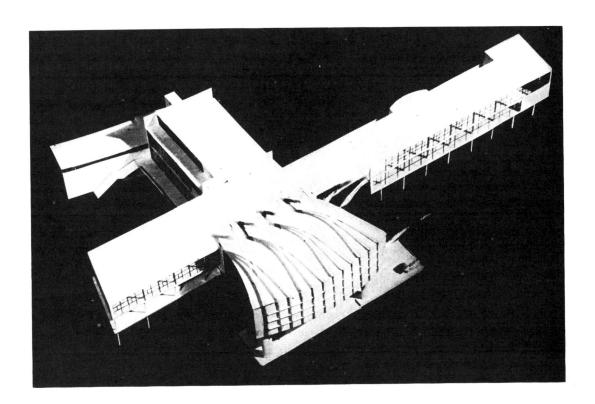

The daring and imagination of Nowicki showed in his earliest work. Model photos above and left show his college thesis, done in 1936, representing an architects' building for Warsaw. The model for a mosque (lower left) and the one (below) of a sports center are also examples of work done before the war changed everything in Poland, including architectural thinking. The sports center was completed in time to be destroyed by the first bomb to hit Warsaw. It was built, incidentally, without the little projecting wing; in fact, the model was actually done to show how awkward this part of the specifications would be

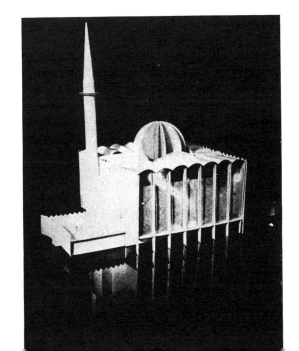

NOWICKI'S WARSAW WORK

FOR NOWICKI, as for most of the young architects of Europe in the nineteen-thirties, Le Corbusier had found the answer to the problem of modern form. But during the desolate period of the war, he and the architects about him in Poland underwent an experience Le Corbusier had not prepared them for, the resurrection of national sentiment, the desire to recapture the ties — once so easily tossed aside — with their own national past. As a result, the structures Nowicki designed during the war, offices in the Warsaw business quarter, were outwardly classic buildings: classic in feeling if not in detail, with individual windows treated in a repeating pattern, severe and well ordered.

This mode of architectural treatment contrasted with the boldness of the urban pattern; for here Nowicki had willingly absorbed all that modern planning could give: the superblock, the pedestrian scale within that block, buildings only four stories high to reduce congestion, with only an occasional tower for vertical accent; and he had conceived of using the dismaying heaps of rubble of ruined Warsaw, by placing these buildings on a mound formed of this very rubble, with the avenues running in channels below the levels of the blocks. The structures themselves, it is true, were conceived on a modular basis; but then classicism itself, strictly interpreted, always had a modular basis.

This return to classic order gave Nowicki practice in the planning of free-standing buildings, visible on four sides, set apart by gardens and pedestrian malls. But even at this period Nowicki's inventive genius could not rest content with a classic solution, however well it fitted the modular necessities of prefabrication. In his sketch for a public forum, a connecting link in space between the business quarter and the Cathedral across the river, he indicated a circular

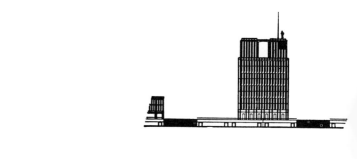

painter and those of the architect: they were interested in drawing, not as symbol and expression, but as a means of opening the young architect's eyes "to the nature of his surroundings," as Nowicki recorded, and to "teach him to see things as structures. To this end a drawing was built, with skeletons of structural lines exposed. In many instances even the use of shades and shadows was forbidden." In other words, drawing, as practiced in the Warsaw Polytechnic, was primarily a means of exact analysis, intellectual as well as visual, and in the end an organ of structural synthesis. In each case, the purposes of architecture defined the method of teaching. That discipline was one of the solid foundation stones of Nowicki's education, and his skill with pen and pencil made it possible for him in later life to translate his architectural ideas swiftly into the third dimension, treating plan and elevation as one, a trait he admired in Frank Lloyd Wright's freehand sketches.

Nowicki's talent as an architect matured slowly, or perhaps it would be more accurate to say that his singular aptitude and originality were at first only slowly noted by others. So many personal qualities were in his favor that his professional potentials were perhaps overshadowed by his social graces.

When his future wife met him at school she had no doubt of his architectural genius; but, as so often happens in academic life, it was she who often carried off the prizes, and it was to her, rather than to her future partner, that her professors looked as to a future architect of distinction. And perhaps her teachers were not altogether mistaken, for from the beginning to the end of his professional career theirs was the closest of partnerships; so close that they had a common signature for the work they did together in illustrating books and designing fabrics. As sympathetic critic and catalyst, if not always reagent, the wife played a productive part in the husband's work.

Nowicki's years of professional study were punctu-

building, with its roof held in suspension from the steel posts about the perimeter, placed like the candles in a birthday cake. These Warsaw designs are notable, not only because their human scale contrasts with that of Le Corbusier's City of the Future, extravagantly emphasizing its man-dwarfing heights, but because they are conceived in four dimensions, with a constant change in relationships due not merely to pedestrian movement itself but to changes in levels and angles of approach.

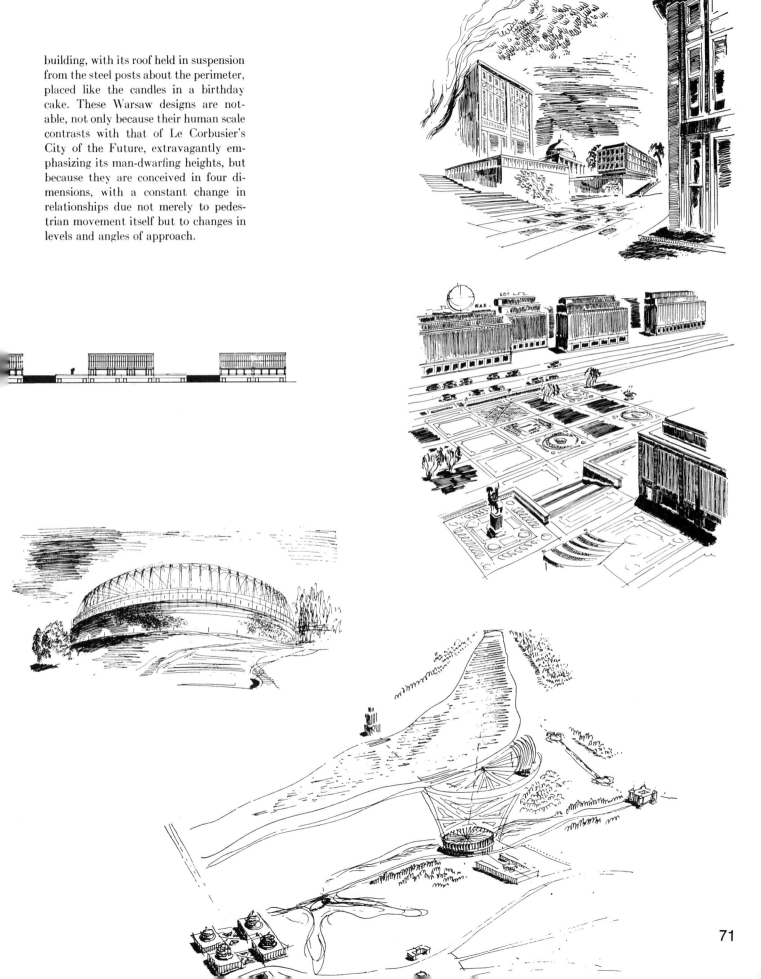

ated by wide travel. Before he was graduated in 1936, he had travelled, sketchbook in hand, over most of Europe, as far as Athens. He even visited Brazil before it became an architectural exhibition piece. His first-year course in Greek and Roman history caused him to spend a whole vacation in Rome, confining his explorations wholly to the historic ruins of the Forum. After that his prescribed course gave a year to medieval history, and two years to contemporary history, starting with Bramante and ending with Le Corbusier: all this in addition to the history of Polish architecture, in which much attention was paid to the traditional wooden structures with their ingenious and highly wrought forms. So thorough was this teaching, so well knit was it with personal explorations, that Nowicki had, as a constant standard of reference, the entire architectural and civic past of Europe, and not a little of America. There was nothing in his education that would confuse originality with

enough money to go travelling. This strenuous professional training was mixed with an equally strenuous and dashing social life: brilliant formal dances, elegant rather than Bohemian, or skiing parties in the Carpathian mountains over long weekends. The pace was swift; the training rugged; the vitality high — all facts that stood Nowicki in good stead during the grim days of the occupation and the even darker days of the "premature" uprising — that uprising the Russians prompted and then betrayed, so that their political rivals, liberal or socialist or conservative, should all be liquidated before their occupation.

The Warsaw Polytechnic in the nineteen-thirties was, like almost every similar school in the West, in process of transition; but that very fact perhaps gave Nowicki the best of both worlds. On one hand was well-knit curriculum uniting traditional architecture, with its humanistic background, and engineering with its scien-

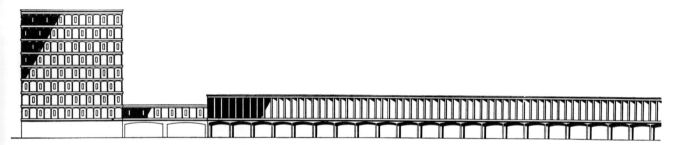

Modular design was a principle much stressed in Nowicki's work, as a basic discipline of architecture. This is a textile mill building for the mill town of Zrardow, Poland

deliberate illiteracy, or would treat contemporary forms as if they existed in an architectural void, like a space ship cut loose from the gravitational pull of history. From the beginning of the course, the students of architecture at the Polytechnic had both a sound and exhaustive training in engineering, and they were encouraged to work on building projects or find a job in a professional architect's office. To make this "work-and-learn" program easier, the students were not kept to the close time-schedule of an American school. Instead of a series of short problems, they had only two or three designs to work on each year, at their own pace. What counted was the finished work. Their professors set the problems and criticized the results. What happened between was the student's business.

So effective was the general education of the architects that in competition with regular Beaux Arts students the architectural students walked away with the honors in poster-making and other forms of commercial art; indeed, it was in this fashion that many of them eked out their wages or allowances and got

tific and technical methodology. At the same time the students' minds were opened to a new flood of critical ideas, esthetic images, social projects advanced by the new leaders of architecture, Le Corbusier, Oud, Gropius. As happened in America, it was the students, rather than the faculty, that clamored to be released from archaic historical patterns: Le Corbusier, in a series of eloquent books and a few buildings that photographed rather better than they functioned, had opened up for them a new world of form. Their professors, when the students submitted a new design might say indulgently, as one of them habitually did: "This is an interesting solution. It contains many good *and* original elements. Unfortunately, what is good is not original, and what is original is not good."

As with most of his fellow students, Le Corbusier was at first Nowicki's god: the house he designed for his parents in the country was pure Le Corbusier, almost to the last detail. Le Corbusier gave this generation a formula, almost as elementary as a painting by Mondrian, for achieving modern form: the result was crisp, elegant, photogenic, easily identifiable without reference to any quality except the esthetic one. One built in concrete, or covered brick with stucco to make it look like concrete; one divorced the building from the ground by setting it on columns; one used a flat roof and flat windows that formed a continuous surface with the wall; one avoided ornament and one ostentatiously used a machine form, like a chickenwire fence, as a final symbol of emancipation from the past, of identification with the mechanized present. If the result could not always stand up under inspection as architecture, it was at least identifiable as a symbol of the modern. A machine for living. Was not a truly modern life one dominated by scientific principles and dedicated to the machine?

Nowicki never wavered in his personal loyalty to Le Corbusier, and the esthetic appeal of Le Corbusier's formalism, the latest expression of a cartesian logic that had been born in Alberti and Bramante, long before Descartes himself, never ceased to appeal to him. So it says something for Nowicki's early maturation as an architect that after passing under the discipline of Le Corbusier, he followed exactly the opposite course to that of his master: he sought out the work of Auguste Perret, to pick up all the threads that Le Corbusier had dropped in his attempt to carry into architecture the painter's esthetic of the Cubist and the Purist.

As a beginner Nowicki sought release from historic forms in the two-dimensional freedoms of the painter; then he returned, with Perret, to the four-dimensional problems of architecture, and submitted to the discipline of the structure itself as a work of engineering, not scene painting, and to the highly articulated plan for the orderly and economic arrangement of the functions to be served. Nowicki admired in particular Perret's use of ferro-concrete, and saw in his work the true continuation of the great Gothic builders whose adventurous engineering had been dismissed in the formal designs — usually so unadventurous, if not regressive, in their technical demands — of the Renaissance painter-architect. In both Le Corbusier and Perret, Nowicki was attracted to the spirit of discipline: but in Le Corbusier it was the discipline of the eye, while in Perret, so-to-say, it was the kinesthetic discipline of the hand and the body as a whole, with the eye cooperating, not dominating. Loving Le Corbusier, he could understand the contemporary meaning of a Palladio, a Vignola, a San Gallo: their buildings, when he beheld them in Italy, exactly met his highest expectations.

Through Perret, coming after Viollet-le-Duc, Nowicki achieved a new insight into the Gothic, a moment in architectural history to which Le Corbusier, in his earlier days, was characteristically blind. By this means Nowicki was prepared for the revelation that came to him when finally, in 1947, he visited Frank Lloyd Wright at Taliesin in Spring Green. For here was an architecture, he confessed to his wife, for which neither Le Corbusier nor Palladio had prepared him. Though as a student he knew every detail of Taliesin by heart, the living reality overwhelmed him. Le Corbusier's buildings, at best, lived up to their photographs: Wright's masterpieces in their richness of organic form, went far beyond anything that two-dimensional reproduction could convey. What Perret had begun in Nowicki's life, Wright was to complete, though to the end he would be irritated by Wright's idiosyncrasies in detail, and by the same token for Le Corbusier's kind of formal elegance was perhaps deepened by his later acquaintance with the formally impeccable buildings of Mies van der Rohe, in Chicago.

2. The Ordeal of the Occupation

From his professional beginning, in 1936, things went Nowicki's way. He not only became an associate professor of architecture at his own Polytechnic, but his private practice soon was an important one: he received

Prefabrication was another principle taken seriously by Nowicki. This model of an office building was a study of design possibilities in prefabrication

73

METAMORPHOSIS OF A CHURCH DESIGN

Nowicki's first church design (upper left) is not too far from traditional churches seen in Poland. The larger one (above and left) is a great step forward. Though modular design again introduces a classic note, the wall is entirely separate from the roof, which is supported on tall mushroom columns from within the church. Outwardly the building maintains a sympathy for the traditional church already on the site, and the symbolism of the cross is strongly brought out. Third in this series of churches, designed in Nowicki's Warsaw days (opposite page, section below) represents a still more imaginative use of the mushroom column, and a freer interpretation of church symbolism

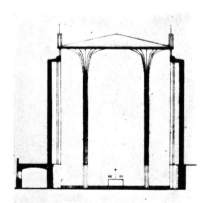

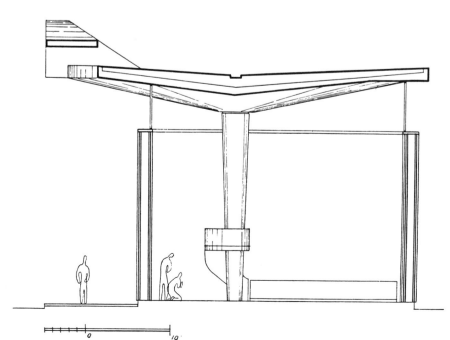

prizes in competitions for office buildings, housing units, houses of worship, the Pavilion for the World's Fair in 1939.

Still, Nowicki had only three years in his professional career, when war came. In September 1939, he was in fact on training maneuvers, as a lieutenant in charge of an anti-aircraft battery. Even at that late moment, in the country immediately menaced by Nazi Germany, war still seemed an absurd impossibility. Nowicki once told me how, on the day it broke out, the Polish army watched hundreds of German bombers fly over their lines, in the direction of Warsaw, bombers easily identifiable as German, without anyone's believing what his eyes saw sufficiently to give the order to fire on them. In the debacle that followed he made his way back to Warsaw, and during the occupation, he conducted underground classes in architecture and town planning, in the face of the Nazi ban upon such activities, while officially he taught bricklaying — an art he had first to master — in a permitted trade school. Those days

Polish occupation, which had its parallel in other countries, notably in the Netherlands. Cut loose from international life, oppressed by their enemies, deserted by their friends, the Poles turned to their own national traditions, and sought in their own past to find a precedent for the new buildings the nation would one day erect again. Esthetically, the results were formalistic, even archaic; mainly a return to the spirit of eighteenth century classicism; but humanly, this understanding of the national and the regional elements, disregarded in the evolution of machine forms — though they themselves, in fact, often demand regional adaptations for functional reasons — brought them closer to the underlying human needs they served. Perhaps without this wartime evocation of sentiment, Nowicki would not have so easily come to terms with the pride and folk feeling of the people in North Carolina, and not a little by his personal warmth and understanding prompted them to respond so quickly to the call of modern design.

The final lesson of Nowicki's ordeal was that which

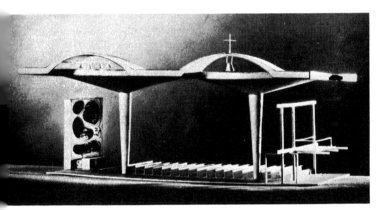

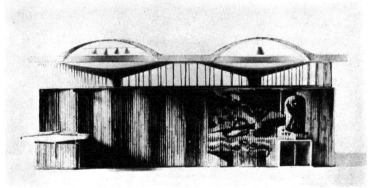

and nights were so filled with horrors that only once did he even give me a glimpse into them: but this sensitive spirit, on whose face every feeling seemed instantly mirrored, underwent daily danger and trial without self-betrayal. This ordeal culminated in a period of guerilla fighting in the woods around Warsaw and finally in his escape to a distant mountain region with his wife and his little son, born during the occupation.

No one can undergo such experiences without being deeply affected by it. Such an ordeal burns away residual weakness and brings out unexpected sources of strength. In Nowicki it deepened his dedication, both to his art and to the needs of his fellowmen; partly perhaps as a refuge from his macabre memories, he threw himself into architecture, as into an asylum and a sanctuary.

But in addition something else had happened in the

his father had taught by his own life: the lesson of citizenship. Nowicki had grown up under a semi-fascist regime, which had felt too much kinship with the phobias and hatreds and repressions of Nazi Germany to alert itself against its intentions and defend itself successfully. In that state, as in America today, the student generation had become non-political, lest too great a concern for freedom and democracy should interfere with their careers. To the end of his days, Nowicki's father reproached himself for not having dedicated himself more completely to warning his fellow citizens of the dangers he himself had clearly seen. By the end of the war, Matthew Nowicki himself realized that there was no escape from politics: the architect, first of all, had a responsibility to his community, to understand its needs and to create forms for their highest fulfillment. That is why, in his program of education, he not merely stressed the value of a humanistic approach to architecture at North Carolina State College but prefaced it with the declaration that "we expect our graduate to become a citizen first and a professional later."

Since, in a totalitarian state, only the members of the party even partly exercise the full prerogatives of citizenship, the transformation of Poland into a colonial dependency of Soviet Russia would automatically have exiled Nowicki, for the claims of communism, with its know-it-all Marxian ideology and its contempt for freedom were foreign to every part of his nature. Nowicki made his escape to America, as it were, through an open door; for his opportunity came before the communists had achieved their coup d'etat, which removed all pretext of Poland's being permitted to exist as a free, multi-party state. Even before this, the communists were numerically strong enough and sufficiently concentrated in their aims to be the dominant political group in Poland. But so great was Nowicki's devotion to his country's good, so unsullied his record in the Underground, so undisputed his genius as architect and planner, that those in authority made him chief of planning for the central area of Warsaw and let him work on his own terms: that is to say, at his own office, at his own time, without stopping when the official day ended. Seeing how poor were the prospects of genuine cooperation, Nowicki seized the chance offered him of coming to the United States as technical adviser to the

"The study of the well-being of contemporary man, which has been introduced into the language of architecture continues to be the inspiration for our work but this time the quality is differently analyzed. It is no longer 'the machine to live in' that stirs our imagination. It is the eternal feeling of a shelter to which we subordinate our creative ideas."

Matthew Nowicki

Polish Embassy, to enlist American interest in the rebuilding of Warsaw, and to establish contacts with the advances in building, engineering and urbanism that had been made since war had blocked communication.

I shall pass over Nowicki's brief period of work as Polish representative in America, first in Chicago, where he devoted himself mainly to awakening public interest in the plans for re-building historic Warsaw, and then in the United Nations, where he was selected to represent the Polish government in the choice of a site for the United Nations. This last responsibility, which took him across the continent to San Francisco, gave him a certain opportunity to show his capacity for leadership, but what was more important, it gave him a first-hand view of the country and some of its leaders in business and government: re-enforcing sympathies and intuitions acquired in youth. As a consultant

to the Director of Planning on the Board of Design, Nowicki came into direct contact with the leaders of the modern movement, a highly diverse group of men, from Le Corbusier to the Uruguayan architect, Vilamajo, whose work independently paralleled that of Perret. As the youngest member of this group, with a more limited achievement in buildings actually built, his influence on his seniors was, unfortunately, negligible: yet perhaps his own development had not, at this point, gone far enough to make him ready to challenge the parti at which their combined talents arrived.

For Nowicki, indeed, the great lesson of this U.N. cooperation was the fact that in spite of the diversity of approach, there was unanimity as to the end to be sought: he felt that in this very unity was proof of the fact that modern architecture had come of age. His own insight into the thousand difficulties that beset this design — an imperfectly formulated program, an insufficiency of funds, the pressure of time that deprived the architects of the benefit of second thoughts — all this would probably have made him lenient toward the defects of the original conception, and generous especially toward that part of the work he had no part in. But in a few years, Nowicki was to indicate, in his sketches for the Parliament Building at Chandigarh, the quality of imagination that was lacking in the design for the entire U.N.

Perhaps the best part of Nowicki's association with the United Nations, in its formative state, was not alone the sense of confidence it gave him as an architect, measuring his own powers against his elder colleague's abilities: rather it was a further lesson in citizenship. Thenceforward, he was no longer merely a Pole, or any other purely national citizen: he felt himself a part of that One World which the United Nations exists to bring to birth. Stirred by his mission in India, one of Nowicki's final thoughts, as reported by Albert Mayer, played with ways of overcoming the architectural disabilities of that country. Out of this came his proposal that America should as a gesture of friendship set up a complete architectural and engineering school in India. This would be part of a larger movement that would bring men of the highest calibre, adept in human relations as well as professional services, on such missions as his own, to devote a few years of their lives to the helping of other peoples, and being enriched, as Matthew Nowicki himself was enriched, by the lessons they would in turn teach him.

That dedication to the service of a United World makes Nowicki, not merely a man of his generation, but a man of the century to come. Meanwhile, his services to the United Nations, as architect, gave him the means to sever his official relations with Poland and to start on a new career as architect and teacher. It is to his ideas as a teacher that the next article in this series is addressed.

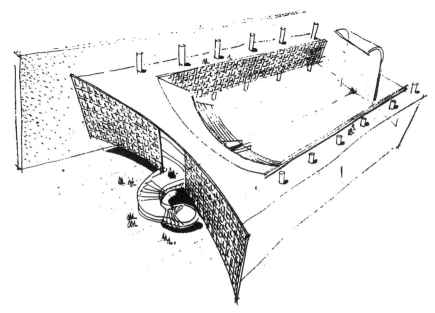

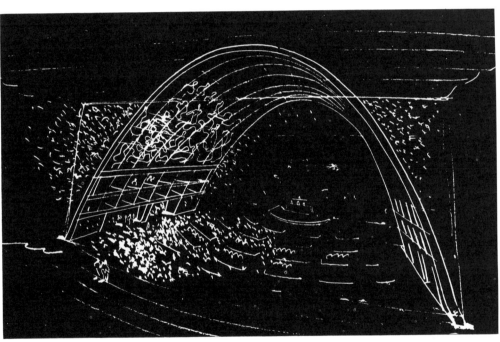

Nowicki was one of the younger, perhaps less assertive, members
of the U N Planning Commission, but his facile pencil was frequently busy, and his imagination always active. These are a few of
many sketches done for the problem of the Assembly

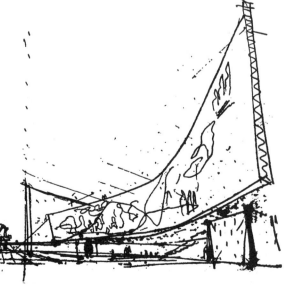

Part II MATTHEW NOWICKI AS AN EDUCATOR

Diagrammatic outline of Nowicki's proposed curricula for architectural education at North Carolina State College

Study Periods	ORGANIZATION OF STUDIES						
5	Landscape Design V, VI, VII	Arch. Design VII, VIII, IX Instructional Assistance	Foundations Building Codes Office Procedure	Drawing XI, XII	Philosophy of Design	City Planning I, II, III	Elective
4	Landscape Design II, III, IV Landscape Construction Planting Design	Arch. Design IV, V, VI	Architectural Structures Building Products Office Procedure	Drawing IX, X	History of Architecture IV Human Behavior Urban Sociology		American or English Literature; Or Advanced Military Elective
3	Landscape Design I Plant, Materials, Nursery Practice Landscape Construction	Architectural Design I, II, III	Construction Drawings I, II. Design of Structures, Sanitary, Electrical, Heating, Air Conditioning, Equipments of Bldg.	Drawing VI, VII, VIII	History of Architecture I, II, III		Modern Language; Or Advanced Military
2		Design IV, V, VI	Topographics Materials Structures Statistics Strength of Materials Material Testing	Drawing III, IV, V	History of Landscape Architecture		Military Science Sport Activities
1		Design I, II, III	Mathematics	Drawing I, II	Contemporary Civilization Contemporary Science		English Composition Military Science Fundamental Activities Hygiene
CHAIRS	Landscape Design	Architectural Design	Structures	Descriptive Drawing	Humanities and History	City Planning	Unrelated Subjects

MATTHEW NOWICKI, the architect whose Arena already stands forth as one of the monuments of modern form in America, had just reached the age of thirty-five when he came to America. His education, his apprenticeship in architecture, his ordeal as a Polish citizen under the Nazi occupation and its Russian successor, were now behind him. He stood at that Dantean midpoint where the energies are at highest level and the human shape, spiritually even more than physically, has taken form. More than six feet tall, with a long face whose slightly rounded outline contrasted with the firm, lean lines of his body, usually dressed in light gray tweeds, he was a man to attract attention. Gay, affable, scrupulously polite to the point of formality, he was at home in every kind of society. Without rigorous discipline, the affability might have been too indulgent, the sensitiveness might have been too fragile or painful, the politeness might have sacrificed truth to sociability; but in fact, none of these things happened, for an underlying gravity of purpose and an immense capacity for work kept every part of his being focused on architecture.

Nowicki was as far as possible away from the Renaissance ideal of the dilettante, the gifted amateur too enamored of balance to give his last ounce of energy to any specialized profession. But the fact was that

"Perhaps the very essence of Nowicki's contribution as an architect lay in the fact that he began and ended with the human being to whose purposes he gave structural order and symbolic expression."

Nowicki achieved balance by a reversed process: so concentrated was he on the problems of architecture and city planning, so central was this interest, that it rayed out into every other department of life and brought every other human need or aptitude intuitively to bear on it. In that sense he would describe architecture as "a way of life more than a profession."

No matter where one might begin in conversation, I cannot remember half an hour in his company when the talk did not go back to architecture: yet what always impressed one, was not so much the wealth of architectural perceptions and ideas, as the humanity that accompanied them. No one could have demanded higher standards of work from his students: following his example they would habitually work far into the night, at some sacrifice of sleep and perhaps health; but what he asked from them he demanded of himself, and the impression that he left on them was not of hardness and rigor and discipline, but of his quick, warm responses as a human being.

This tension of opposites, this alternation of expression and inhibition, of releasing passion and restraining intellect, is, I am sure, one of the stigmata of genius;

and Nowicki showed it in the highest degree, and was sufficiently conscious of its meaning to give that tension and interplay a place in his educational philosophy. With lack of form in every sense — lack of moral standards, lack of taste, lack of intellectual backbone, lack of a sense of the occasion — he was impatient to the point of contempt. He had no use for the bohemianism that masquerades as freedom, for the puerile self-indulgence that equates the bizarre with the original. Finally, the quality that pervades all one's impressions and memories of Nowicki is the quality of a deep joy, a joy in work, a joy in action, a joy in thought, a joy in friendship.

Nowicki's almost compulsive concentration upon work, even in a plane or on a hospital bed, would perhaps have been disturbing if it had not been perpetually accompanied by this inner joy, and relieved by the warmth of his response to the people around him. None rejected that warmth except those who enviously felt overshadowed by his genius; for, as Albert Mayer has recorded, "his bubbling humanity never failed him in even the most distressing and frustrating situations." At thirty-five, then, Nowicki had achieved a rare union of talent and character. He was ready at last for a rounded lifetime of work; and in five short years he indicated in outline what that lifetime might have brought forth.

The New Teacher and The New Curriculum

These first few years in America, so important in giving Nowicki afresh the feel of his adopted country, had one serious defect: they gave him no chance to practice his art on his own. This did not prevent him in his spare moments from designing imaginary buildings, like the charming little church (herewith illustrated) with its roof set on two mushroom columns, completely detached from the outside walls. Nor did it prevent him, in the winter of 1947–48 from serving as visiting critic in Pratt Institute. By this time the Communist coup in Poland had revealed to him the impossibility of going back to his native country; and since the era of or-

A brochure for School of Design, North Carolina State College; text and format by Mr. and Mrs. Nowicki

Some heretofore unpublished drawings by Nowicki for a State Museum for North Carolina (this project was held in abeyance and probably will not be built). One problem was to design a museum that would not clash with the Capitol (by Ithiel Towne), which would indeed leave the capitol as the dominant structure. Accordingly the facade was designed as an unbroken mass

ganized suspicion and inquisitorial demoralization had only begun to darken the American horizon, he was attracted without reserve by the old and seemingly solid virtues of our country: its democratic manners, its social egalitarianism, its respect for human variety, its spirit of adventure. The decision to apply for American citizenship coincided with his call to the School of Design at North Carolina State College in Raleigh: a happy stroke of Dean Henry Kamphoefner's, then in the act of renovating a sadly run-down institution. In the two brief years he spent there, beginning September 1948 — all that remained of his life — he made a powerful impression upon his students and upon the people of Raleigh, and was rising on a floodtide of varied architectural activity. With his architectural work, during this period — work that ranged from Brandeis University to Chandigarh — I shall deal in another article.

Here I propose to examine Nowicki's contribution as teacher; for, though his ideas never fully prevailed at the School of Design, the proposals he made for a new curriculum there go far toward stating the problems of architectural education today. In one sense, they complete the revolution that has been taking place; but in another, they offer constructive proposals for overcoming the weaknesses that have disclosed themselves, and restoring, in a new form, some of the elements that had proved their value in the past.

Architecture, for Matthew Nowicki, must itself be taken as Plato described it — as a pedagogical art. "The architect," he observed, "is continuously instructing others by means of his words or designs how to create architecture . . . An architect must be an interpreter and promoter of new ideas beneficial to the life of men," and in this process, he emphasized, the client had a part to play hardly less important than that of the architect; indeed, he sometimes went so far as to say that no great work of architecture was ever created without a great client. This meant that the architect, though a teacher, also must be capable of learning: "the humility of the truly great must be part of his professional ethics," and even if Nowicki made tolerant exceptions for wayward genius, he kept that ideal for himself. This does not mean, it goes without saying, that Nowicki had anything but impatience for those callow bumptious clients — there was one such official at Chapel Hill — who approach the architect with their own drawings of the desired building and ask him, as their grandfathers might have asked a menial servant,

The now-famous Arena at the North Carolina State Fair. done in association with WilliamHenley Deitrick

merely to add the practical details. Nor did it mean that he abdicated the responsibilities of leadership in favor of some pseudodemocratic solution by "compromise in committee" or by majority vote. On matters of taste, judgment, creative insight, he exercized no Pecksniffian humility; he knew that his own professional qualifications demanded the full respect of his clients, as surely as their human needs and preferences in turn demanded his own acceptance.

Nowicki's approach to this fundamental matter, the relation of architecture to the client and the community, comes out very well in his attitude toward one of North Carolina's cherished monuments, the excellent Capitol designed by Ithiel Towne. In association with William Henley Deitrick, he was given the task of designing a monumental state museum, to be placed within the general ambit of the capitol grounds. Knowing that the people of North Carolina would want, if possible, to keep the Capitol a dominating structure that would set the tone for the neighborhood, he conceived the façade of the museum in scale with the State House, and in stone. And since the new structure could not, as a modern building, honestly keep to the classic system of fenestration, he designed the wall as an un-

broken mass of stone, and relied on artificial lighting and ventilation to serve the building's uses. Respect for the client did not demand that he should design a sham-classic structure; but respect for modern principles of design did not demand, either, that he distract attention from the central monument by great expanses of glass or by a surface treatment in violent contrast in form or texture to the beloved building. That kind of understanding won friends both for modern architecture and for the School of Design, during those early years when the principles of contemporary form were as yet neither understood nor accepted by any large number of people in the South.

In conceiving the role of the School of Design, Nowicki had two large but related ends in view: the introduction of humanism and regionalism into the architectural curriculum, to counterbalance the detached and impersonal requirements of the scientific and technical approach, even when interpreted with esthetic sensitiveness by a Le Corbusier of a Mies van der Rohe. In outlining the new curriculum, he put first and foremost:

"Man —
    "The creator and the final reason for human creation

> "*The unchanging module of scale and proportion in art*
>
> "*As unchanging since the beginning of his race as are his emotions, instincts, and basic needs, and*
>
> "*Man —*
>
> "*The promotor of constant change, different in every century, decade and year, reflecting the varying ways of his individual and social life in the ever-changing forms of his creation.*"

Next to man — and note that this reverses the order in which Frank Lloyd Wright has cast the processes of architecture — comes

> "*Nature —*
>
> "*The source and the medium of creation — demanding subordination and granting freedom of its expression*
>
> "*The birthplace of all structure*
>
> "*An unchanging message for constantly changing interpretation*

and finally

> "*Time —*
>
> "*The yardstick of human memory and the module of space*
>
> "*The bridge to the beneficial experience accumulated by the generations.*"

With these postulates as a basis, Nowicki goes on to point out that "the concept of organizing life through the mechanical and technical control of its environment, the School considers as no longer sufficient for the growing maturity of our period." And "as maturity differs from the days of early youth, providing a new set of sometimes unexpected values, so have we changed many of our concepts" in the field of architecture . . . "The study of the well-being of contemporary man, which has been introduced into the language of architecture continues to be the inspiration for our work but this time the quality of this well-being is differently analyzed. It is no longer 'the machine to live in' that stirs our imagination. It is the eternal feeling of a shelter to which we subordinate our creative ideas. It seems to us that as much as every architecture is and has always been art of an abstract form, with hardly a formal precedent in nature, so its allegiance to nature has been and still might be expressed through the use of a symbol. The school feels that those symbolic values were underestimated by the philosophy of the passing period, and the conscious revival of their importance, in the new form to be created, is aimed at in the educational program of the school. . . . As much as the mechanized concept of values has been the outcome of the mechanized life of a metropolis, so the coming chapter of our culture might be inspired by the regional approach to life."

To do justice to the variety and fullness of human needs, Nowicki proposed to unite architecture, landscape architecture, and city planning — and in due time all the other related arts of design — into a "single frame for the changing picture of the life of man." This led him to propose a fourfold division of the curriculum: a chair of design, a chair of structures and technical subjects, a chair of descriptive drawing, and a chair of humanities, history and regional studies. In that curriculum the chair of design would have the task of ideological synthesis and practical integration. "In terms of philosophy, it tends to impress the student with the humanistic approach to all problems of his profession. Even the elements of form such as scale and proportion extend their further significance into the field of professional ethics. Composition defined as the sense of order in space and life is integrated in the design problem. A habit of methodical thinking is formed."

At a time when most architectural schools, in their abandonment of older academic models, begrudge the time needed for even architectural history, Nowicki's proposals for the chair of humanities are particularly significant. "Starting with a course on contemporary civilization," he observed, "it develops into a course on contemporary science. Physics, biology, chemistry are studied here, not from their technical but for their humanistic value as the basic components of our period. The history of the development of human thought in each of these channels is compared here to give the student a broad approach to his profession. Since his professional studies are not related in a strictly technical way to physics, biology and chemistry, it was considered as more advisable to approach these subjects in the chair of humanities, emphasizing the basic laws involved in their intellectual structure rather than the purely technical formulas."

Similarly, it is through history that Nowicki proposed to deal with the organized landscape, from the garden outward into the region, in order to give the student insight into the human meaning of these transformations. Architectural form he likewise approached in the same fashion, as itself a document in interpreting the social relationships characteristic of every period: this serves as a preparation for an advanced course in sociology and economics. Was that not characteristic of a teacher who, as one of his students, George Qualls, has observed, "gave the impression of a man intent upon completely describing the character of our civilization in terms of architecture." Finally, in the fifth year, he proposed to invite a distinguished scholar to give a course that would synthesize these various studies, and integrate them into a viable philosophy. Doubtless this capstone of the curriculum was the one that needed most reflection and most experimental effort; but the fact that Nowicki treated it as a coordinate department shows the importance he attached to psychology. It was in the final year, incidentally, that Nowicki proposed to institute a course in city planning, as an integral part

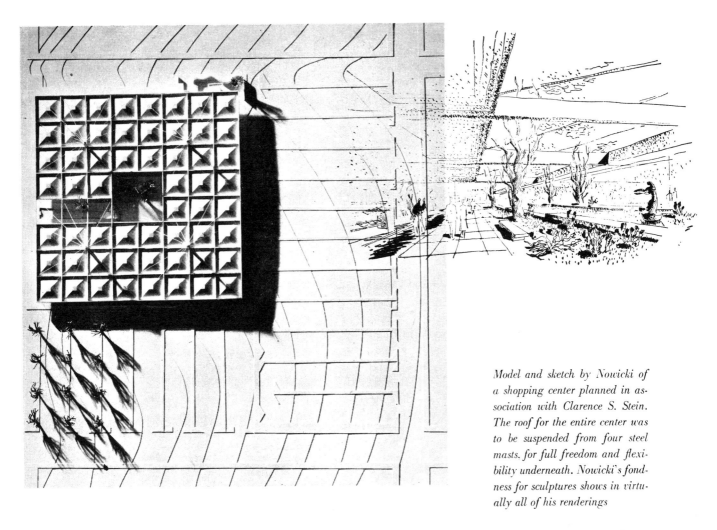

of architectural education; but in practice it turned out that there was a place for planning and group design — indeed a necessity for it — at an even earlier stage.

Beneath these proposals, which Nowicki had outlined in detail, were still other assumptions that derived from his own training and education. One of them was the conviction that no one could be an effective professor of architecture without being engaged in active practice or research. Since this might occasionally lead to absences from school that conflicted with the American academic routine, still another premise that went along with this was the belief, derived from his own education, that a student should be encouraged to greater independence and self-help; so that his work would not depend upon

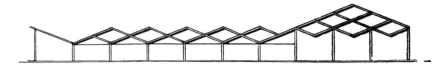

the constant overseership of his professor. The first part of his program had the active cooperation of Dean Kamphoefner, who, in effect, seeded this barren ground with able young practitioners of modern architecture, and, by lending one of his faculty to the State as a one-man reviewing board, succeeded in demonstrating the virtues of a non-traditional approach, in terms of economy as well as unity and order, in carrying through a great building program. Though some of the local architects may have feared this competition, the final result was to bring more work to the local members of the profession since their clients were less tempted to step over their heads to bring in a more glamorous name — too often only a name — from New York or Chicago. But freedom from academic routine is hard to mesh into the cogwheels of administration. Despite the Dean's tolerance, the fact that Nowicki might work with his students till two in the morning did not offset his unreadiness to punch the time clock, so to say, during the academic week, even if the professional work he was engaged in greatly enriched the student on his return. Though architectural schools keep less rigid hours than other academic departments, there is still room for greater flexibility here to free both teacher and student, if Nowicki's premises are worth building upon.

The best of curricula, worked out on paper, is still only a half-formed thing. Before it can come to life it needs the assistance of a group of teachers who understand and sympathize with its main aims; and then it needs further working out detail by detail in each co-operating course, shaped and re-shaped in the act of teaching, tested out by the effects it produces — or fails to produce — on the student. This is a long and difficult process even if there is no current of opposition, no effort to overlay the plan with a radically different set of interests and purposes. After five years, one can perhaps make further decisions as to what courses must be dropped or taught differently for lack of suitable teachers; what courses are out of harmony with the equipment and training and purposes of the students; and what courses promise with whatever further modification, to succeed.

In music, the notes do not give one the composer's form without an able player, and the player indeed plays in vain unless the audience, by its participation and response, completes the effort. So in teaching. In the form outlined in the first new catalog of the School, the vision and interpretation were Nowicki's own: they did not yet represent the philosophy of the component members of his department. With sufficient time for experiment, for persuasion, and for bringing in more sympathetic colleagues, Nowicki's new curriculum might have become a reality. The professor who understood his ideas and purposes most intimately succeeded with Nowicki's aid in shaping a new course in basic design that has already begun to serve as a model in other institutions; and so, by friendly intercourse and a continued sharing of ideas Nowicki might have hoped, in the course of time, to infuse the School of Design with some of the discipline and the love of adventure that his own life-experience and education had given him.

What was perhaps most difficult for contemporary Americans to accept in Nowicki's architectural philosophy, as expressed in this curriculum, is precisely what was most characteristic in his work, and most vital for a rehabilitation of our civic and educational life: the union of law and order with adventure and freedom. Repeating some words of Herbert Read's to the effect that "law and art are forces of culture, which unite men as individuals in independence and freedom," Nowicki observed: "Independence, freedom, law, and art seem to be the goals of our life. Creating a climate for their growth might be considered as the aim of contemporary education." The intellectual confusion "that often replaces freedom and the rigid academicism when order degenerates to formula" he considered equally dangerous for education.

For Nowicki discipline, "self-consciousness, law and order" are the supplements we need to freedom and experiment. This dynamic union of opposites in method was similar to his bringing together of the technologies and the humanities, of the regional and the universal elements, in projecting the goals of architecture. In his own work this reconciliation and union, this productive marriage, had, in fact, already taken place. To Nowicki it was clear that the romantic and the classic, the dionysian and the apollonian, the experimental and the historic are the permanent components of anything that can be called civilization, or high creative achievement. Once that perception becomes general, a new curriculum on the lines that Nowicki proposed will, perhaps, with whatever modifications experience and practice may bring with it, become the foundation for architectural education. Since it was, in effect, the translation into more general pedagogical terms of his own education, enriched by his own growth as a man and his own experience as an architect, it had a special merit: it had already produced one outstanding student.

Nowicki's interest in structural ideas and forms produced a wide variety of designs, many of them complicated and daring. One of the simpler schemes was this design for a synagogue

Perhaps an important element in his structural innovations was daring. Nowhere is that quality so apparent as in this scheme for a shopping center for Columbus Circle, New York, a great doughnut set up above the traffic at a busy intersection, where pedestrians would appreciate a new route

Part III   NOWICKI: HIS ARCHITECTURAL ACHIEVEMENT

MATTHEW NOWICKI was one of the most creative architects of his generation; but this fact alone was not enough to make him seem destined to be the great architectural leader of our time. In the realm of design there are perhaps half a dozen people who might have remained on a par with him; Oscar Niemeyer, in Brazil for example, or Eero Saarinen, in the United States, to mention only his close contemporaries. What gave Nowicki a special place was a combination of things: a sound and many-sided education, discipline and practice in both architecture and city planning, and the teacher's gift of formulating his ideas and communicating them to others. He had passed through all the phases of the modern movement: classicism, eclectic nationalism, the cubist mannerism of Le Corbusier. In designs as different as those for the State Fair Arena and the State Museum in Raleigh he showed how varied were his resources in facing each new situation.

But in the very last months of his life, on his visit to India, Nowicki was pushing beyond these earlier approaches to one more richly human, more genial to the spirit if not to the eye. His intuitions of form in India, visible only in a handful of sketches would, I think, have modified still further the change that was going on in his ideas during the last few years of his life. The result would have been no one-sided universalism, like that of the International Mannerists or the Mechanical Functionalists, but a genuine universalism in which the warm, the intimate, the personal attributes of a local culture would have mingled with the ideas and forms that are common to all men in our time. In other words, Nowicki's architectural development pointed the way of the coming age — if the promise of that age be not wrecked forever by irrational hate and genocidal violence.

Nowicki, with his own sense of self-discipline, went perhaps as far as anyone can go without losing himself in the Ice Queen's palace of sterile formalism to which the

Nowicki's last important project was the design of Chandigarh, India, with Mayer & Whittlesey, where he was "pushing beyond these earlier approaches to one more richly human . . ." His Indian work will be the subject of the next and final article

brilliant Mies van der Rohe has led himself and his disciples. One of the best examples of this method of approach is the design for the *Architectural Forum* School of 1950: a design for two new types of school building, radically different in both plan and construction from those which the California school has produced. Nowicki here set himself the problem of achieving the utmost economy: to this end he created a building with maximum interior space in relation to the perimeter: an interior that, since it had been based on the modular principle, could be reorganized at will. This led, inevitably, to the design of a classroom much more deep than wide, and to light that classroom — and the rest of the building — he had the bold idea of placing monitors about the roof, so that a great part of the lighting would come from overhead. These monitors were to be Plexiglas bubbles, a means not available in 1950 but actually used in 1953. When he translated this design into a circular school, with an auditorium at the center, he created a maximum amount of usable space with a minimum expenditure on the perimeter. The economy in construction costs, to say nothing of lighting and heating, of such a building, gave justification for this kind of construction. Whether in every other way it was sound would have required the testing of practice. Nowicki's solution of the problem of modular construction and pre-fabrication was different from that which has been applied to the schools of Hertfordshire in England; and here, as well as in another series of buildings in which he had a hand in designing, I feel that Nowicki's sense of human values would have corrected any errors his fidelity to principle might have produced.

During the vacation period of 1949, Nowicki had a few happy weeks working in intimate collaboration with his opposite American number, Eero Saarinen, on the design of a series of buildings for Brandeis University. The two men liked each other and worked harmoniously as friends; so that it would probably be difficult to determine what each of them contributed to the layout and design of these buildings. The fact that the pen and ink sketches of the Brandeis project are unmistakably in Nowicki's charming idiom does not indicate that they were his solitary contribution, in the sense that his original designs for the Museum and the State Fair Arena at Raleigh show that Nowicki had produced these designs. But the point is that at this particular moment in his own development, Nowicki's desire for economy and esthetic elegance committed him heartily to this mode of design. Some of the buildings show a superb command of the spatial elements, in places where planes and colors, the play of light and dark, are the main architectural facts to be considered. But some of the other buildings are, frankly, a disappointment, possibly because the module had become an inflexible master, rather than a servant. The formal treatment of the façade in the

faculty apartment buildings, with vast panes of glass on the lower floors, despite the formidable New England winters and the lack of visual privacy, and the bleak insufficient window, badly placed, on the upper floor, point to one of the weaknesses of this mode of approach. These buildings are neither genially at one with the landscape, nor are they the best possible answer to human requirements; nor are they, for that matter, so conceived that they could be adapted to other purposes, without radical alterations: so they have the inflexibility of the module itself without the flexible functional rearrangement that the very indifference to specific needs is supposed to create.

Now it happens that Nowicki himself was one of the first to analyze the problems that his own proposed school scheme and Saarinen's designs for Brandeis had created. In his last published essay he posed the problem raised by Sullivan's old formula that form follows function; and pointed out that modern design, whether one liked it or not had become a style, and that when a style is achieved the architect's choices are, by that fact, limited, so that in fact function follows form.* As before noted, for Nowicki this form was based, essentially, on the acceptance of the module; and the choice of the module meant not functional exactitude, but functional flexibility. A building, conceived in this fashion, sacrifices exact conformity to the needs to be served at any one time in order to be ready, through this very indifference and anonymity, to serve other needs and later times.

The line of thought that Nowicki opened in this essay needs to be followed even further than he took it, though that short essay is rich in historic perceptions and interpretations. Nowicki realized that what we call the modern movement had taken shape around the middle of the nineteenth century, notably in the Crystal Palace, under the influence both of engineering practice and a fresh theoretic appreciation of gothic construction. That movement, had it been followed through, would have resulted in buildings whose plan and structure would have been closely adapted to every physical need and whose ornament would have been derived from the exposure of the constructive elements, as in a Gothic church. But at a critical moment, Nowicki pointed out, the modern movement had taken a different direction, under the influence of cubist painting: for the desire of the cubists for extreme simplicity and purity had led to a denial of the new, often complicated, constructive elements, as in earlier Renaissance architecture, and the desire for a cubist organization of planes — "areas in color and immaterial paint" — had led to the renuncia-

---

*See *"Composition in Modern Architecture"* and *"Function and Form"* in The Roots Contemporary American Architecture, *edited by Lewis Mumford.*

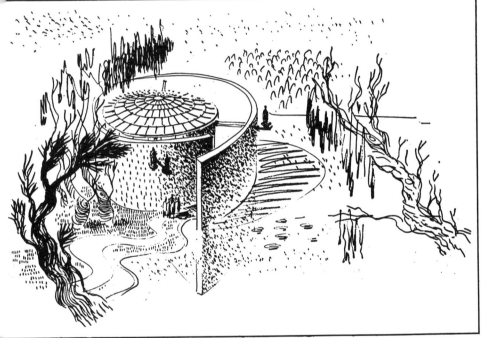

". . . Nowicki had a few happy weeks working in intimate collaboration with his opposite American number, Eero Saarinen, on the design of a series of buildings for Brandeis University . . . The fact that the pen and ink sketches are unmistakably in Nowicki's charming idiom does not indicate that they were his solitary contribution . . ."

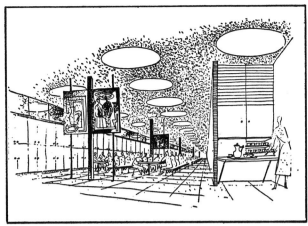

". . . at this particular moment in his own development, Nowicki's desire for economy committed him heartily to this mode of design (Brandeis buildings). Some of the buildings show a superb command of the spatial elements. . . ."

These buildings (still Brandeis) might be taken to represent the full development of Nowicki's response to the more academic theories of modern architecture. In the text Mumford shows that Nowicki went onward from this point to "point the way of the coming age"

tion of function. The inescapable elements of construction were hidden behind planes and partitions that had only a formal significance. The one connecting link with the older constructivism was in the use of the machine-made element, not as a functioning part, but as a symbolic element: he pointed to the two stacks at the entrance to the Salvation Army shelter in Paris, through which only minor ducts were carried, though they dominated the design. In that case, form did not follow function: it parodied function and distorted it for purely visual satisfaction.

As Nowicki saw it, the next phase in the development of modern design was the divorce of spatial relationships from both physical function and its formal imitation: the determinant was no longer the physical requirement of structure but the human requirement of beauty and order. Under such a mode of design, the actual character of the structure would not be revealed, in any particularity, by plan or elevation: but in response to human need, symbol and decoration would again become an integral part of design.

Though Nowicki's logic led him to his analysis, he was not, I think, altogether convinced by it; for I remember more than one discussion in which, after formulating these ideas, he would say: "But who knows? Perhaps the best way now would be to return to mid-Victorian functionalism and apply that logic to the designs which would take in psychological functions as well as physical ones." For he knew that the phrases functional exactitude and functional flexibility could be defined in a somewhat different fashion from that which he explored in this essay. He realized that the exact shaping of a building for all its functions, mechanical, biological, social, esthetic, resulted in an individual work of art that could not, without wholesale destruction of its organic unity of plan, be adapted to any other purpose. On the other hand, when one designed a building for flexibility — so that it might be made over completely from within, or used for different purposes without such remaking — it sacrificed its organic fitness and rightness: by almost meeting a dozen possible demands, it failed to meet completely any one of them. If one abandoned the notion of quick fabrication, easy adaptation to new functions, and early replacement, one also lessened the need for a kind of building based on functionally interchangeable parts.

Just as Nowicki had found that the classic and the romantic elements are present in all architecture, so, I think, he would have found, in the end, that functional exactitude and functional flexibility are necessary components of every building. There is in fact no either/or because both must be regarded. The problem of the architect in our time is to design buildings that can be made over, in each generation, so as to conform to new needs and new feelings and ideas. But that does not mean that he must design a library so that it may become a supermarket, or build a court house so that it might become an office building. Indeed, the very quality of architecture as an art, its expressiveness, depends in no little degree upon its unique synthesis of its manifold human functions.

What Nowicki's two papers on modern architecture brought out, and what his work was to bring out even further, is that the ultimate arbiter of function is the human being that the building serves: his needs for an orderly world, for esthetic satisfactions, for a response in his environment to his feelings, his emotions, his interests. Perhaps the essence of Nowicki's contribution as an architect lay in the fact that he began and ended with the human being to whose purposes he gave structural order and symbolic expression. Not that he served those purposes blindly or passively: he felt it the duty of the architect not merely to carry out his clients' wishes but to clarify them, to enlighten them, to bring out the latent possibilities that he himself, as designer, commanded. When he observed that architecture was a "pedagogical art" he brought everyone concerned with building, from the immediate client to the ultimate spectator, into that common area: not forgetting the architect himself.

Perhaps the best example of his talents in this respect came out in his practice in North Carolina; particularly in the project which came to him in association with William Henley Deitrick in the design of the buildings and grounds of the State Fair at Raleigh. This opportunity to interpret the "spirit of the Fair" and to design a series of free-standing buildings, was very close to Nowicki's heart. Responding to the generous hospitality of his Southern neighbors, appreciating the genial simple ways he had found among them, he saw a chance to add to the gaiety as well as the dignity of their life by an architecture worthy of democracy: a new architecture such as Whitman had foretold. From the first, his relations with the Director of the Fair, Mr. J. S. Dorton, were warm. Though modern architecture was still almost an unknown quantity in North Carolina, Nowicki's enthusiasm, his friendliness and humanity, wakened confidence in it; and in his approach to the architectural problem of the Arena, he showed a boldness, he confessed to his wife, that America itself had brought out in him. He had escaped from the European cliché of post and beam, he realized: hence his great constructivist notion of enclosing the arena in two gigantic parabolic concrete arches, intersecting close to the ground, to support the roof and frame the grandstands. About the quality of Nowicki's creation there is no dispute; for here all his long discipline as architect, as structural engineer, as planner united to create, with an exquisite simplicity of means and high constructive audacity, a building that sings, as only great architecture can sing.

PLAN OF CIVIC CENTER

CIVIC CENTER

The Life, the Teachings and the Architecture of Matthew Nowicki

Part IV NOWICKI'S WORK IN INDIA

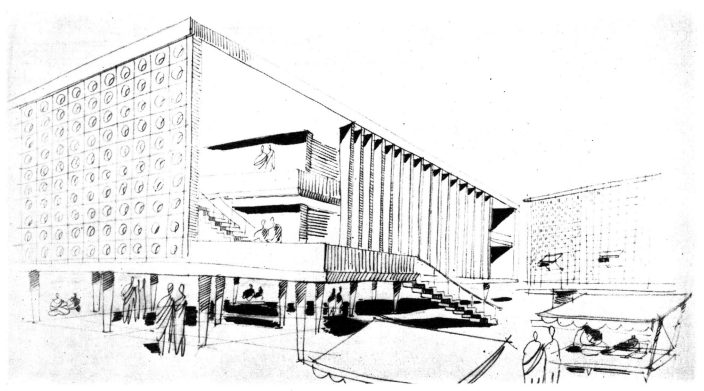

Design for an office building in Chandigarh, capital city of the Punjab

EVEN WHILE he was teaching, designing the State Fair Arena, and working out the fundamental conception of the design for the State Museum at Raleigh, Matthew Nowicki had embarked on work that drew even more fully on all his powers: that which he undertook, as consultant with Mayer and Whittlesey, for the design of the new capital of the Punjab, in Chandigarh, India. This collaboration came about largely through the earlier friendship he had formed with Clarence Stein, an old colleague of Mayer's.

That this great opportunity in India should have been, by accident, the occasion of Nowicki's death on his return flight is a double tragedy, for India gave Nowicki that which had hitherto been lacking among the younger architects, although for long there had been evidence of it in the work of Frank Lloyd Wright, and there were fresh indications of it, even before, in the later work, for example, of Oscar Niemeyer in Brazil. Those two and a half months in India not

merely knit together his education and experience, up to that point, but prepared the way for a new integration which would, I think, have had a decisive effect, not only upon his own designs, but on the course of modern architecture. In one form or another, it is indeed bound to come, unless the machine overrides human purposes and a pathological nihilism brings civilization itself to an end.

India, with all its contrast of magnificence and poverty, was, it goes without saying, a shock to Nowicki. But it was the human lesson of Hindu culture, as conveyed in its rich buildings, whose ornament and symbolism so intimately, yet overwhelmingly, dominate the whole, that made their impact upon him. After a week's motor trip to some of the great cities and monuments of Indian architecture he wrote his wife: "I learn so much here." That a Westerner had much to learn from Indian architecture and town-planning was something that Sir Edward Lutyens, the planner of New Delhi,

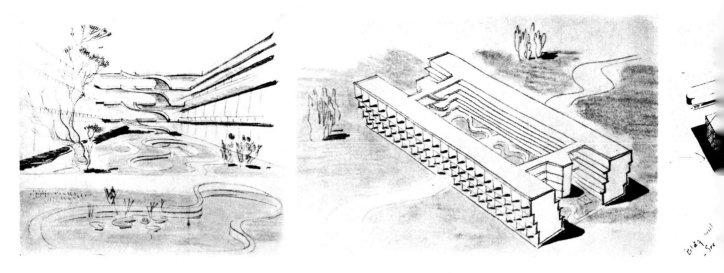

would have raised his eyebrows over, though forty years before Patrick Geddes, whom Lutyens dismissed as a "crank", had made that the very basis of his many town-planning proposals in India.

But there was more in Nowicki's admission than a becoming receptivity, on the part of a Westerner, to the ideals and forms of the East: it was also an admission, on the part of a mind committed to the modern, that the machine age, in its anti-historicism, anti-regionalism, anti-humanism, was not the last word in human culture. As I have pointed out, this reaction took place in Europe under the Nazi occupation; but in a form that was limiting, rather than releasing, to the human spirit, so that it was with some embarassment that Nowicki would refer to this sentimental return — and indeed, in the work of the Dutch architects, like Oud and Dudok, it was, alas! accompanied by an esthetic falling off from the clarity and formal elegance of their earlier designs. But here in India, still teeming with an emotional and sexual life so strong that it had once pervaded even the paintings of the Buddhist monks in the Ajanta caves, here that aspect of man's nature could not be so easily rejected, on grounds of mechanical function, formal purity, or esthetic elegance. At this point one of Nowicki's greatest qualities came to the front: his readiness to question old assumptions, to learn from new experiences; for that was one's main assurance of his relatively unlimited capacity for growth.

During the late winter of 1950 Nowicki had begun working with Mayer and Whittlesey on the city plan for Chandigarh. About the broad concept of the scheme, such as the use of the superblock and the neighborhood unit, the collaborators were in general agreement: so, too, with the need for concentrating the open air

markets. But Nowicki in a letter written to Albert Mayer in March, found himself challenging other assumptions. "I come back," he said, "to my very strong feeling that we admire the plans of beautiful cities mostly for the clarity of their concept. In planning a city for ages of its future growth, it seems to me that we must continuously beware of trends in our present taste that might not be appreciated in future. . . . The only unquestionable element in our thinking is cold logic and its striving for the utmost economy. Within this logic . . . one must secure the greatest possible flexibility for unpredictable future changes." Therefore, it has to further "what I would call functional flexibility, which is very much different from functional exactitude."

Nowicki then went on to distinguish in the city two functions, an everyday function and an occasional — as he called it "holiday" — function, and he held, almost as if Horatio Greenough's thoughts had taken possession of him "that if there is a cheaper way of providing well for these functions it is also going to be more beautiful. . . . This is so, I feel, because the concepts of economy and beauty derive from the same sources." All this led to his questioning any departures in the general street plan which would, in the interest of variety, create more than a minimum number of roads: "diversity of plan should be secured not through the diversity of size of the superblocks, but the diversity of their space treatment. It should be not a quantitative diversity, but a qualitative one." Following up this, he suggested that the path system within the superblocks should vary as much as possible and that there no prevailing system is needed or even desirable.

As for the holiday function of the city, here Nowicki's

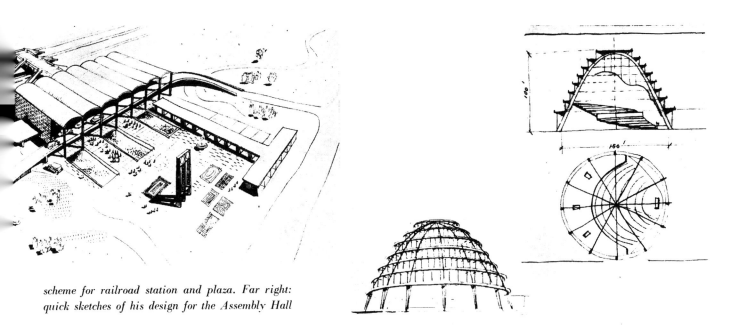

scheme for railroad station and plaza. Far right: quick sketches of his design for the Assembly Hall

bold concepts were equally clear. "The everyday function [working and dwelling] is responsible for the pattern texture of the city plan. The holiday function is responsible for the basic conception of the great scale composition. It is through the diagram of the holiday function that one can best express a plan of a city. The holiday function unites the city," and thus it became a graphic symbol of its plan. "I know," continued Nowicki, "no better example to quote than the axis, Place de la Concorde, Etoile, and the Bois de Boulogne. The perfection of Paris is related to the simplicity of this composition. The greatness of the holiday function was, I feel, underestimated in the recent city planning where the element of recreation was decentralized and confined within the texture. . . . In planning the holiday function for the entire city, it is legitimate to strive for magnifying of the space, which means that there should be a complete continuity of one composition, instead of dividing it into related parts. . . . In our plan there should be a continuous park system tying all parts of the city with the hill, the great park, the public forum, and the capitol area. The holiday function can depend very largely on a mass pedestrian movement, just as the everyday function depends on mass transportation. This difference should express itself in planning. Speed is needed in the repetitive movements. Leisure might be advisable in occasional movements of a greater significance where the process of getting to a destination is as important as reaching it."

In putting forward these ideas, Nowicki was countering a long prevailing American tendency to seek deliberate variations to overcome the inadequacies of the gridiron plan and "the lack of diversity in the creation of modern architecture. We love irregularity because we have too much boring regularity around.

Here the abuse of a notion is confused in our minds with the notion itself." But to him it seemed that a city "always has been and will be a 'modular problem' based on a repetitive function. This is the basic problem of a city. The plans of old cities of India, Africa, Greece, Rome, etc., were based on a regularity of design because there was a regularity of purpose. Every conscious planning effort was to create an order. The clarity of this order was always admired by posterity and comprehended in the same way as it was intended by the planner. The picturesque was introduced by time and not the planner. A perfect city was the result of time, and I am afraid no planner can make it so without the help of time. I feel that it would be a mistake to attempt to create a perfect city incorporating in it a notion of diversity that the perfect cities, as we know them, have. A logical and true city plan is always a modular diagram, expressing a certain philosophy and principle of life (true for a certain period) applied to specific conditions. The amount of sensitivity in applying the diagram will be responsible for legitimate variations. But the main objective should be order, not diversity." In the whole literature of planning, I cannot recall a page where so much has been said in so few words.

The concept of a clarified geometric order for the main outlines of the city plan, with its resultant functional flexibility, contrasted with a more subtle, humanistic approach to the details of the neighborhood, allowing for small contours in laying out a footpath, preserving a tree here, altering the axis of a group of houses to take advantage of prevailing winds or a view, in short, enriching the texture of the plan through a pliant sense of human need. In the second approach was "functional exactitude," with its sense of the

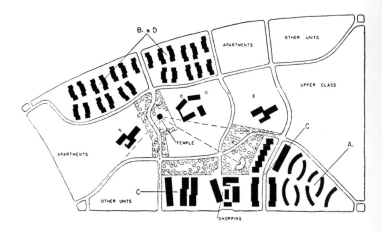

unique and the individual. In finding a place for both kinds of design within the new city Nowicki's theory of design went far beyond that of most of his contemporaries, above all, that of Le Corbusier, whose original sense of the intimate texture of daily life had been so lacking, and whose oversimplified handling of the entire city in terms of abstract spatial elements handled on a grandiose scale has had such a dehydrating effect upon housing and planning throughout the western world. In his planning, as in his architecture, Nowicki exhibited binocular vision, which brought together order and variety, logic and emotion, the universal and the local.

The main decisions about the plan of Chandigarh had been made before Mayer and Nowicki left for India, open to such changes as a fresh view of the site would bring. But when Nowicki arrived in the Punjab, it turned out that the work that was supposed to have been finished by the Indian bureaus simply had not been done: the staff from the chief engineer in charge down was demoralized and no adequate assistance was available. Plainly there was no possibility of doing the great tasks that had lured Nowicki to India, — working out in detail the layout of the great city squares and the design of the Capitol buildings. Though filled with anxiety promoted by the Korean war, which had just broken out, Nowicki accepted these frustrations and disappointments in a cheerful spirit. He spent the greater part of the summer, almost alone, planning a single superblock and carrying through, to the last detail, the plans and elevations of the houses. When he met Albert Mayer in Delhi, six weeks later, he amazed his colleague, himself no sluggard, with the sheer quantity of work he had produced — drawings "full of gaiety, almost as a cartoonist's drawings are," and "the flow of imagination through it all, as though the work and thinking had been quite unhurried, quite undistracted by the other complications of the Punjab situation," as Mayer put it. In all that he had done, as in his conception of the city proper, in its "holiday" aspect, Nowicki had an original contribution to make, not only to the immediate project but to town planning thought in general. In putting forth his ideas here I do not mean, however, to underestimate the fruitful give and take between the three architects responsible, or the extent to which their more intimate knowledge of the site would not, in the end, have led to further readjustments in the master plan and the siting of the public buildings.

Samuel Butler used to say that the test of a writer is: Can he name a cat? The test of an architect is: Can he design a minimal dwelling house that will still show the quality of his mind? By that test, Nowicki's place as an architect would be established alone by his varied house plans for minimal income groups. In the general planning of the superblock, in line with his own analysis of the need for texture, Nowicki avoided both the obsolete continuous street pattern that dates back to the seventeenth century, and the repetition of formal cul-de-sacs, as used in Radburn. Instead, he introduced the utmost possible variety in the grouping of the dwelling houses, in the treatment of their façades, in the succession of footways and open spaces that led from the dwellings to the more public activities of the neighborhood, the schools and the local bazaars. All these new designs, worked out to all but the last detail, provide evidence — no less striking than his stunning sketches for the Capitol building — of how much he had taken in of Hindu culture.

In none of these designs is there any reproduction of the outward forms of Hindu architecture: instead he had assimilated the spirit of the culture that had produced these forms, and he had translated that spirit into modern terms. Genius is the only word for that quick intuitive perception of the whole, the flash of creative synthesis that could fuse the regional and the universal in a new form. No one who examines these plans and sketches can doubt that genius is the only quality that could account for the results.

In a sense, Nowicki's Indian designs adequately speak for themselves; so that any interpretation of mine would be redundant. Yet I cannot resist pointing out one of his innovations in housing, which I think that the planners of future American housing estates would do well to ponder. Four years ago I looked at these plans without fully understanding their significance; then recently in the course of a fresh analysis of the problems of modern family life in relation to housing, I had the illusion of formulating a new answer to the problem of how to house people who need to exchange services with each other, and to have a common place for their little children to play in safely; how at the same time to recover that sense of intimacy and enclosure which some of the most desirable quarters in historic cities possess and that almost all open developments — whether modeled after Unwin or Le Corbusier — so deplorably lack. When I came back to Nowicki's Indian plans, in the course of preparing this article, I discovered that he had already outlined the answer: groups of ten or twelve houses, grouped like a bracket

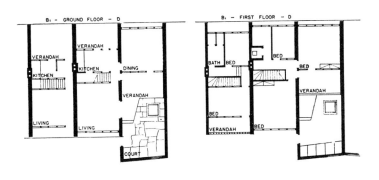

GROUND FLOOR   FIRST FLOOR

VERANDAH

BEDROOM   BATH

KITCHEN

BEDROOM

OPEN COURT   OPEN COURT

LIVING ROOM   BEDROOM   SHOWER

B₁ - GROUND FLOOR - D   B₁ - FIRST FLOOR - D

VERANDAH   VERANDAH

KITCHEN   KITCHEN   DINING   BATH   BED   BED   BED

VERANDAH

LIVING   LIVING   BED   VERANDAH

COURT   VERANDAH   BED

Superblock L 37, basis of Nowicki's scheme for Chandigarh, he designed in detail during his summer in India. He sought both order and diversity, but above all he worked toward the delineation of individual neighborhoods and a sympathy toward the Hindu's way of life. This sympathy can be seen in the plans of the dwelling units and in the character of the façades. The textures recall, but do not attempt to reproduce, the intricate ornamentation of the Hindu house

or a parenthesis, within which was a pool of common space, under the shade of a tree or two.

So much for the layout of this new group: one that gives expression to the most elementary social unit, the group of families, as Gaston Bardet puts it in his excellent description of the successive echelons of occupation, from family groups to the city as a whole. But look at the plan of these houses, with their inner court, open to the sky, where so much of the life of an Indian family takes place; and not least, note the character of the façades, with their self-ornamented openings which recall, but do not attempt to reproduce, the intricate handicraft ornamentation of the upper class Hindu house. To emphasize the fresh and original quality of Nowicki's approach here is not to underestimate a similar change that other architects, in contact with the more vivid esthetic and emotional responses of so-called primitive peoples, have experienced: witness some of Sert and Wiener's designs for South American housing. Indeed, is it not the fresh sense of color, the liveliness in the detail, that partly redeems the otherwise clumsily procrustean interior plan of Le Corbusier's famous Marseilles habitation? But there is a richness of invention in Nowicki's Indian work that has surely not been surpassed — and usually not even approached — in any of the work of his contemporaries.

The aftermath of this lonely charette at Simla in the foothills of the Himalayas was tragic, both as respects Nowicki's work and his life. The contribution that he had made to India — much to his spiritual enrichment, no doubt, but also at bitter personal sacrifice — was tossed aside by the officials responsible for Chandigarh. The excuse for this shift from an American team of architects to a French and British team — Le Corbusier and the Maxwell Frys — seemed reasonable

enough: it was necessary to get assistance that could be paid for on a sterling basis; and in the shiftover, Le Corbusier had even accepted Mayer's suggestion of admitting a friendly competition between the two teams, by retaining Nowicki's completely worked out plans for one of the superblocks. That decision, which would have put two different theories of planning to a practical test, was apparently soon forgotten; and though Le Corbusier retained the main lines of the master plan as worked out by Mayer and Whittlesey and Nowicki, he re-introduced the concept, as antiquated as it was anti-functional, of the old fashioned corridor avenue for shopping, instead of the concentrated markets planned by Nowicki for the core of the neighborhood. (In a few short years, Le Corbusier seems even to have forgotten the C.I.A.M. conference on the function of the Core.) As it turned out, then, the trip that cost Nowicki his life was to be a vain one.

This outcome of Nowicki's India work is all the more ironic because, if one were forced to put in a word the new synthesis which Nowicki had achieved, one would say that it was a union of Le Corbusier and Frank Lloyd Wright, the two opposite poles of the modern spirit, one formal, cartesian, rational, mechanistic, cubist and classicist; the other vital, full-blooded, constructively inventive, organic and romantic. But this pat description, though true as far as it goes, is nevertheless inadequate: the fact is that Nowicki's promised work transcended both his masters. For in his new unity there was a third element, imperfectly developed in either of the two great geniuses who have dominated the modern movement — the capacity of a deeply sympathetic, passionate, and loving man to understand, through his own joy and suffering, the needs of other lives, and to interpret those needs freshly in terms of forms that do justice to every aspect of life. To nature, as interpreted by Wright, to science and the machine as interpreted by Le Corbusier, Nowicki added the missing term — man. Not Le Corbusier's lay figure, Modulor, but the creature of flesh and blood and mind and spirit: the whole man. That quality of mind, a quality bestowed on his architectural forms by the man that Nowicki was, had no place for the childish vanities, the flatulent egoisms, that even the highest genius sometimes displays.

Nowicki's high creative competence was the child of humility and love: the humility of the teacher happy to find he has always something to learn, the love of the artist whose eyes tenderly transfigure the objects he loves, and whose imagination brings forth every ideal possibility. That is why those who examine Nowicki's character, his education, and his life experience will find in it a refreshment and a replenishment — and a challenge to their own further growth. So, too, those who look understandingly on his work will find in it, if I am not mistaken, the clue to an architecture that is still to be born. — THE END

Opposite page: Nowicki's inventiveness, also his facility at drawing, show in the design for the Temple. Top right: the shopping center keeps to the form of the bazaar. Right: the "middle" school, located near the temple at the center of the superblock. The Civic Center, a "clue to an architecture that is still to be born"?

BOOK FOUR

The Future of the City

1962-1963

"The key to a fresh architectural image of the city as a whole lies in working toward an organic unit of urban order which will hold together its component parts through successive changes in function and purpose from generation to generation. While such an archetypal image can never be fully realized, this concept of the city as a whole, restated in contemporary terms, will help to define the character of each institutional structure."

THE FUTURE OF THE CITY

No one in our time has considered the city as seriously, as continuously, and as penetratingly as has Lewis Mumford. ARCHITECTURAL RECORD *is pleased to publish this series of articles in which Mr. Mumford will cap his great series of books on the city with some positive suggestions for architects and planners. First, he exposes the faulty thinking that has produced the "miscarriage of the city"; he goes on to show what is needed to "effect a synthesis . . . of the physical, biological, social, cultural and personal components."*

1.

THE DISAPPEARING CITY

Nobody can be satisfied with the form of the city today. Neither as a working mechanism, as a social medium, nor as a work of art does the city fulfill the high hopes that modern civilization has called forth—or even meet our reasonable demands. Yet the mechanical processes of fabricating urban structures have never before been carried to a higher point: the energies even a small city now commands would have roused the envy of an Egyptian Pharaoh in the Pyramid Age. And there are moments in approaching New York, Philadelphia or San Francisco by car when, if the light is right and the distant masses of the buildings are sufficiently far away, a new form of urban splendor, more dazzling than that of Venice or Florence, seems to have been achieved.

Too soon one realizes that the city as a whole, when one approaches it closer, does not have more than a residue of this promised form in an occasional patch of good building. For the rest, the play of light and shade, of haze and color, has provided for the mobile eye a pleasure that will not bear closer architectural investigation. The illusion fades in the presence of the car-choked street, the blank glassy buildings, the glare of competitive architectural advertisements, the studied monotony of high-rise slabs in urban renewal projects: in short, new buildings and new quarters that lack any esthetic identity and any human appeal except that of superficial sanitary decency and bare mechanical order.

In all the big cities of America, the process of urban rebuilding is now proceeding at a rapid rate, as a result of putting both the financial and legal powers of the state at the service of the private investor and builder. But both architecturally and socially the resulting forms have been so devoid of character and individuality that the most sordid quarters, if they have been enriched over the years by human intercourse and human choice, suddenly

New York City, Lower Manhattan

Ewing Galloway

Los Angeles, from Mount Wilson

Venice, by J. M. W. Turner

The Bettmann Archive

"There are moments, in approaching [our cities] by car when, if the light is right and the distant masses of buildings are sufficiently far away, a new form of urban splendor, more dazzling than that of Venice or Florence, seems to have been achieved."

Ewing Galloway

The Bettmann Archive

Florence

seem precious even in their ugliness, even in their disorder.

Whatever people made of their cities in the past, they expressed a visible unity that bound together, in ever more complex form, the cumulative life of the community; the face and form of the city still recorded that which was desirable, memorable, admirable. Today a rigid mechanical order takes the place of social diversity, and endless assembly-line urban units automatically expand the physical structure of the city while destroying the contents and meaning of city life. The paradox of this period of rapid "urbanization" is that the city itself is being effaced. Minds still operating under an obsolete 19th century ideology of unremitting physical expansion oddly hail this outcome as "progress."

The time has come to reconsider the whole process of urban design. We must ask ourselves what changes are necessary if the city is again to become architecturally expressive, and economically workable, without our having to sacrifice its proper life to the mechanical means for keeping that life going. The architect's problem is again to make the city visually "imageable"—to use Kevin Lynch's term. Admittedly neither the architect nor the planner can produce, solely out of his professional skill, the conditions necessary for building and rebuilding adequate urban communities; but their own conscious reorientation on these matters is a necessary part of a wider transformation in which many other groups, professions and institutions must in the end participate.

FORMLESS URBANIZATION

The multiplication and expansion of cities which took place in the 19th century in all industrial countries occurred at a moment when the great city builders of the past—the kings and princes, the bishops and the guilds—were all stepping out of the picture; and the traditions that had guided them, instead of being modified and improved, were recklessly discarded by both municipal authorities and business enterprisers.

Genuine improvements took place indeed in the internal organization of cities during the 19th century: the first substantial improvements since the introduction of drains, piped drinking water, and water closets into the cities and palaces of Sumer, Crete and Rome. But the new organs of sanitation, hygiene and communication had little effect on the visible city, while the improvements of transportation by railroad, elevated railroad and trolley car brought in visual disorder and noise and, in the case of railroad cuts and marshalling yards, disrupted urban space as recklessly as expressways and park-

New York City, Wall Street

Ewing Galloway

Los Angeles, Broadway

Venice, The Piazzetta, by A. Canaletto

The Bettmann Archive

If our skylines can bear comparison with those of older and equally famous cities, the street-level view cannot. "Too soon one realizes that the city as a whole does not have more than a residue of this promised form in an occasional patch of good building. . . . The illusion fades in the presence of car-choked streets, the glare of competitive architectural advertisements, the studied monotony of highrise slabs. . . ."

Florence, the Loggia dei Lanzi

ing lots do today. In both the underground and the above-ground city, these new gains in mechanical efficiency were mainly formless, apart from occasional by-products like a handsome railroad station or a bridge.

In consequence, the great mass of metropolitan buildings since the 19th century has been disorganized and formless, even when it has professed to be mechanically efficient. Almost until today, dreams of improvement were either cast into archaic, medieval, classic or renascence molds, unchanged except in scale, or into purely industrial terms of mechanical innovations, collective "Crystal Palaces," such as H. G. Wells pictured in his scientific romances, and even Ebenezer Howard first proposed for a garden city shopping mall. In America, despite the City Beautiful movement of the Nineties, urban progress is still identified with high buildings, wide avenues, long vistas: the higher, the wider, the longer, the better.

Current suggestions for further urban improvement still tend to fall automatically into a purely mechanical mold: gouging new expressways into the city, multiplying skyscrapers, providing moving sidewalks, building garages and underground shelters, projecting linear Roadtowns, or covering the entire area with a metal and plastic dome to make possible total control of urban weather—on the glib theory that uniform conditions are "ideal" ones. So long as the main human functions and purposes of the city are ignored, these subsidiary processes tend to dominate the architect's imagination. All the more because the resulting fragments of urbanoid tissue can be produced anywhere, at a profit, in limitless quantities. We are now witnessing the climax of this process.

The great exception to the routine processes of 19th century urban expansion was the replanning of the center of Paris. Paris became in fact *the* model 19th century city. Here, in a consistent organic development that began under Colbert and was carried to a temporary climax under Baron Haussmann during the Second Empire, a new central structure was created—first in the handsome monumental masonry of the Seine embankment, and then in the great boulevards and new parks. By creating a new outlet for sociability and conversation in the tree-lined promenade and the sidewalk café, accessible even to older quarters that were still dismally congested and hygienically deplorable, the planners of Paris democratized and humanized the otherwise sterile Baroque plan. The beauty and order of this new frame, which at once preserved the complexities of the older neighborhoods and opened up new quarters threaded with broad public greens, attracted millions of visitors to Paris and—what was more important—helped increase the daily sat-

New York City, Sixth Avenue, ca. 1909

New York City, Queens
Martha Washington Ho

Levittown, Long Island

Boston, Fitzgerald Expressway, 1959

In the 19th century: "... the improvements of transportation by railroad, elevated railroad and trolley car brought in visual disorder and noise and disrupted urban space as recklessly as expressways and parking lots do today." In the 20th century: "... suggestions for further urban improvement still tend to fall automatically into a purely mechanical mold, as gouging new expressways into the city ..."

New York City, Park Avenue

Ewing Galloway

"*What has passed for a fresh image of the city turns out to be two forms of anti-city. One of these is a multiplication of standard, de-individualized high-rise structures. . . . The other is the complementary but opposite image of urban scatter and romantic seclusion often called suburban.*"

Ewing Galloway

isfaction of its inhabitants.

But while Paris improved its rich historic core, it lost out in form, as badly as London or Berlin, Philadelphia or Chicago, on its spreading periphery. The vitality and individuality that had been heightened by the boulevards, parks and parkways of Paris were dependent upon historic institutions and many-sided activities that the new quarters lacked. Left to themselves, these residential quarters were deserts of pretentious monotony. Today central Paris, too, is being annihilated by the same forces that produce the vast areas of urban nonentity that surround the living core of our own big cities. These forces are choking Paris today as they have choked cities in the United States, as new as Fort Worth and as old as Boston.

Not the weakest of these destructive forces are those that operate under the guise of "up-to-date planning," in extravagant engineering projects, like the new motorway along the Left Bank of the Seine—a self-negating improvement just as futile as the motorways that have deprived Boston and Cambridge of access to their most convenient and potentially most delightful recreation area along the Charles. This new order of planning makes the city more attractive temporarily to motor cars, and infinitely less attractive permanently to human beings. On the suburban outskirts of our cities everywhere in both Europe and America, high-rise apartments impudently counterfeit the urbanity they have actually left behind. Present-day building replaces the complex structure of the city with loose masses of "urbanoid" tissue.

This formless urbanization, which is both dynamic and destructive, has become almost universal. Though it utilizes one kind of structure in metropolitan renewal projects and a slightly different kind in suburbia, the two types have basically the same defect. They have been built by people who lack historical or sociological insight into the nature of the city, considered as anything but the largest number of consumers that can be brought together in the most accessible manufacturing and marketing area.

If this theory were an adequate one, it would be hard to account for the general exodus that has been taking place from the center of big cities for the last generation or more; and even harder to account for the fact that suburbs continue to spread relentlessly around every big metropolis, forming ever-widening belts of population at low residential density per acre, ever further removed from the jobs and cultural opportunities that big cities are by their bigness supposed to make more accessible. In both cases, cities, villages and countryside, once distinct entities with individuality and identity, have become homogenized masses. Therewith one of the main functions of architecture, to symbolize and express the social idea, has disappeared.

THE MISSING URBAN IDEA

During the last generation an immense amount of literature on cities has belatedly appeared, mostly economic and social analysis of a limited kind, dealing with the subsidiary and peripheral aspects of urban life. Most of these studies have been entirely lacking in concrete architectural understanding and historical perspective. Though they emphasize dynamic processes and technological change, they quaintly assume that the very processes of change now under observation are themselves unchanging; that is, that they may be neither retarded, halted nor redirected nor brought within a more complex pattern that would reflect more central human needs and would alter their seeming importance.

For the exponents of aimless dynamism, the only method of controlling the urban processes now visible is to hasten them and widen their province. Those who favor this automatic dynamism treat the resultant confusions and frustrations as the very essence of city life, and cheerfully write off the accompanying increase in nervous tensions, violence, crime and health-depleting sedatives, tranquillizers and atmospheric poisons.

The effect of this literature has been, no doubt, to clarify the economic and technical processes that are actually at work in Western urban society. But that clarification, though it may help the municipal administrator in performing his daily routines and making such plans as can be derived from five-year projections, has so far only served to reinforce and speed up the disruptive processes that are now in operation. From the standpoint of the architect and the city planning, such analysis would be useful only if it were attached to a formative idea of the city; and such an idea of the city is precisely what is lacking.

"Idea" comes from the original Greek term for "image." Current proposals for city improvement are so imageless that city planning schools in America, for the last half-generation, have been turning out mainly administrators, statisticians, economists, traffic experts. For lack of an image of the modern city, contemporary "experts" covertly fall back on already obsolete clichés, such as Le Corbusier's Voisin plan for Paris. Following the humanly functionless plans and the purposeless processes that are now producing total urban disintegration, they emerge, like the sociologist Jean Gottmann, with the abstract concept of "Megalopolis" —the last word in imageless urban amorphousness. And unfortunately, people who have no insight into the purposes of urban life have already begun to talk of this abstraction as the new "form" of the city.

The emptiness and sterility of so much that now goes under the rubric of modern city design is now being widely felt. Hence the interest that has been awakened by books like Jane Jacobs' *The Death and Life of Great American Cities,* with its keen appreciation of some of the more intimate aspects of urban life, and with its contrasting criticism, largely deserved, of radical human deficiencies in the standardized, high-rise, "urban renewal" projects.

But unfortunately Mrs. Jacobs, despite her healthy reaction against bad design, has, to match her phobia about open spaces, an almost pathological aversion to good urban design. In order to avoid officious municipal demolition and regulation, she would return to Victorian *laissez faire*; in order to overcome regimentation, she would invite chaos. Mrs. Jacobs has made a sentimental private utopia out of a very special case—a few streets in a little urban backwater—a special neighborhood of New York that happily retained its historical identity longer than any other area except Brooklyn Heights. In any large sense, she lacks an image of the modern city. Her new model is only the old muddle from which less whimsical planners are belatedly trying to escape.

The fact is that 20th century planning still lacks a fresh multi-dimensional image of the city, partly because we have not discussed and sorted out the true values, functions and purposes of modern culture from many pseudo-values and apparently automatic processes that promise power or profit to those who promote them.

What has passed for a fresh image of the city turns out to be two forms of anti-city. One of these is a multiplication of standard, de-individualized high-rise structures, almost identical in form, whether they enclose offices, factories, administrative headquarters or family apartments, set in the midst of a spaghetti tangle of traffic arteries, expressways, parking lots and garages. The other is the complementary but opposite image of urban scatter and romantic seclusion often called suburban, though it has in fact broken away from such order as the 19th century suburb had actually achieved, and even lacks such formal coherence as Frank Lloyd Wright proposed to give it in his plans for Broadacre City. As an agent of human interaction and cooperation, as a stage for the social drama, the city is rapidly sinking out of sight.

If either the architect or the planner is to do better in the future, he must understand the historical forces that produced the original miscarriage of the city, and the contemporary pressures that have brought about this retreat and revolt.

2. YESTERDAY'S CITY OF TOMORROW

In a previous article I dealt with the continued dissolution of the city into an amorphous, over-mechanized urbanoid mass, lacking both esthetic identity and social character. Even the biggest metropolises seem fatally doomed by this process, if we allow it to continue. Private transportation by motorways, during the last two decades, instead of assisting the reorganization and reintegration of urban life on a regional scale, has only lengthened distances, slowed down transportation within the city, and dispersed useful facilities that were once close at hand and constantly available. Therewith the city and all its organs have been dissolving into the formless nonentity miscalled Megalopolis.

THE INFLUENCE OF THE SUBURB

Meanwhile the major reaction against the misdemeanors of the city has been the escape to Suburbia. For more than a century, families that were content to do without the social advantages of the city profited by the cheap land and the natural landscape to create a biologically more adequate environment, with full access to all the things now missing from the city: sunlight, untainted air, freedom from mechanical noises, ample lawns and gardens, accessible open country for walks and picnics; finally, individual houses, specially designed for family comfort, expressive of personal taste.

This impulse to have closer contact with the rural scene was fed by the literature of the Romantic movement, from Rousseau on to Thoreau; but it did not originate there. For the rich families of Florence, Rome and Venice, in the fifteenth and sixteenth centuries, did not wait for either romanticism or the railroad age to build their country villas in Fiesole, in Frascati, or on the Brenta. What marks the modern age is that both the impulse and the means of achieving it have become universal.

Though the ultimate outcome of this suburban retreat on a large scale has proved to be a non-city, if not an anti-city, just because of the very isolation and separation it proudly boasted, one must not underestimate its architectural results or its great human attraction; in fact, no adequate image of the emerging city will arise until these are both fully reckoned with. From William Morris's Red House to the shingle-houses of H. H. Richardson, W. R.

Emerson, and their colleagues, from Frank Lloyd Wright's prairie houses on to the work of Voysey, Parker, and Baillie-Scott, from Olmsted's Riverside and Roland Park to Unwin's Hampstead Garden Suburb, most of the fresh forms of domestic architecture and planning grew out of the suburb. This still holds true today: not merely in houses, but in shopping centers, school complexes, industrial parks. Apart from purely industrial architecture, like the cotton mills of Manchester or the early skyscrapers of Chicago, no other environment has proved so encouraging to positive architectural expression as the suburb.

Though the original values of the suburb have been fast disappearing in the welter of the ever-spreading conurbation, the image that was left behind has had an influence upon urban planning. This is the image of a new kind of city, the "City in a Park"; more open in texture than the more crowded cities of the past, with permanent access to gardens and parks for all the inhabitants of the city, not just for the dominant minority. That influence has expressed itself in three different conceptions of the contemporary city, advanced by three distinguished architects and planners, Raymond Unwin, Frank Lloyd Wright, and Le Corbusier. Though radically different in their human background and purpose, all three conceptions have a common denominator: an unqualified demand for more space. In this article I shall confine myself to the work of Le Corbusier. If space and speed, mass production and bureaucratic regimentation were all that were necessary to form a new image of the modern metropolis, Le Corbusier would already have provided an adequate solution.

LE CORBUSIER:
DESTROYER AND INNOVATOR

Most architects, during the last thirty years, and certainly most architectural and planning schools, have been dominated by the powerful propaganda and experimental achievement of this singular man of genius, Le Corbusier. If anyone put forward what seemed a fresh and original conception of the City of Tomorrow, it was this redoubtable leader. Though that conception has gone through a series

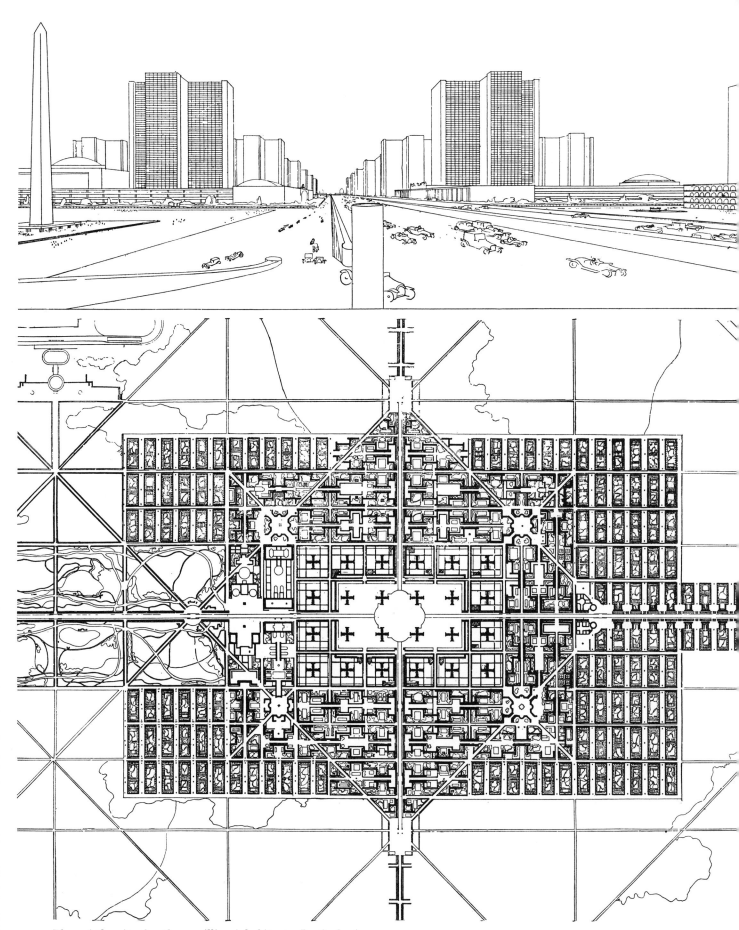

Plan of the city for three million inhabitants, Le Corbusier

"While Le Corbusier's image of the city is still often regarded as the last word in modern design, it combines, in fact, the three chief mistakes of the nineteenth century"

of changes, corresponding to changes that have taken place likewise in his architecture, certain main features stand out, and will probably for a while continue to have influence, even if the master should abandon them. And though no one city, except Chandigarh, shows the full range of his influence, his thought has run so closely along the grain of our age that fragments of it are scattered everywhere.

The chief reason for Le Corbusier's immediate impact lies in the fact that he brought together the two architectural conceptions that separately have dominated the modern movement in architecture and city planning: the machine-made environment, standardized, bureaucratized, "processed," technically perfected to the last degree; and to offset this the natural environment, treated as so much visual open space, providing sunlight, pure air, green foliage, and views.

Not the least attraction of Le Corbusier's thought to his contemporaries was that in bringing these two together, he paid no more attention to the nature of the city and to the orderly arrangements of its constantly proliferating groups, societies, clubs, organizations, institutions, than did the real estate broker or the municipal engineer. In short, he embraced every feature of the contemporary city except its essential social and civic character. This failure to understand the function of the city as a focal meeting place extended to the C.I.A.M., which commissioned a book on the city in which the functions of the city that concerned the planner were reduced to Housing, Work, Recreation and Industry; and it was not until this group produced its symposium on the Heart of the City that the city's special social attributes, as a meeting place, were at last recognized.

In his first presentation of the City of the Future, Le Corbusier over-emphasized its new mechanical facilities, and equated urban progress with geometrical order, rectilinear planning, and mechanized bureaucratic organization. Enchanted by the possibilities of modern steel and concrete construction, Le Corbusier first presented a picture of a modern city like Paris, transformed into his new image: an image of free-standing, 60-story office buildings, set in open spaces, as the central feature, with multiple high speed transportation routes at many levels, feeding into this center, and long series of apartment houses, uniform in height, forming an undifferentiated residential district outside the bureaucratic core. This new unit would hold three million inhabitants, the equivalent of Paris. Le Corbusier's "Voisin" plan (1922-1925) was superimposed on the center of Paris: he proposed to tear down the historic core of Paris, as confused, unsanitary, pestilent, preserving only a few ancient monuments, and packing all its multifarious activities into uniform structures.

In his readiness to demolish the historic quarter of Paris and replace it with these towering isolated buildings, Le Corbusier's imagination worked like a bulldozer on an urban renewal project. In the name of efficiency, he paid no attention to the actual functions and purposes of the structures he proposed to re-house, or to historic buildings that by their individual character give form and continuity to the life that goes on within them. In short, he ignored the main office of the city, which is to enrich the future by maintaining in the midst of change visible structural links with the past in all its cultural richness and variety. In proposing prudently to preserve a handful of historic buildings as isolated monuments, Le Corbusier overlooked the fact that no small part of their value and meaning would disappear, once they were cut off from the multitudinous activities and associations that surrounded them; that in fact it was people, not space, that they needed if they were even properly to be seen.

In placing his emphasis on the vertical, rather than the horizontal elements of city design, Le Corbusier was fascinated, not only by the general possibilities of technology, but by the desire to give a more rigorous Cartesian expression to the American skyscraper. He had returned, most probably without any consciousness of it, to the form of the early Chicago skyscrapers, and had removed, not merely the romantic pinnacles and setback towers that had followed, but the visual jumble and congestion. His novel proposal was to combine the new order of height with something that had never been seriously suggested before, a palatial increase of open space, in the form of a park, between the buildings.

In that simple act, Le Corbusier wiped out the complex tissue of a thousand little and not so little urban activities that cannot be economically placed in tall structures or function efficiently except at points where they are encountered at street level and utilized by a multitude of people going about their business at all times of the day.

The extravagant heights of Le Corbusier's skyscraper had no reason for existence apart from the fact that they had become technological possibilities; the open spaces in his central areas had no reason for existence either, since on the scale he imagined there was no motive during the business day for pedestrian circulation in the office quarter. By mating the utilitarian and financial image of the skyscraper city to the romantic image of the organic environment, Le Corbusier had in fact produced a sterile hybrid.

But perhaps the very sterility of Le Corbusier's conception was what has made it so attractive to our age. In American cities tall buildings came into

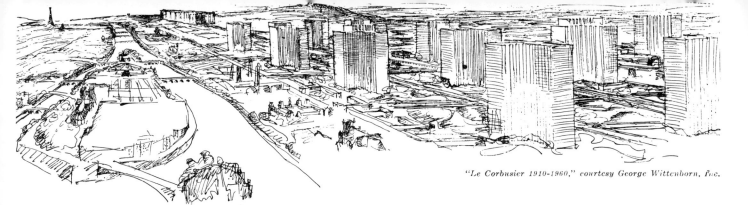

"Le Corbusier 1910-1960," courtesy George Wittenborn, Inc.

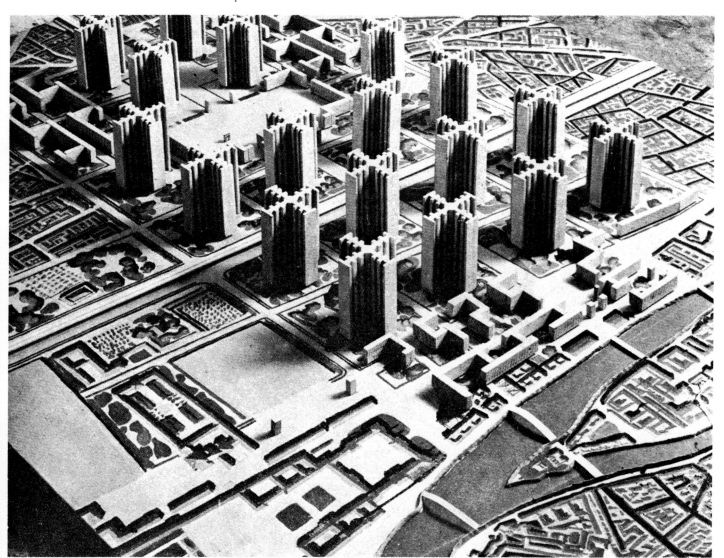

Voisin Plan for Paris, Le Corbusier, 1925

existence not simply as a convenience for business enterprise, but as a mode of increasing land values and the opportunities for highly profitable large-scale building and speculation; and even when the business towers provided too little floor space in proportion to elevator space to be profitable, they served by their very extravagance as a form of commercially valuable advertisement. The tall building was accepted in America as a standardized substi-

tute, with convertible units of space, for more functional plans and elevations that might require a more generous—that is expensive—allotment of land along with a more exacting design.

By stressing the visual openness between tall buildings, offsetting the low coverage with ever higher structures, Le Corbusier seemed to have satisfied two hitherto irreconcilable conditions: higher densities with higher rents on one hand, and greater exposure to light and air, along with a greater sense of open space, however unusable except to the eye. This pattern could be reduced to a mechanical formula and repeated anywhere precisely because it paid so little attention to the variety of human needs and the complexities of human association. That failing largely accounts for the present success of Le Corbusier's formula. But applied to urban renewal projects it has proved a disastrous success, on which Jane Jacobs has said almost the last word, though her own counter proposals, to increase densities and encourage haphazardness, are equally unsound, and quite as willfully negligent of urban realities.

MISPLACED OPENNESS

Le Corbusier's early images of the city were supplemented by later designs that could be carried out on a more modest scale: his plan in the Nineteen Thirties for the little town of Nemuors in North Africa, with its geometric grouping of domino structures, set the fashion for high-rise slabs. Both images in turn have had a massive impact upon the minds of today's architect-city planners. The post-war housing estates of the London County Council record that influence at its best, sometimes in more ingratiating forms than he had pictured,—as in the Alton estate at Roehampton, on land already richly landscaped by the original suburban owners—but also at its worst, as in their over-emphatic repetitions of his Unity House slab in another area.

In the United States the standard urban renewal projects fostered by the Federal government have been designed in a similar socially heedless fashion. Le Corbusier meanwhile has kept on modifying his original proposals, which were exclusively metropolitan and bureaucratic. In more recent statements since 1945 he has envisaged small, better balanced, more self-contained communities, as complementary members of the metropolis; and in Chandigarh he even took over from Albert Mayer and Matthew Nowicki, the first planners, the outlines of the Radburn plan, with its series of neighborhood superblocks and its inner green walkways.

But the gigantic scale of that city demands a completely motorized population: that is the mischief of excessive openness. Though Le Corbusier's buildings are low, his walks are long, and the central public buildings swim in space under a torrid summer sun whose heat further penalizes pedestrian circulation. The misplaced openness of Le Corbusier's new capital turns the great buildings and monuments into isolated works of sculpture, exhibited as in a high outdoor museum. They are meant to be visited piously or admired occasionally at a distance: not to serve as intimate architectural companions in the daily traffic of the city, visible at all times, with sufficient detail to hold the eye and refresh the spirit even under intimate inspection. In its excessive, official openness this plan vies with Walter Burley Griffin's purely suburban conception of the Australian capital of Canberra.

Le Corbusier was of course right in thinking that the functions of business and transportation could be better handled in structures especially designed to fit modern needs; he was right, too, in thinking that a basic pattern of order is essential to the full enjoyment of the city, particularly in our own age, in which a multitude of sensual and symbolic stimuli—print, sound, images—at every hour of the day, would produce overwhelming confusion if the general background were equally confused. So, too, he was correct in thinking that the skyscrapers of New York or Chicago should be thinned out, if they were to be visible from street level, or the traffic avenues were to remain usable; and further, that sunlight, pure air, vegetation, along with order and measure, were essential components of any sound environment, whether urban or rural.

But in his contempt for historic and traditional forms, Le Corbusier not merely lost continuity with the past but likewise any sense of how much of the present he was also losing. His new conception of the City in a Park misconceived the nature and functions of both city and park.

The monotony of Le Corbusier's favored forms has expressed the dominant forces of our ages, the facts of bureaucratic control and mechanical organization, equally visible in business, in industry, in government, in education. That fact itself constituted one of its attractions. But until Le Corbusier theoretically destroyed the historic tissue of the city, with its great complexity of form and its innumerable variations even within the fixed geometry of the gridiron plan, the prevailing bureaucratic pattern had been modified by many human, sometimes all-too-human, departures. The old skyscrapers of Wall Street or the Loop may have been anarchic in their efforts to pre-empt space or claim attention, but they did not present the faceless conformist image of present-day Park Avenue. As for urban compositions that have been more directly influenced by Le Corbusier's idea of the City in a Park —the collection of office buildings in the Pittsburgh Triangle, for example—they might as well be in a suburb as in the city itself. Even the open space around these buildings has become meaningless in terms of light and air, for all-day fluorescent lighting and air conditioning flout the one benefit that would justify this type of plan.

THE SUB-URBAN METROPOLIS

Unmodified by any realistic conception of urban functions and urban purposes, apart from the bureaucratic process itself, Le Corbusier's City in a Park turns out in fact to be a sub-urban conception. By its very isolation of functions that should be closely connected to every other aspect of city life, and by its magnification of the forces that govern metropolitan life today, it can be detached from the organic structure of the city and planted anywhere. Even the space around Le Corbusier's skyscrapers has an ambivalent function, for the City in a Park has now taken a more acceptable, commercially attractive form, and has become a City in a Parking Lot.

When we follow this whole process through, we discover that the freedom of movement, the change of pace, the choice of alternative destinations, the spontaneous encounters, the range of social choices and the proliferation of marketing opportunities, in fact, the multifarious life of a city has been traded away for expressways, parking space, and vertical circulation. It is not for nothing that so many of the new urban housing projects, filled with 20-story skyscrapers, are called villages: the conformities they demand, the social opportunities they offer, are as limited as those of a village. These islands of habitation in the midst of a sea of parking lots may have densities of 500 inhabitants a residential acre, and be part of a megalopolitan complex holding tens of millions of inhabitants, but the total mass still lacks the complex character of a city.

In short, the City in a Park does nothing to foster the constant give and take, the interchange of goods and ideas, the expression of life as a constant dialogue with other men in the midst of a collective setting that itself contributes to the animation and intensity of that dialogue. The architectural blankness of such a city mirrors the only kind of life possible under it: over-all control at the top, docile conformity at the bottom.

BASIC URBAN FALLACIES

While Le Corbusier's image of the city is still often regarded as the last word in modern design, it combines, in fact, the three chief mistakes of the nineteenth century. These misconceptions destroyed the classic form of the city, as it had existed almost from the beginning, and replaced it with a succession of urban and suburban wastelands: anti-cities.

The first mistake was the over-valuation of mechanization and standardization as ends in themselves, without respect to the human purpose to be served. The second was the theoretic destruction of every vestige of the past, without preserving any links in form or visible structure between past and future, thereby over-magnifying the importance of the present and at the same time threatening with destruction whatever permanent values the present might in turn create, and nullifying any lessons that might be learned from its errors. This is the error of the "disposable urban container." Finally, Le Corbusier's concept carried to its extreme the necessary reaction against urban overcrowding: the mistake of separating and extravagantly over-spacing facilities whose topographic concentration is essential for their daily use.

Now that a sufficient number of adaptations of Le Corbusier's leading concepts are in existence, we begin to have an insight into both their social and their esthetic limitations; for the two are in fact closely connected. The visual open space that this planning produces has no relation to the functional open space, space as used for non-visual purposes, for meeting and conversation, for the play of children, for gardening, for games, for promenades, for the courting of lovers, for outdoor relaxation. At the high density of 250-500 people per acre, what seems by the trick of low coverage an ample provision of open space turns out to be miserly.

The esthetic monotony of these high-rise dominoes is in fact a reflection of their social regimentation: they do not represent, in architectural form, the variety that actually exists in a mixed human community; uniformity and conformity is written all over them. Such freedom, such family intimacy, such spontaneous utilization of the natural environment, and such architectural identity as even the old-fashioned railroad suburb offered has been forfeited without any equivalent return.

The City in a Park, as so far conceived by Le Corbusier and his followers, is a blind alley. Yet its basic ingredients, the more adroit use of present-day mechanical facilities and the constant respect for the natural conditions for health and child nurture, must play a part in any better image of the future city. Neither high-rise structures, vertical transportation, spatial separation, multiple expressways and subways, or wholesale parking space will serve to produce a community that can take advantage of all the facilities modern civilization offers and work them into an integrated urban form. Even when assembled together in orderly fashion they still do not constitute a city. Before the architect can make his contribution to this new form, his private services to his client must be combined with a better understanding of the nature and functions of the city as a device for achieving the maximum amount of human cooperation and crystallizing in more durable and visible form the whole creative process.

3. MEGALOPOLIS AS ANTI-CITY

FLIGHT FROM THE CITY

The bureaucratic ideals of standardization, regimentation and centralized control have left their mark on all our urban planning for the last half century: the city, to paraphrase Aristotle, has become Organization Man writ large.

In reducing the realities of living organisms and human societies to calculable financial abstractions —square feet of rentable space, acres of traffic interchanges, miles of superhighways, millions of taxable real estate—the constructors and administrators of our modern, machine-conditioned metropolises have overlooked the essential task of the city. That task is to provide the maximum number of favorable opportunities for large populations to intermingle and interact, to interchange their human facilities and aptitudes as well as their economic goods and services, to stimulate and intensify by frequent contact and collaboration many common interests that would otherwise languish.

This neglect of the corporate activities and personal participations of the city, derives from a new situation. Except for the extractive industries, production and consumption can now be carried on almost anywhere. The more mechanized and automatic the economic operations, the less need they have of the city's human abundance and cultural variety. More than half a century ago the prophetic eye of H. G. Wells pointed out in "Anticipations" that, with the railroad and the motor car—and soon, he foresaw, the airplane—the population would become "delocalized" and mobile. He pictured detached villas and factories spread all over the countryside, entirely released from the gravitational field of the big city.

This pressure toward total dispersion has been embodied in two different concepts of urban design that still keep on cropping up. The earliest was that of the Spanish engineer, Soria y Mata: he proposed in the eighties to create a continuous "linear city" by extending the existing centers systematically along their major routes of transportation, to form continuous urban belts. This idea was revived in

1910 by an American engineer, Edgar Chambless, in a book called "Roadtown", and the notion in turn was reformulated once more by Le Corbusier, before it was given a grim practical expression in some of the Soviet Russian industrial settlements of the thirties.

In an entirely undirected but diagrammatic fashion, Roadtown has automatically grown up along the major highways of America; an incoherent and purposeless urbanoid nonentity, which dribbles over the devastated landscape and destroys the coherent smaller centers of urban or village life that stands in its path. Witness among a thousand other examples the Bay Highway between San Francisco and Palo Alto. Roadtown is the line of least resistance; the form that every modern city approaches when it forgets the functions and purposes of the city itself and uses modern technology only to sink to a primitive social level.

THE BROADCAST "CITY"

The other model for urban dispersion was that put forward by Frank Lloyd Wright in his design for Broadacre City, with the square western section and quarter-section doing duty for the purely linear traffic-road. This plan took a self-sufficient family dwelling as the unit of urban development, and placed it on a plot of from one to three acres, repeating this unit, as one might easily do on the flat prairie, with similar rectangular plots spatially regimented to serve such minimal social institutions as might survive. On the scale of Broadacre City, less than 800 families—at most some 3,000 people—would occupy a site as large as New York's Central Park.

This fantasy of Wright's was based on both his wholesome appreciation of the hygienic and domestic values of rural life, and his Jeffersonian contempt for the many-sided corporate and institutional life of the city. In the name of the first, he was ready to shrink the acreage of productive soils and break down the special human values of the rural

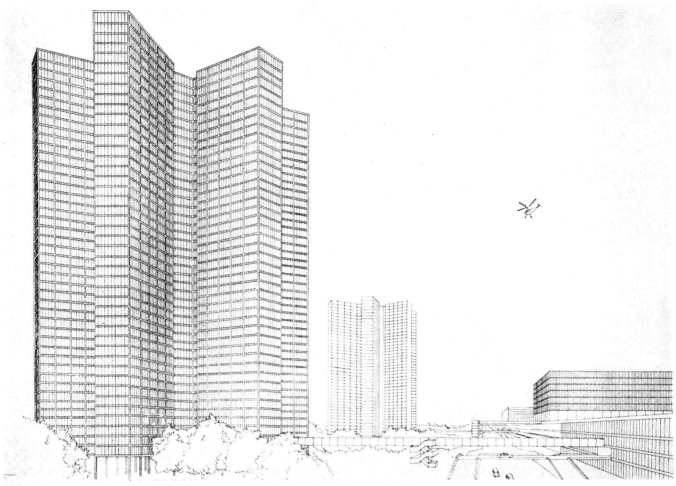

Metro-Linear: Reginald F. Malcolmson's recent study based on linear principles

landscape, with the functional divisions of meadow, pasture, and woodland, of cultivated land and wild land, in order to give every house and family a subsistence garden; and he was no less ready to break down the natural coagulations of life in villages and country towns, in a new fashion that made every social activity call for long distance transportation and therefore the incessant use of the motor car.

Wright's handsome disciplined designs for Broadacre City were never carried out except in piecemeal form. But the idea itself has indirectly had a devastating success, since it merely represented in a coherent pattern the random forces, mechanical and financial, that have been disintegrating the city.

In short, what Wright proposed as "the City of the Future" proved to be what his countrymen, during the next thirty years, would turn into our dismal sub-suburban present, abetted as they have been by exuberant highway building and expansive motor car production. The upper income group image of urban dispersion is the green ghetto of the exurban community, just far enough beyond the metropolitan center and its spreading suburban belt to be able to zone its territory for housing at a mini-

mum density of one family to the acre. The high price of such remote lots automatically turns the farmer into a real-estate speculator, and results, as in California, in the slaughter of the orchards, vineyards, and market gardens that once gave both health and delight—to say nothing of fresh food— to the nearby urban communities. Every year, according to Dr. Marion Clawson, a million acres of agricultural land are taken over for housing, largely scattered in green acres, and another million acres are withheld from farming through speculation and social erosion.

The result is not a new kind of city on a super-metropolitan scale, but an anti-city; not merely destitute of urban attributes, but inimical to the most important of them—the unification of specialized vocations and interests in order to produce a more stimulating and creative common life. And instead of producing the maximum amount of freedom and spontaneity, this scattering of the metropolitan population over the remoter parts of the countryside confines its working members for ever longer periods to a mobile cell, traveling ever longer distances to the place of work or to achieve even a few of the

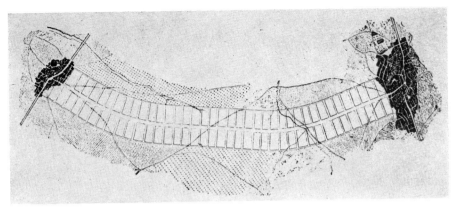

Soria y Mata's plan for a "linear city" in the 1880's

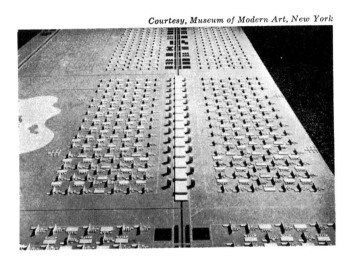

"Roadtown is the line of least resistance; the form that every modern city approaches when it forgets the functions and purposes of the city itself and uses modern technology only to sink to a primitive social level."

social and interpersonal relations that the city once provided at one's elbow.

On the surface Frank Lloyd Wright's ideal of the self-sufficient rural household in a thinned-out pattern of settlement might seem to be a large-scale domesticated fulfillment of Thoreau's Walden; but actually he had projected in elegant geometric form a regime as antithetic to Walden as Skinner's "Walden Two" or his own later "skyscraper a mile high." Walden was at least attached to Concord, and Concord in turn to Cambridge and Boston: so even in isolation Thoreau partook of the multi-dimensional social life of the city.

ARCHITECTURAL LURE OF THE ANTI-CITY

The anti-city that is now being produced by the reckless extension of standardized expressways, standardized roadside services, and standardized residential subdivisions—all greedily devouring land —dilutes to the point of complete insolvency all the valuable urban functions that require a certain den-

sity of population, a certain mixture of activities, a certain interweaving of economic necessities and social occasions. Despite all that, this negative image has proved, especially during the last two decades, to be a highly attractive one; so powerful that many people already identify it, despite its brief history and meager promise, with the "American way of life."

The reason is not far to seek, for the anti-city combines two contradictory and almost irreconcilable aspects of modern civilization: an expanding economy that calls for the constant employment of the machine (motor car, radio, television, telephone, automated factory and assembly line) to secure both full production and a minimal counterfeit of normal social life; and as a necessary offset to these demands, an effort to escape from the over-regulated routines, the impoverished personal choices, the monotonous prospects of this regime by daily withdrawal to a private rural asylum, where bureaucratic compulsions give way to exurban relaxation and permissiveness, in a purely family environment as much unlike the metropolis as possible. Thus the anti-city produces an illusory image of freedom at

123

Photo from "The Living City" by Frank Lloyd Wright, published by Horizon Press, New York 10

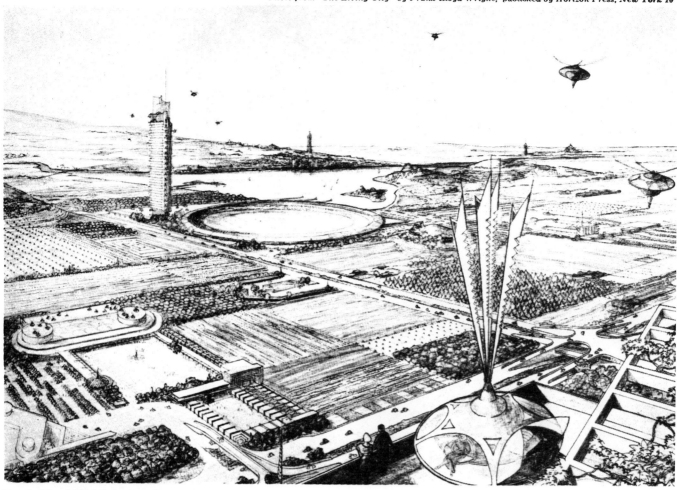

Frank Lloyd Wright's Broadacre City

the very moment all the screws of organization are being tightened.

Though the anti-city, almost by definition, is hardly imageable, its scattered parts are often esthetically attractive and humanly rewarding. Moreover, as a practical expedient, the anti-city has at its disposal the combined forces of highway engineers, motor car manufacturers, real estate developers, and lending institutions: all the more favored because its very randomness avoids the need for disciplined cooperation and municipal coordination. Because the anti-city is by nature fragmentary, any part can be built by anybody anywhere at any time. This is the ideal formula for promoting total urban disintegration.

Not the least factor in this development, certainly in America, is the persistent residue of the curious pioneer belief in space and mobility as a panacea for the ills of social life. In a recent discussion of the siting of a new university in California, which has been endowed with thousands of acres at the outskirts of a small, well-situated coastal town, I found I was almost alone in favoring a compact development in close proximity to the existing facil-

ities of the town. Most of the administrators, under the current doctrine of space for space's sake, favored a much looser grouping of buildings, miles away from the center of the town, with a faculty housing subdivision even more remote and more segregated. Characteristically, this scattering would necessitate the building of a special motor road and the sacrifice of valuable university land to parking.

When the sense of the city's reason for existence is lacking, there is nothing to keep the parts from spreading ever further away, not merely from the metropolitan centers but from each other. This has become the "space age" with a vengeance: in architecture space has become a substitute for urbane design. In opting for the anti-city, the architect and the business man play into each other's hands. Great business enterprises tend more and more to operate like self-sufficient feudal enclaves, watchfully regulating the activities of their employes in the interest of their health, working efficiency, and future promotion. By moving into the open country, a corporation can plan self-contained facilities, on land hitherto unbuilt on, and occupy acres at a lower price than the city demands for square feet. In this new

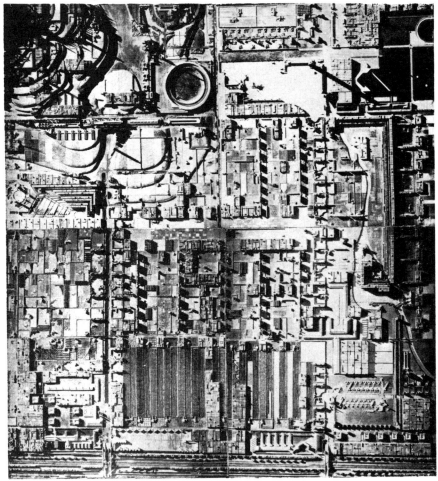

"Wright's handsome disciplined designs for Broadacre City were never carried out except in piecemeal form. But the idea itself has indirectly had a devastating success, since it merely represented in a coherent pattern the random forces . . . that have been disintegrating the city."

anti-urban pattern, each agency has its own self-contained plant, surrounded by broad acres of parking lot, often with its own bowling alley, its own medical clinic, its own hospital; while its employes draw upon the marketing facilities of a shopping center equally insulated in space.

These conditions have proved highly attractive to the architect, too. Even if he does not share Frank Lloyd Wright's delight in the rural background as such, he too easily falls for the attraction of empty acres upon which his individual creation will stand gloriously alone: no longer cramped by inadequate frontages, by insufficient land, or by too exacting urban building codes and zoning regulations; no longer in danger, either, of being defaced or obliterated by the building next door. The archetypal model for this overspaced existence is the airport.

This lonely eminence is a powerful lure; all the more so because the new rural office buildings, the new industrial parks, sometimes even the new shopping centers, above all the new schools and college campuses can in fact often show a much higher level of design than their constricted metropolitan equivalents. Apart from the architect's freedom, one of

the reasons for his readiness to desert the city is that with land so cheap, a proportionately greater part of the budget can be spent on the building and the landscaping. Unfortunately, this distinction too often is nullified by the immense paved void of parking lot, and the esthetic result is sullied by regiments of motor cars in the foreground.

Actually, the conditions provided by the anti-city are not so favorable in the long run for any purpose as either the architect or the business man imagines. This spatial openness, on close examination, proves to be social enclosure and constriction; and too often the architect himself, in obedience to the dominant bureaucratic principle, nullifies the advantages of his ample acres by designing a sealed-in, air-conditioned building, whose blank, Venetian-blinded façade turns its back on the landscape and mocks its very openness with a tightly closed inner court. Alternately, the plethora of space may go to the architect's head and cause him to produce loose, rambling plans and vacuous incoherent structures, as overspaced as his parking lots. What the modern architect needs for a better model is an image of variety and multiformity and social complexity and con-

"Not the least factor in this development, certainly in America, is the persistent residue of the curious pioneer belief in space and mobility as a panacea for the ills of social life."

centration that neither the bull-dozed landscape of Roadtown nor the systematic dispersal of Broadacre City provides. Only the city can bring him back this image or the life that it stands for.

HOMOGENIZED URBANITY

Both Roadtown and Broadacre City have provided such persistent images for the "City of the Future" that one must pause for a moment to show how, despite their professions of spatial and social liberation, and their effort to bring urban settlements closer to the agricultural and recreational areas of the countryside, they actually have only introduced the typical vices of the overgrown and over-regimented metropolis in a new form. For first of all, both concepts attempt to break down the most fundamental of all organic limitations: the functional limits of growth. Every organic form has, as Aristotle pointed out, an upper and lower limit of growth; and this applies, as he also pointed out, even to purely physical utilities, like ships, because if a ship is too big it is not maneuverable or seaworthy, and if it is too small it cannot carry a sufficient cargo.

In the case of cities, this natural limitation had, until the 17th century, rarely been overpassed: except for a few Romes and Babylons, the city by its very size and form expressed the need for social concentration.

Not merely do these anti-urban concepts destroy the social forms of the city, they likewise destroy the natural variety in the size and architectural structure of communities, a variety determined by a multitude of conditions: local population, agriculture, topography, productive industry, transportation, and cultural affiliations. There is a great choice in the style of life as between a solitary villa, an agricultural hamlet, a country village, and a country town on one side, though they all have the common attribute of ample areas for gardens and for play, and these in turn are different from the more urban styles of the small industrial town, the suburb, the seaport, the small provincial city with a base of its own, the satellite town, dependent upon the metropolis, and the metropolis itself, with its historic concentrations of culture. As long as this wide range of settlement is maintained, with its corresponding assortment of sizes, all limited by function and need, every type of human character, every

Connecticut General Life Insurance Company headquarters outside Hartford, Conn. Architects, Skidmore, Owings & Merrill

kind of industrial and cultural interest, can be satisfied somewhere. To concentrate on a single urban type, even though it be as big and far-reaching as a New York, a London, or a Tokyo, is to wipe out a valuable store of human potentialities.

Since form is conditioned by these other factors, the greatest wealth of architectural and town planning forms is possible. The anti-city image has only one form: a negation of complexity, ecological variety, and intimate social cooperation. Each fragment duplicates, with massive monotony, the limited premises upon which the negative image was based.

Finally, these images of total urban dispersal destroy by their very premises another significant organic characteristic, which in the city takes a special institutional form: the power of the attractive nucleus to serve as a magnet for concentrating a diversity of functions and purposes. Without such a nucleus, aided by many sub-nuclei, urban life lacks organs for mixing, meeting, mobilization. The essence of the city is its ability by its very form to focus human activities, and to make visible by symbolic magnification the true nature of the human condition and the human prospect. Historic cities, above all great metropolises, thanks to the accumu-

lations of time and sentiment, have powerful nuclei, which magnetize not merely their own inhabitants but people from distant regions. For many occasions their magnetic field has now become planetary. The absence of such social foci in the anti-city actually puts an end to necessary urban functions and imposes a uniform pattern of life, derived at second or third hand from some distant metropolitan center that still retains the surviving vestiges of the city's social properties.

The total result of these defects is to do away with natural variety, with urban individuality, with human choice. But from the standpoint of the other essential function of the city, as a container of human culture, the diluted and homogenized environment of the anti-city proves an even greater sociological absurdity. For the capacity of the urban container should vary with the total amount of experience and culture that must be transmitted from generation to generation. Part of this heritage is carried forward in institutional and symbolic form, represented by buildings, archives, records, libraries, for which the city serves as permanent storehouse; and an even larger part of it is transmitted directly through human agents, by daily

127

face-to-face transactions and conversations, by direct observations and imitations, and by chance encounters as well as deliberate meetings. The size and design of the urban container must vary directly with the size and complexity of this total heritage.

If our civilization is worth while maintaining, with all its vocational differentiation and cultural variety—historic, scientific, religious, humanistic—two urban conditions must be laid down: one, a many-dimensioned container capable of maintaining this richness and complexity and of distributing, over wider areas in space and time and over larger populations, the cultural wealth that urbanization both stores and helps to increase. The other condition is the creation of highly attractive focal points —cities in the historic sense, striking in form and character—where a diversity of organizations, institutions, associations, along with primary family and neighborhood groups, necessary to maintain this complex social order, can come together and profit by the constant give-and-take.

No secondary modes of intercourse, neither the printed page, the telephone, nor television, can take the place of that direct face-to-face intercourse whose occasions the city, when it remains close to the human scale, multiplies. Without an urban container deliberately planned for such intercourse, the dominant economic and technical pressures of our time tend to form a multitude of over-specialized, non-cooperating, and non-communicating enclaves, whose spatial remoteness and social segregation favor the totalitarian automatism of our time.

As an instrument for disrupting the processes of culture and ultimately arresting human development, the anti-city seems little less than a slow-acting equivalent for a nuclear catastrophe. The reduction of organic social complexity in the anti-city makes its scattered population incapable of carrying on its tasks with greater mental stimulus than that of a village: the mechanical conformity that this life exacts, by its utter dependence upon remote centrally controlled and secondary modes of intercourse, is quite as deadening as the social conformity of the tradition-bound village—and much harder to escape.

Even if the anti-city embraces a population as numerous as Gottman's Megalopolis—that is, the whole population of the Atlantic seaboard—the total cultural capacity of this atomized container would still be less than that of any single metropolis in a healthy state. Though the isolated institutional parts might be as hyper-productive as those computers whose data is already too abundant to be assembled and interpreted, the cultural creativity that fosters further human development is bound to drop, within a generation or two, toward zero.

The first institutions to feel the effect of this failure will be the great corporations that are now so often, singlehandedly, escaping from the overgrown metropolis. Not least does this hold for the various research agencies whose members, from day to day, see only their own kind, hear only echoes of their own ideas, and more and more live in a mental isolation-ward inhabited only by other specialists, equally cut off from human realities. In sheer self-defense, the directors of these institutions will have to send their staffs periodically, as the Bell Telephone Company has been sending its too sedulously trained junior executives, back to the university, to have a therapeutic injection of dynamic ideas that the city once spontaneously generated.

In view of all this, the nature of the modern city needs to be re-examined: a new pattern of urban integration more capable of utilizing the immense energies that modern man now commands must be invented. We can no longer think, in old-fashioned terms, of a "metropolis of three million people," for that no longer corresponds to the range of urban co-operation; nor shall we improve the situation by thinking of a pseudo-metropolis of thirty million, for such an agglomeration would effectually wipe out one of the most important components of the city: the natural landscape and all its appropriate cultural and recreational uses. We must rather seek a new over-all pattern for both the small-scale and the large-scale unit.

The large unit must be on a regional scale: sufficiently big to stabilize the essential rural occupations and provide a permanent green matrix, within which further urban colonization may take place. This concept, not of a *metropolitan* region dominated by a single center and continuous in structure with it, but of a regional framework capable of embracing cities of many sizes, including the central metropolitan center and giving each urban unit the advantages of the whole, has still to be worked out. But I have sketched in its main outlines under the title, "The Invisible City," in "The City in History." This larger structure, unlike the present clumsy magnification of the old Stone Age container, is rather an open network, comparable to the electric power grid, which utilizes both small and big units to form a greater interdependent system.

With a regional grid, the smallest urban unit will be able to make demands and draw on all the resources of the largest unit in a two-way system of intercourse and cooperation. But to create such a larger system, one must begin with a reorganization of small units, by introducing balance, self-government, organic growth, and a dynamic, self-renewing form into the neighborhood, the precinct, the city, and into all the institutional components of the city, which have become clumsy and disorganized through unregulated over-expansion. The first effective steps toward creating such local units have already been made; and I shall consider them next.

4. BEGINNINGS OF URBAN INTEGRATION

REGIMENTATION AND CHANCE

The two favored images of the city today are the products of a complementary process of regimentation and disintegration. One of them is the City in a Parking Lot, a collection of high-rise slabs and towers linked by multi-laned expressways; the other is the Anti-City, a by-product of urban decomposition, which in the pursuit of nature denatures the countryside and mechanically scatters fragments of the city over the whole landscape.

Whether the urban container explodes upward, in profitably congested "urban renewal" projects, or explodes outward, in suburban and exurban subdivisions, the result is an increasingly homogenized urbanoid mass that lacks the complex social and cultural attributes of the city, at the same time that it levels down the geological and ecological character of the natural landscape and lowers its agricultural potential.

The problem of finding an adequate form for the modern city is increased by the very powers the highway engineer and the architect command when they willingly serve the economic forces making for disintegration. Today the chief mode of urban destruction comes from misdirected construction. This paradox cannot be resolved by holding that formlessness is the determining feature of contemporary urban form. Yet some of our younger architects and planners have been making sketches for an anti-city on the assumption that randomness, accident, deformation, fragmentation—like crime, violence, extermination—have the same order of value as function, purpose, integration, health, moral character or esthetic design.

This tendency finds ample support, unfortunately, not merely in the fashionable *avant-garde* literature and drama of our time, but in the practice of some of the most sensitive contemporary painters and sculptors who keep on telling us that the only order possible is willful disorder, that the only valid image of man himself is a horror-skeleton derived from the Nazi extermination camps, and that the only

imageable urban form, apart from a collective underground shelter, would be the deliberate equivalent of the debris left by a nuclear bomb. Elizabeth Close's satiric commentary on "Design by Chance," published in the May number of the Journal of the American Institute of Architects, is too close to reality to be funny. If a chimpanzee, a psychotic, and a museum-qualified painter are equally capable of achieving a "modern" painting, the forces that are now vomiting the wreckage of the city over the landscape are doubtless sufficient to produce the "modern" form of the city—formless by intention.

If we are not to follow these irrational forces to their methodical conclusion—the effacement of human culture and the annihilation of man himself—the explosive elements that are now at work must be harnessed to a different and more human set of purposes. As with the mixture that composes gunpowder, the individual components in this urban explosion are in themselves innocuous: motor transportation, mass production, instantaneous communication, automation, are all potentially effective agents for human development, provided that it is the welfare of man, not the untrammeled expansion of his mechanical instruments, that one has in view. Even their explosive mixture, again like gunpowder, may prove serviceable for better human purposes provided we have adequate social instruments to control the explosion, and a rational target to aim at.

The paramount urban problem today is to invent an adequate urban container which will do for our complex and many-sided culture what the original Stone Age container did for the far simpler cooperations and communications of earlier societies. This problem cannot be answered, then, merely by pointing to the existing metropolis, or the conurbation, or the "megalopolis," and calling one of these the new container, though these big units do in fact point to the scale in which an effective multi-centered container must be conceived, and the vast range of specialized functions and human purposes that must be brought together.

More than a generation before all the dimensions

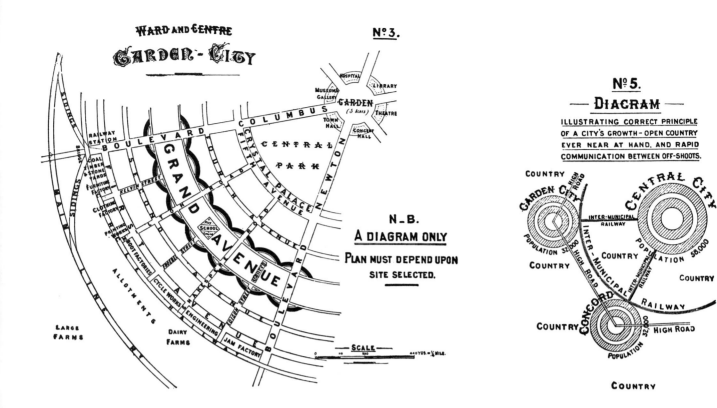

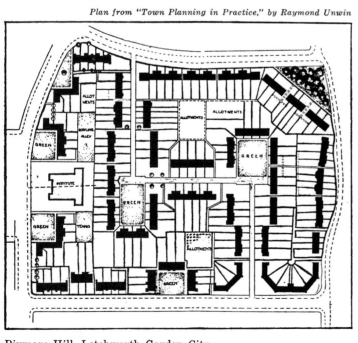

Plan from "Town Planning in Practice," by Raymond Unwin

Pixmore Hill, Letchworth Garden City

Early plan of Sunnyside Gardens

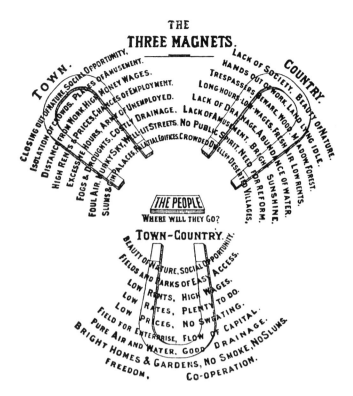

"... the first tentative step toward an answer was made by Ebenezer Howard ... His dry little prospectus—it is little more than that—"Garden Cities of Tomorrow," first published in 1898, started many fresh ideas sprouting in other minds; and some of the original seeds that remained dormant are now ready at last to germinate."

"The first translation of Howard's idea (far left) ... was the work of Raymond Unwin and Barry Parker ... carried further (left) by Clarence Stein and Henry Wright in Sunnyside ..."

of this problem had become visible, the first tentative step toward an answer was made by Ebenezer Howard. In his concept of the garden city, he restored many of the essential elements that the city, in its mechanical expansion and dispersion, in its human regimentation and biological depression, had lost; for he returned to the human scale, and he conceived of a means of increasing size and complexity of social relations without destroying this scale.

GROWTH AND FORM OF THE CITY

The projector of this urban form was not an architect, a planner or a painter, but an inventor of machines. His dry little prospectus—it is little more than that—"Garden Cities of Tomorrow," first published in 1898, started many fresh ideas sprouting in other minds; and some of the original seeds that remained dormant are now ready at last to germinate.

If I feel obliged once more to outline Howard's leading ideas, it is only because the popular view of them, even in planning circles, is often based, not on his proposals, but upon the strange aberrations of his critics, whose resistance takes the form of attributing to him preconceptions, methods and goals precisely the contrary to those he held. Even Howard's followers have sometimes given to his tentative proposals a rigidity of form and a finality of purpose he did not himself value; for his was an experimental mind, and the worst homage one could do to his way of thinking would be to assume that his experiment is already fixed and finished.

What Howard proposed was both a new image of the modern city and an organic method of handling its continued growth. The new image was that of a city limited in size, not by natural obstacles or poor economic resources or military necessity, but by a deliberate social intention and by the very nature of the contents and purpose of the plan. He sought to handle the problem of continued population growth by continued colonization in a series of self-contained towns with a sufficient variety of industrial, agricultural, and professional occupations to give work to the larger part of their own populations.

These new cities, in contrast to the current mode of urban expansion, were to be limited in area, in density and in population. Howard estimated that the desirable size for such a town would be about 30,000, with 2,000 more inhabitants engaged in market gardening and other rural occupations in the permanent greenbelt that surrounded it and gave the community its visible definition. The number of acres and of people he deemed adequate was a first approximation. It is not any single population

Aerial view of Radburn, New Jersey

Fairchild Aerial Surveys, Inc.

figure, but the desirability of establishing limits for the concrete, visible urban form that is important.

The main feature of Howard's idea, apart from the limitation of population and area, was a notion that he himself introduced with the very concept of the new city: the city was not only to be small enough to be manageable and accessible, but big enough to have variety and diversity. At this point he made a decisive departure both from the plans of "industrial villages" that were being built by a few British manufacturers, bent solely on improving housing conditions of their workers, and from the ordinary residential suburb, wholly dependent for diversity upon a distant urban center.

Howard's prospectus was so fully given over to the practical details of launching such a city that he himself barely sketched in its more fundamental ideas. But if the words "balance" and "organic

unity" and "social mixture" are lacking in Howard's book, they underlie the whole conception, and I do him no injustice in emphasizing them, though he himself rather stressed the municipal ownership and control of the land, as a means of maintaining the new pattern.

In outlining a more organic form of the city, Howard sought at the same time to unite town and country: he rightly understood their interdependence and complementarism. In proposing more spacious surroundings both for the buildings and the town as a whole, Howard was only democratizing a process that the aristocracy had long observed in establishing their own quarters in the city. The luxury of space, particularly the luxury of great parks and gardens, was historically the great aristocratic contribution to the city; and Howard felt, again rightly, that for the sake of health and de-

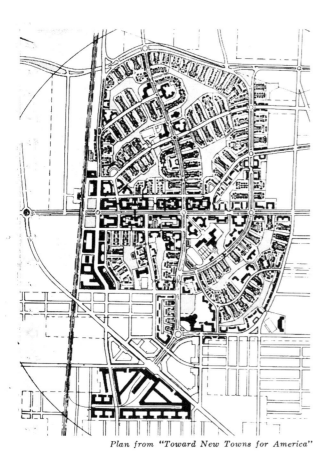

Plan from "Toward New Towns for America"

"To Unwin's demonstration, carried further by Clarence Stein and Henry Wright in Sunnyside and Radburn (here shown) we owe in large part the adoption of the superblock . . ."

again rightly, that for the sake of health and delight the garden and the park were an integral part of every quarter of the city.

In the 19th century this spacious mode of planning had been achieved only in the health spa and the suburb; but by now it has become a basic requirement of all urban design. Howard felt, indeed, that one of the great benefits of building new towns on a large scale would be to reduce the pressure of metropolitan population sufficiently to make it possible to replan every part of London, and make it as attractive and habitable again as it still is around its green core of parks and tree-filled squares

In aiming to deal with the dual problems of congestion and overgrowth Howard had, almost by accident, rediscovered the essential nature of the city itself. The main ingredient of this conception was a population large enough to be diversified; diversified enough to be economically and socially balanced,

and balanced sufficiently to permit most of the daily needs of the community to be satisfied within the city's limits, and yet have secure immediate access to the open country.

But Howard was no small town isolationist. Not for a moment did he suppose that a single community of 32,000 people could satisfy all modern man's social and cultural needs, or provide a sufficient variety of economic opportunities. Nor did he underestimate the special advantages of large numbers and plentiful capital resources, though he suspected that the great metropolis exacted too high a price for supplying them. On the contrary, in his chapter on "Social Cities" Howard pointed to a higher order of organization: a new kind of openwork metropolis, with 10 such communities grouped around a larger city at the center, bound closely by public rapid transit, commanding a population within the range of 350,000.

Here Howard suggested that such a constellation of cities or "town clusters" would have social and cultural advantages that no small town could offer. But he saw—as many advocates of continued metropolitan expansion and dispersion still do not see —that as the size of the total regional population increases, its component parts must be gathered together in more concentrated and coherent containers, built to a human scale, with sufficient autonomy to assume responsibilities and make demands, as no scattered, disorganized population can.

To make order again out of the present metropolitan explosion we must begin with its antithesis: a small-scale urban implosion or assemblage of urban elements. Only by first unifying the parts can a larger whole, the "urban grid," a highly organized regional network of cities and urban institutions, come into existence.

THE GARDEN CITY AS TRANSLATED

If I have correctly interpreted the significance of the Garden City, why is it that Howard's leading ideas have often been violently caricatured or disdainfully ignored? Apart from sheer human perversity, there are two reasons for this. The first is that Howard, as a public character, was a far bigger man than his book; and it was his genius for action as well as a certain meagreness of sociological and historic background that kept him from expressing in more effective literary form the full implications of his ideas. That task was left largely to his followers, particularly Unwin, Purdom, Osborn and Stein.

The second reason was that Ebenezer Howard had no pretensions to being a planner and he of-

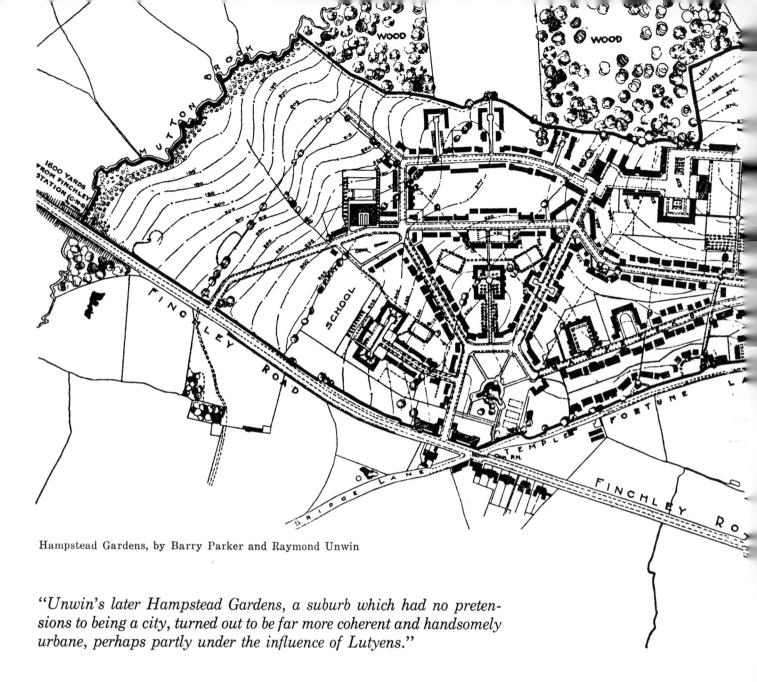

Hampstead Gardens, by Barry Parker and Raymond Unwin

*"Unwin's later Hampstead Gardens, a suburb which had no preten-
sions to being a city, turned out to be far more coherent and handsomely
urbane, perhaps partly under the influence of Lutyens."*

fered no plans: all his illustrations are plainly la-
beled as diagrams. In so far as he himself suggested
any concrete forms for the new city, they were
closer in spirit to Paxton than to William Morris,
and were more or less adaptations of the common
forms of his own time: a central park as in London;
an elongated glass shopping arcade, like that built
in Milan or many other European cities; a green
belt, collectively owned, such as had always existed,
though usually without public protection, around
country towns and railroad-suburbs. As to the residential area, if Howard had an image of the city,
it was nearer to that of an early Victorian development in London, Ladbroke Grove, than to the cities
that came actually to be built as demonstrations of
his idea.

The first translation of Howard's idea into an ac-

tual urban form, was the work of Raymond Unwin
and Barry Parker, two young planners who did not
fully share Howard's old-fashioned delight in Victorian invention and mechanical progress: for they
were under the corrective humanizing influence of
William Morris, and were more interested in recap-
turing the genial older traditions of domestic architecture than in finding a fresh, striking image for a
new kind of city as a whole.

As an historian of city design and a planning the-
orist, Raymod Unwin was the outstanding figure
of his generation, for he carried further the pioneer
innovations of Frederick Law Olmsted, and since
he had both the literary facility and the cultural
background that Howard lacked, his vision of the
new town carried greater authority. Unwin's analysis of the human insufficiency and economic waste of

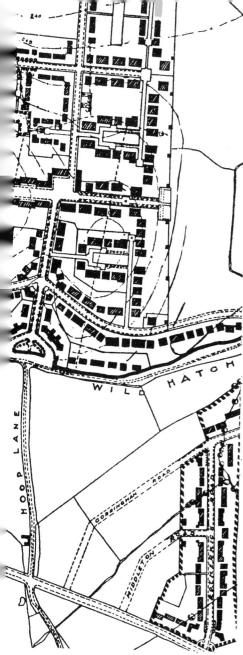

Plan from "Town Planning in Practice"

the "standard bye-law street" imposed by English legislation to achieve a minimum of sanitation and order is a classic little pamphlet: for he showed in residential neighborhoods that capital was being wastefully sunk into an excessive number of streets, paved for heavy traffic that did not exist, and mechanical utilities that were not needed, which could have been turned to better account by eliminating a large number of through streets and converting the space so saved into playgrounds and gardens.

To Unwin's demonstration, carried further by Clarence Stein and Henry Wright in Sunnyside and Radburn, we owe in large part the adoption of the superblock, which has liberated the architect from the rigid constraints of the building lot, the narrow block and the uniform building line.

Unfortunately, the plan for Letchworth Garden City was uninspired. In leaning backward to avoid the stark simplicity of Howard's diagrams, the planners managed to avoid any positive visual expression of the idea itself. And though much of the domestic architecture was more fresh and vigorous than anything of comparable cost being built at the time, and an occasional factory, set in the midst of these houses, like the Spirella corset plant, was admirable in design, the total architectural effect was mediocre, and as far as the idea went, esthetically unconvincing. Neither the plan nor the structures articulated the differentiated but balanced structure of the new city. Visually the garden displaced the city.

As a result of this architectural indecisiveness, the handsomely cultivated gardens and open spaces far outshone the architecture and served as the identifying mark of the new idea, though the garden was only one of many ingredients in Howard's new urban formula. In form Letchworth Garden City now seems a cross between a modernized country town and a spread-out contemporary suburb. Unwin's later Hampstead Gardens, a suburb which had no pretensions to being a city, turned out to be far more coherent and handsomely urbane, perhaps partly under the influence of Lutyens. In a word, the still-fermenting New Town wine was poured, at the beginning, into a too familiar suburban milk bottle. That archaic image has retarded the acceptance of the idea itself.

This overemphasis upon the gardens and open spaces was doubtless a natural reaction against the dreary deserts of pavement, with trolley poles and lamp standards taking the place of trees, that stood as sterile symbols of mechanical progress. But by its very over-emphasis it shifted attention from Howard's main idea, which was that of social manifoldness, balance of urban and rural opportunities, functional completeness. As a result the Garden City came to be tied up in many people's minds, even in those of its most powerful proponents, with a general housing standard of 12 to 14 houses per residential acre. This notion was further stereotyped by Unwin himself, for as chief architect to the English Ministry of Health, Unwin introduced this standard on a national scale for public housing estates. He advocated this density for the sensible but limited purpose of providing a subsistence garden for every working class family. And it is this standard layout, not the garden city, that spread everywhere in England from the nineteen-twenties on.

Though Howard himself experimentally promoted group housing design for communal living, the single-family house-and-garden of fixed dimensions became a standard, or rather an over-standardized, requirement. When Welwyn Garden City was built

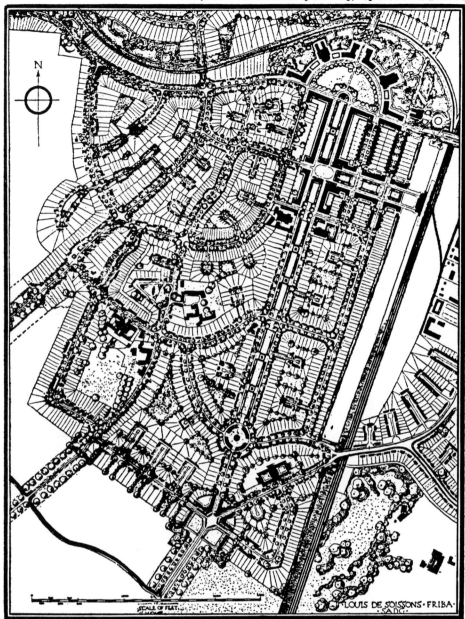

A section of Welwyn Garden City

"When Welwyn Garden City was built . . . the Georgian revival was in full swing, and the planner, Louis de Soissons, achieved greater charm and coherence . . ."

some 15 years later, the Georgian revival was in full swing, and the planner, Louis de Soissons, achieved greater charm and coherence here than Letchworth possessed. Yet, except for the admirable industrial zone, the emphasis was again on private functions and traditional forms and ample greenery, rather than on association and intercourse, on public functions, on focal meeting places and social intermixture, all of which call for the pedestrian scale and a more close-textured design.

This failure to convey a more coherent image probably slowed down the acceptance of the idea, but in recent years it has been partly corrected. Indeed, at the very moment that Letchworth was being built, Tony Garnier, in his ideal plans for a new industrial city on the Rhone, was often closer in his

architectural forms to the fresh image of the new town than were Unwin and Parker. A generation later Ernst May, once an assistant of Unwin's, came still closer to a valid form in the satellite settlement of Römerstadt, near Frankfurt-am-Main. Today the planners of the New Town of Cumbernauld, near Glasgow, though they have over-reacted against both the excessive spacing and neighborhood segregation of the first batch of British new towns, are approaching in architectural form—without resorting to high-rise structures—the compactness that is needed to make daily encounters and mixtures between people and groups not merely possible but inevitable. In time, both lack of historic structures and lack of modern examples will be overcome: the new image itself will come clear.

5. SOCIAL COMPLEXITY AND URBAN DESIGN

THE UNIT OF URBAN ORDER

The key to a fresh architectural image of the city as a whole lies in working toward an organic unit of urban order which will hold together its component parts through successive changes in function and purpose from generation to generation. While such an archetypal image can never be fully realized, this concept of the city as a whole, restated in contemporary terms, will help to define the character of each institutional structure.

In general outline, though not in dramatic architectural form, such a unit was first achieved in the British New Towns, for these were the first towns since the Middle Ages to attempt to incorporate in a unified whole all the necessary features of the social and natural environment. Contrary to prevalent opinion, England's two pioneer New Towns, originally called Garden Cities, built by private corporations under the restriction of limited dividends, have been an economic success. Though their growth was at first slow, it was sound. And in far more rapid fashion, the 15 British New Towns built since 1947 in accordance with Ebenezer Howard's principles, now with government aid, have been even more strikingly successful. In many of their factory precincts, and in some of their new town centers, they vie with Coventry, Rotterdam, and Vällingby in delineating the beginning of a fresh urban form. Already nearly 500,000 people live in these salubrious towns, planned to contain from 15,000 to 90,000 people each; and ultimately they will hold a million. In the past year, three more New Towns have been started in Britain.

Plainly Howard's method of nucleating and integrating urban functions, in units scaled to human needs and purposes to which bureaucratic and mechanical functions are subordinated, has proved viable even under a regime more or less committed to expanding these separate functions and profiting by their continued growth. The new quarters in existing cities that have achieved anything like a comparable gain in health, social diversity, family-centered amenity, and varied economic opportunity are those which, like the rebuilt Borough of Stepney in London, have followed most closely the New Town formula of mixture, balance and limitation of density.

Today the municipal corporation of Glasgow, which for long obstinately resisted the new idea of urban growth by colonization instead of the usual method of congestion and conglomeration, has reversed itself. Glasgow is now controlling its further population growth by building new towns; and its first full-size town, Cumbernauld, is now approaching completion. If there has been any flaw in this development it is only that it has proceeded so rapidly that the planners and architects—too often bound by obsolete standards imposed by the Ministry of Transport and local government authorities —have not been able to incorporate the results of past experiments and recent urban experience in their designs.

Now this organic principle of urban growth and organization does not apply only to that part of the population which can no longer be packed into the existing metropolitan centers. One of the great causes for the wholesale exodus now taking place into the suburbs is that those who can make a choice are no longer content to put up with depleted physical environment and the often degraded social conditions of our "great American cities." If the big cities hope to hold their population and continue to perform those special functions that depend upon large numbers of people, they themselves must have some of the spaciousness, the order, and the variety in their intimate, small-scale units that the New Town concept has brought into existence. Fortunately the method Howard initiated can be applied equally to the redevelopment of the existing metropolitan centers.

137

". . . 19th century boulevard . . . has long been obsolete . . ."

*". . . but its latest specialized form,
the expressway . . .
must be routed out . . ."*

". . . the mistakes of monotransportation in urban areas . . ."

ALTERNATIVE URBAN PROGRAMS

Limitation of numbers and density, mixture of social and economic activities, internal balance, the interplay of usable open spaces with occupied spaces, the restoration of parks, gardens, and green walkways as integral parts of the urban environment—these are the keys to overcoming the congestion and disorganization of the big city and restoring its general habitability. So essential are these processes in creating new urban forms that many critics who parade as Howard's sworn enemies have nevertheless adopted his guiding principles under another name.

Thus in "Communitas," Paul and Percival Goodman, after shelving Howard respectfully as a bourgeois back number, restate a major part of his thesis as their own original contribution. Thus Le Corbusier, after contemptuously dismissing the British garden city, comes forth with his own "Vertical Garden City" as an alternative and uses the advanced mechanical facilities of a skyscraper to achieve the all-too-limited associations of a mere village. Thus again Dr. E. A. Gutkind, whose recent book on "The Twilight of Cities" spurns the Garden City and the New Town as an obsolete Victorian concept, projects as alternative a multitude of garden townlets, or infra-garden cities, as his way of handling regional dispersal.

Even Jane Jacobs, after characterizing Howard as a would-be destroyer of the city, proposes to restore the essential urban qualities that have been lost through over-congestion and over-expansion by dividing the metropolis into self-governing "districts," with their own local economic enterprises and social opportunities. Mrs. Jacobs' districts are designed not merely to welcome the diverse activities that Howard insisted on for the Garden City, but they turn out even to have the same suggested population, some 30,000. That number, incidentally, is the very size that Leonardo da Vinci hit upon when he proposed to the Duke of Milan to relieve the congestion and foul disorder of 16th-century Milan by designing 10 cities of 30,000 population each.

In short, Mrs. Jacobs atones for her sedulous ignorance of Howard's work by unconsciously becoming his disciple, at least for half his urban program. And for similar valid reasons the recent Royal Commission report on the government of London proposes to reorganize that unwieldy mass into semi-autonomous boroughs of approximately equal size, around 200,000, all co-operating within a larger regional framework. This gives support to Mrs. Jacobs' suggestion that 100,000 is perhaps the right size for a "district" in a big city like New York; but here again she touches on the upper limits of the actual New Towns!

No adequate image of the emerging city can be formed without reference both to the most enduring and valuable features of historic cities as well as to the fresh departures and fresh opportunities that our modern age, with its immense stores of knowledge, wealth and power, has opened up. Not least, we must carefully evaluate the many experiments in urban design made during the last century, from Ladbroke Grove (London) to the latest suburban shopping center.

Yet as a result of the ferment in planning thought that Howard started, we can now draw the following conclusions. First, the useful, manageable, visible, reproducible, and—not least important—humanly lovable city must range somewhere between 30,000 and 300,000 people. Beyond that size, if we are not to enter the realm of de-personalized mechanisms, the unit of organization becomes not the city but the region. Second, its own area and population must be limited in order to be able to set a limit to its component parts. The maintenance of diversity and balance between all essential urban functions, biological, economic and cultural, is the only effective means of controlling the insensate dynamism of separate institutions that, concerned solely with their own expansion, tend to separate themselves from the whole.

Like personalities and organisms, cities are devices for reducing the now otherwise limitless energies at our command to just those quantities that will promote a self-governing and self-developing mode of life. Localized oversize in any single institution, whether it is a business corporation, a hospital or a university, is a sign that the city has ceased to perform one of its most essential modern functions: the control of one-sided growth.

Thus the new conception of the city, as a balanced organization maintaining unity in diversity and continuity in change, is essential for controlling excessive quantities, whether of population or physical power. For having achieved the first glimpse of this organic principle of urban order, Ebenezer Howard will perhaps be remembered even longer than the "first" Greek town planner, Hippodamos. Though many historic cities embodied this idea, this is the first age in which it has come clearly into consciousness.

THE NEXT STEPS IN DESIGN

Those of us who are pursuing further the train of constructive thought that Howard so largely started and Raymond Unwin and Barry Parker first carried out, cannot be content with any present embodiments of their ideas, though we no doubt have a duty to defend them from libelous caricature and

". . . the green walkway . . . must be restored as a separate system . . ."

". . . it requires time, not merely an individual lifetime, but many collective lifetimes . . ."

ignorant abuse. Still less do we wish to make the existing New Towns a standard pattern for all urban integration, duly codified by law. Such a stereotyping of the idea would eliminate the very richness and variety of concrete detail that is inherent in the notion of a city. For the city is nothing less than a collective personality whose character reflects its unique combination of geographic, economic, cultural and historic factors. As William Blake put it, "One law for the lion and the ox is oppression."

Admirable though the New Towns of Britain have proved, in contrast with the raucous disorder and standardized blight of so many metropolitan areas, no existing examples can be considered as final. Many rectifications and improvements remain to be made both in detail and in their general pattern. And meanwhile, some seemingly decisive innovations made elsewhere, like the American suburban shopping center and the specialized industrial park, have already disclosed their own grave liabilities, which stem mainly from their boasted detachment from the city. Apart from this, thanks to a century of historic investigation whose results have at last come to a head in the works of Pierre Lavedan, Ernst Egli and myself, the essential value of old forms can now be properly appreciated, and some of these forms, hitherto rejected as obstacles to "progress," can be preserved either to maintain continuity or to serve as a departure for further renovations. For much has recently been learned about the social nature of the city and the meaning of its diversity that suggests further revisions, adaptations and innovations. Some of Mrs. Jacobs' fresh observations on these matters deserve to be heeded, even by those who are not drawn to her planning proposals.

But first we must remove a current superstition. The notion that the form and content of the city must primarily serve its technology turns the true order upside down. Perhaps the primary function of the city today is that of bringing technology itself into line with human purpose, reducing speed, energy, quantification to amounts that are humanly assimilable and humanly valuable.

Along these lines there has been a considerable amount of fresh architectural and social invention, which awaits embodiment in the larger framework of the city. Thus the separation of fast-moving vehicles from the pedestrian—the Radburn principle, or more anciently, the Venice principle—not merely facilitates these two complementary modes of circulation, both still necessary, but releases building from the old uniform lot-and-block pattern. This makes it possible to plan superblocks and precincts and neighborhoods so as to serve a variety of functions related in space and form to the needs of the users,

rather than to an arbitrary street pattern. That gives the architect in the city proper some of the freedom in composition that he has had only in the suburbs. So, too, the new pedestrian shopping mall, as in Coventry, Rotterdam, and Stevenage, has already demonstrated advantages that neither the old shopping avenue, nor the isolated suburban shopping center, wallowing in a sea of parking space, can provide.

Still other innovations call for critical assessment and doubtless for further modification or for alternative solutions. Some of them, like the urban greenbelt, the Radburn plan of a continuous internal park, or the Perry conception of the balanced neighborhood unit, have now been sufficiently tested to provide useful data for judgment. Not least the notion of a single ideal residential density calls for further reconsideration; for, even before the Architectural Review's polemic against "prairie planning," it had become clear, as I pointed out in 1953, that the British New Towns had been overspaced, and that the hygienic and recreational advantages of abundant open spaces must be integrated with the social and domestic needs for cohesion, intimacy, and spontaneous association, which demand somewhat higher densities and the preservation of the pedestrian scale.

For all their notable improvements, the over-all designs of the British New Towns are at last ready for detailed and discriminating criticism on the basis of their actual performance. One of the principal factors to be reconsidered is their density. As a result of a uniformly low residential coverage, under mandate of legislation, along with an over-plenitude of wide roads and verges, to say nothing of the acres of playing fields demanded by education authorities, plus neighborhood greenbelts, which are actually more often wide wedges, the planners of New Towns have even forfeited the domestic convenience of the neighborhood unit itself. This space wastage must be challenged even more severely in many current American projects, from new university campuses to the new project of El Dorado Hills near Sacramento, California, which has been conceived as a collection of semi-urban villages that more or less correspond, in fact, to Dr. Gutkind's ideal pattern. All this calls for more judicious criticism than it has yet received from any quarter in the light of a more social conception of the city.

Meanwhile many older inventions in planning call for fresh expression. The 19th-century boulevard or parkway, in which pedestrians and vehicles shared the same space, has long been obsolete, but its latest specialized form, the expressway, must be routed out of the city, if the city is to have a life of its own. Once the expressway enters the city, it undertakes

*. . . part of what was modern 50 years ago
by now vitally historic . . ."*

". . . the fashionable current model . . ."

". . . what looks brightly modern
only for the year in which it was built . . ."

an impossible task of canalizing into a few arteries what must be circulated through a far more complex system of arteries, veins, and capillaries: only the fullest use of the whole system, restored for general circulation, with public vehicles undertaking the major burden, will rectify the mistakes of mono-transportation in urban areas. As for the discarded element in the boulevard—the green walkway—it must be restored as a separate system, detached from wheeled vehicles, as is now being done in the Society Hill district of Philadelphia. For the same reason, that other by-product of the boulevard, the sidewalk cafe—now ruined by the noise and fumes of motor traffic—must take refuge in tiny neighborhood parks, such as those in Central Athens, though they might easily survive as a socially enlivening feature in the interior of a superblock.

These many innovations and rectifications call for increasing integration in formal designs, which will set a new pattern for each part of the city. But to demand a clean-minted urban image from the work of a single architect, or even a single generation, is to misunderstand the essentially cumulative nature of the city. An organic image of the city requires for its actual fulfillment a dimension that no single generation can ever supply: it requires time, not merely an individual lifetime, but many collective lifetimes. Neither as a seemingly unchangeable spatial object outside of time, nor as a disposable container, good only for the brief period necessary for financial amortization, can the city perform its essential function. The now popular concept of the city as a disposable container, to be replaced at a profit every decade or every generation, in order to feed an expanding economy, denies the most valuable function of the city as an organ of social memory; namely its linking up the generations, its bringing into the present both the usable past and the desirable future.

No organic urban design for any larger urban area accordingly can be completed once and for all, like a Baroque city established by royal fiat, by wiping out all existing structures and replacing them by the fashionable current model. This futurist method would put the city at the mercy of five-year-old knowledge and five-year-old minds, and the resulting loss of memory is no less a serious impairment to the life of the city than the loss of memory in people whose brains have been injured by shock or senility. In a sense, then, there can be no single modern architectural form of the city. Part of what was modern 50 years ago is by now vitally historic and as worthy of sedulous preservation as any ancient building in so far as it still serves new uses, while other examples of what was once modern have long been obsolete and should be removed; indeed, what looks brightly modern only for the year in which it was built is usually out of date before it is finished.

MODERNITY AND CONTINUITY

In contrast to the position taken by Paul Ylvisacker and others, a more organic view of the city holds that the greater the inherent dynamism of science, technics, and finance, today, the greater need there is for a durable urban container. For as I pointed out in "The City in History," when the container changes as rapidly as the contents, neither can perform their necessary but complementary functions. Here at last we have, I believe, an essential key to sound urban and architectural design today: it must not merely welcome variety and complexity in all their forms, environmental, social, and personal, but it must deliberately leave a place for continued rectification, improvement, innovation and renewal. When soundly designed, such an urban form will be fulfilled, not spoiled, by the increment of each succeeding generation, as the medieval city was in fact improved by interpolating squares and buildings that mirrored the new spatial order of the Renaissance.

Now the cities of the past often overemphasized continuity. Their builders entombed life in all-too-massive permanent structures and in even more rigid routines that resisted growth and prevented the necessary modifications each generation must make. But the cities of today have just the opposite vice: while their neglected quarters fester, their favored "dynamic" areas are too ephemeral to foster human growth and cultural continuity. Once time and organic complexity are taken seriously as components of design, it is plain that the replacement of outworn areas is a delicate process; and while it must go on constantly in small measures, it must not be fatally limited to superficial reformations that do not interfere with any fresh larger designs. Among the many postwar plans for rebuilding half-ruined cities, those made for Manchester by its town surveyor, Rowland Nicholas, have stood out by reason of the fact that its proposals for the redesign of partly wrecked areas, filled with obsolete buildings and wasteful streets, were conceived as a complex process in time: demolition and rebuilding were provided for in a series of stages, covering a period of 40 years. Such planning, which does justice to the future without forgetting the past, happily exemplifies an organic approach that can handle, and profit by, any degree of complexity and diversity.

This analysis perhaps clarifies the failure of Howard's concept of the Garden City or New Town to find at once an appropriate architectural expression.

Our age tends to think of complexity in purely mechanical terms, and to reduce social and human relations to simplified abstract units that lend themselves easily to centralized direction and mechanical control. Hence the brilliantly sterile images that Le Corbusier and Mies van der Rohe projected, images that magnify power, suppress diversity, nullify choice, have swept across the planet as the new form of the city. This identification of modern form with uniform high-rise buildings, which one finds too often even in recent surveys of modern architecture, should be as outmoded as the bureaucratic animus to which it pays homage. Such over-simplification of form is now eating the heart out of our projects of urban renewal, and has had even more disastrous results in such new cities as Brasilia.

By contrast, a new image of the city which does justice to all its dimensions can be no simple overnight job: for it must include the form-shaping contributions of nature, of river, bay, hill, forest, vegetation, climate, as well as those of human history and culture, with the complex interplay of groups, corporations, organizations, institutions, personalities. Let us not then unduly regret our slowness in arriving at an expressive and unified form for the modern city.

The minds that are fully at home in all these dimensions of modern life are few, and in any quantity they have still to be formed. Certainly they are not yet being equipped and disciplined by our leading architectural and planning schools; nor are there enough leaders in business and government to provide them the opportunities they need. Yet once a more organic understanding is achieved of the complex interrelation of the city and its region, the urban and the rural aspects of environment, the small-scale unit and the large-scale unit, a new sense of form will spread through both architecture and city design. In both spheres, instead of creating closed and complete forms, there will be a deliberate attempt to provide space for further constructive effort and development.

SUMMARY

This series began with the obvious proposition that even our biggest and richest cities today fall short of the ideal possibilities that our age has opened up. We have not had the imagination nor the forethought to use the immense energies modern man now commands: our architects have frittered them away on constructive trivialities and superfluities that have often defaced the environment without improving the human condition or the architectural form. To counteract this miscarriage of effort, we looked about for a fresh image of the city, as conceived by the influential planners and architects of the last half century, Le Corbusier, Frank Lloyd Wright, and Raymond Unwin; and we found that the only model that did justice to the complexity of the city was that offered in purely diagrammatic form by Ebenezer Howard, the founder of two Garden Cities. Because the New Town principle was not invented during the last five years, the more fashionable academic minds regard it as obsolete and flirt with a formless "Megalopolis" as an ultimate form. Yet even the new towns that have been built on Howard's abstract principles have hardly as yet provided a fresh image, in terms of present day potentialities and the present needs of the emerging city.

Part of the reason for all these shortcomings became evident when we considered that organic complexity requires the dimension of time; and that even in the design of the British New Towns not sufficient time has yet elapsed to incorporate and integrate all that we know now about the nature of cities, and the value of the various urban inventions that have been produced during the last century. Thus we see that a truly modern design for a city must be one that allows for both its historic and social complexity, and for its continued renewal and reintegration in time. No single instantaneous image, which reflects the needs of a particular moment, can encompass the feelings and sentiments that bring the generations together in working partnership, binding the past that has never died to the future that is already in question.

This interpretation of urban form indicates that the same cultural factors underlie both the possibility of renewal in existing cities, however big, and the building of new towns, however small. As energy and productivity increase, a larger proportion will be available for the humanization of man; and this task, despite many ominous contrary indications today, is still the essential task of the city. Only those who seek to respond to this challenge will be able to give the city an adequate architectural form: a form that will bring within the range and grasp of every citizen the wider world on which his life and well-being depend.

BOOK FIVE

Essays

1937-1968

"This, then, is the task for today and tomorrow: to restore and eventually to elevate even higher than ever before the organic and human components that are now missing in our compulsively dynamic and over-mechanized culture. The time has come for architecture to come back to earth and make a new home for man."

**What went wrong with the dreams of
a truly modern style in architecture
which would express the realities of our age?
Only, says a noted critic, that they came true:
now we have discovered the limitations
of the machine, and the time has come to develop**

ARCHITECTURE AS A HOME FOR MAN

Not the least part of my architectural education came from my walks through New York's Lower East Side, whose tenements, in their congestion, their darkness, their foul interiors, fully equalled if they did not surpass those of Juvenal's Rome. The absence of space, order, intelligent design, even sunlight and fresh air—the sense of all the human qualities that were missing—taught me, by contrast, what to demand in every work of humane architecture.

These solitary walks were the foundation of my architectural education; and if I have had anything fresh to say about modern architecture or about city design, it is because I have continued these walks throughout my lifetime: not as a sightseer or tourist, looking for notable buildings worthy of three or at least two guidebook stars: but as a man who sought to take in visually and make the fullest possible use of the life about him. To quote Ulysses: "Much have I seen and known: cities of men and manners, climates, councils, governments." For in my ideal scheme of education, this mode of seeing and knowing must both precede and supplement the knowledge we receive from books, statistics, or computers.

Even the worst buildings one encounters in this fashion are still human documents; and as for the greatest, they are of the same stuff that poems and symphonies are made of, not merely vivifying one's limited experience, but uniting one with a tradition that goes back at least as far, architecturally speaking,

149

"...a world that dated not...from the beginnings of architecture...but from the birth of Charles Edouard Jeanneret and Frank Lloyd Wright..."

as the painted caves of Lascaux and Altamira—and probably, if we had any record of older cultures, much farther.

The art of becoming human and its relationship to architecture

In the end I have come to recognize only one supreme art, the art of becoming human: the art of expressing and intensifying one's own conscious humanity by appropriate acts, fantasies, thoughts, and works. So closely are esthetic form, moral character, and practical function united in my philosophy, that the absence of one or the other of these qualities in any work of architecture turns it for me into a hollow shell, a mere piece of scene-painting or technological exhibitionism, like Buckminster Fuller's tetrahedral domes—not a fully-dimensioned building that does justice to all the varied demands of life.

My architectural interest has never been primarily in the formal structure as such: if so, I would have spent much more time learning from Viollet-le-Duc, Guadet, and their successors. My interest has rather been in buildings as a many-sided expression of the human mind: not just its intelligence and practical mastery, but its feelings, its prophetic aspirations, its transcendent purposes. If you wish masterly technical criticism in architecture, you must seek it, not in my own work, but in that of my great American predecessor, Montgomery Schuyler, whose admirable critiques of Richardson, Roebling, Louis Sullivan, J. W. Root and Frank Lloyd Wright I had the privilege of making known to the present generation.*

Le Corbusier and the machine: at once "Cartesian" and "Baroque"

Now my career as architectural critic runs parallel, curiously, with another mind that was to exercise a much greater influence over the past generation, the late and much lamented Le Corbusier; for he, like myself, was some-

*For a bibliography of Schuyler's articles in the RECORD (1891-1917), see January 1956, 284, 288.

thing of an amateur, a term I use in no derogatory sense; and in the eyes of his first master, Auguste Perret, he remained an amateur to the end. Le Corbusier's walking tour through Europe played the same part in his architectural awakening that my peregrinations around New York did for me; and at the moment he and Ozenfant were formulating a new esthetic derived from the machine, I published, in 1921, an article on "Machinery and the Modern Style," based on the same premises.

But from the time I read the first edition of his *Vers une Architecture,* I knew that we were, by reason of our different temperaments and education, predestined enemies: he with his Cartesian clarity and his Cartesian elegance but also—alas!—with his Baroque insensitiveness to time, change, organic adaptation, functional fitness, ecological complexity; and, not least, with his sociological naivete, his economic ignorance, and his political indifference. These very deficiencies were, as it turned out, what made his City of the Future such a successful model for world-wide imitation: its form reflected perfectly the financial, bureaucratic, and technological limitations of the present age.

Even when Le Corbusier used the same urban concepts I had redefined and reestablished, such as the Garden City or the New Town, he did so without the least grasp of the social principles that they embodied. And yet, in the right-about-face that Le Corbusier made toward the end of his life, he deliberately turned his back on his original mechanical cliches and slogans, and sought expression in forms that emphasized not rationality but fantasy, not Cartesian order but emotional depth. Had these two aspects of Le Corbusier's mind been equally cultivated from the beginning, I should have been proud to be counted as his admirer and advocate.

Wright: another "victim of his own egotism and arrogance"

I have used the example of Le Corbusier, not to disparage his creative talents, but the better to define my own position during the decade when his vivid polemics, his marvelously suggestive sketches, and his esthetic innovations influenced, indeed dazzled and in fact overwhelmed, the younger generation.

You might gather from this that since I rejected Le Corbusier I accepted wholeheartedly his older rival and polar opposite, Frank Lloyd Wright. But that would oversimplify my position. Wright was for me, and still is, the outstanding architect of the past century: unrivalled for sheer exuberant creativity. And yet, like Le Corbusier, he was the victim of his own egotism and his arrogance. They lived in a world that dated not from the beginning of the Christian era, nor from the beginnings of architecture in Egypt and Sumer, but from the birth of Charles Edouard Jeanneret in the one case, Frank Lloyd Wright in the other.

An architectural generation absorbed in exploiting newness

In this, these architects were typical of their generation; and the principal fault I find in my own early set of ideas, even though I was better grounded in history, is that I, too, believed that modern science and technics had the happy task of wiping out the effete remains of past cultures, as a bulldozer slaughters the trees and levels the ground for a mass building operation, in order to found a new culture on rational, purely scientific principles. I can speak freely about this aberration, since in my youth I was molded by the same positivist ideology. For me, only contemporary life had meaning. As a student I rebelled at the college requirement to learn even a smattering of first-year Latin. Like the elder writers who influenced our whole generation, Bernard Shaw and H. G. Wells, we identified the new with the good, and hailed the New Man, the New Woman, the New Politics, the New History, the New Science: in short, the New World. History, we thought, began and ended with ourselves, and we expected the new to last

forever, as if the will-to-change itself would remain forever unchanged.

Even before the Nineteen-twenties were over, I had modified many of these views: for as soon as I was married, I discovered that the New Woman was still the old Eve, and then that the New Baby was still full of the old Adam, no matter how much one had departed from the older generation's methods of child care.

Did victories over tradition serve the needs of human beings?

But in architecture, engineering and technics, we nonetheless hailed every departure from precedent or tradition as a victory for the modern spirit; and we did not suspect that many of our modern criteria or our modern forms were as inadequate from the standpoint of organic human needs as the stereotyped historic forms that the eclectic traditionalist half-heartedly imitated.

Yet the fact is that the first of the new experimental buildings, by their very contrast with the old, conveyed a sense of vital originality that they can no longer evoke after having been reproduced, with all their faults, a thousand times. Like the old Strada Nova in Genoa, they stood out magnificently, enhanced by the clutter of old buildings around them. There are still a few structures, like the classic Van Nelle factory near Rotterdam, that keep this freshness.

But during the past quarter century blight and confusion have fallen upon modern architecture, as they have fallen upon our whole civilization; and the principal causes of this blight have remained unexamined and uncorrected, chiefly because they are the result of forces and modes of thought which our contemporaries regard as unqualified goods: the expansion of the exact sciences, the socially explosive inventions of nuclear physics and electronics, the achievements of automation and cybernation. These massive transformations in every department of technics now seek to wipe out every human function or purpose that will not conform to the dominant ideology and support its expanding and inflating economy.

"Caprice and random happenings" as a "principle" of current design

Most of our contemporaries are unprepared to face the fact that our rapid scientific and technical progress has resulted in ecological deterioration and social regression: and that the disintegration of our civilization has been in good part caused by our fabulous success in displacing the human personality and denying its autonomy. Mechanical and electronic processes of integration have produced their astounding successes in mass production and mass communication by systematically breaking down ecological complexities and eliminating the human factor. Compulsory consumption, compulsory waste, compulsory direction, compulsory destruction are the marks of this age; and it would be strange if architecture were not threatened by these same forces. When half a century ago we demanded that modern architecture express "modern life," we were too innocent to guess what this demonstration would reveal.

Though the present cult of anti-life might plausibly be traced back to Marinetti and his Futurist following, the full meaning of this attack has become apparent only during the last 20 years. One of the possible responses to the over-mechanized and over-regimented world we have fabricated is becoming more obvious every day: the elevation of caprice and random happenings into the guiding principle of modern design. This, of course, is most conspicuous at the moment in the realm of clothing and costume. Who could have guessed that the effortful inanity of Quant and Twiggy clothes would come from a country that gave the world the utilitarian rationalism of Manchester which so stimulated the mind of Karl Frederick Schinkel?

Up to now architecture, unlike music, painting, sculpture and the drama, has not successfully been turned into a "happening," for the simple reason that a building constructed on such lines would not stay together long enough to be seen, much less lived in. But the effort will surely be made: either by scattering ephemeral plastic envelopes around an underground shelter, or by staging more elaborate architectural happenings under a geodesic dome—thus uniting the two main avant-garde movements in contemporary disintegration: the Hippies and the Buckies. In both movements, the desire to efface or completely replace the human image and the organic environment dominates its leaders. So those who are in retreat from all mechanization, all regimentation, indeed all order, can hardly be distinguished from those who worship and exalt the machine, and who are utilizing the most advanced technology—nuclear power, bulldozers, jet planes, rockets, computers—to achieve the same results even more effectively.

Today's architectural trends: disposable container, space capsule

Architecture today is thus tending to one or another extreme: either the disposable container or the space capsule. Both are designed for mass production, the first in limitless quantities, the second in units of limitless size, like the Mile High Skyscraper, that denial of his own organic architecture, which Frank Lloyd Wright played with toward the end of his life. Our present object of public worship and religious sacrifice, the space rocket, efficiently serves both as space-capsule *and* disposable container. Both extremes, by definition and by intention, are based on purely mechanical, not human, requirements as determined by systems analysis; and both modes are detached from the living past and the potential future: for they are focussed on a present from which the accumulations of past experience and the potentialities of the future have been rigorously excluded. Such architecture, devoid of human associations, is fit only for computers, not for men. To call these structures modern because of their extravagant technical and scientific equipment is to forget all that biology and psychology, archaeology and history have now added to the naive Seventeenth Century picture of a purely physical cosmos. Machine-made man and his machine-made world are both obsolete.

What happens when the old dreams of modern architecture come true?

What, I have often asked myself, has gone wrong with our youthful dreams about a truly modern style in architecture, one which should express the realities of our own age? I have come to the conclusion that only one thing went wrong with those dreams: They came true! In our admiration for the entrancing constructive feats made possible by modern technics, we did not imagine what the world would look like if every part of it was made over into the exact image of the machine: with trees turning into metal rods, flowers that once bloomed and died achieving immortality in plastic forms, and men and women becoming so completely subservient to the machine that the space capsule, at least in the vulgar form of a motor car, would become their ideal habitat, for the sake of which they would ruin their landscapes, poison the air and the water, and destroy their cities. There is no need today for rocket flights to the moon: the face of our own planet will soon be equally sterile, equally hostile to living organisms. Has not Buckminster Fuller actually characterized the space capsule as the most perfect man-made environment? Why look further?

But we owe a debt to modern architecture: its disposable containers and its space capsules have revealed the real nature of our civilization: its compulsive irrationality, its mechanized barbarism, its psychedelic fantasies, sub-human or pre-human in their complete alienation from man's deep creative potentialities and formative achievements. Neither "instant buildings" nor "instant cities" are likely, on their own terms, to have a long life. The cult of power has made us impotent; and the cult of speed has created an environment so uniform that the faster one travels the less the scene changes.

A time for architecture which restores man to a central position

Our generation, which invented the term feedback, should be able to learn from and rectify the mistakes it has made in its one-sided exaltation of technology. We should at last understand that unless we preserve human continuity, and cultivate variety and balance throughout the human environment, our scientific and technical advances will be not merely menacing but meaningless. Primitive man learned, by a thousand magic tricks and games and rituals, to detach himself from nature without forfeiting the many gifts and advantages nature generously offered him. So now with modern man. He must stake out his own inviolable territory, essential to both his inner balance and his creative growth: so detaching himself from the machine as to make it serve his own purposes.

Instead of abasing himself before his electronic and mechanical gods, modern man must restore his own self-respect, his self-discipline, above all his capacity for selecting and achieving goals that conform, not only to economic and technological conditions, but to the needs of his own personality and community, enriched as they are by precious historic fibres that reach far back into his past. Man, as Pico della Mirandola well said, is the maker and the molder of himself. In that process, architecture has been one of the chief means, through symbolic expression and beautiful form, of transforming and making visible to later generations his ideal self: not just his capacity to think, but his capacity to dream, to love, to enjoy and to hope.

This, then, is the task for today and tomorrow: to restore and eventually to elevate even higher than ever before the organic and human components that are now missing in our compulsively dynamic and over-mechanized culture. The time has come for architecture to come back to earth and to make a new home for man.

153

FUNCTION AND EXPRESSION IN ARCHITECTURE

"We, today, know that the machine represents only a fragment of the human spirit"

ONCE UPON A TIME a great motion picture palace was opened; and an array of notable New Yorkers was invited to the first night. For at least ten minutes, but for what seemed the better part of an hour, the audience was treated to a succession of lighting effects, to the raising and lowering of the orchestra platform, and to the manifold ways in which the curtain could be lifted and parted. For a while, the audience was delighted by the technical virtuosity displayed: but when nothing further seemed about to happen, they were bored: they were waiting for the real performance to begin.

Modern architecture is now in a state similar to that of the Radio City Music Hall on the opening night. Our best architects are full of technical facility and calculated competence; but from the standpoint of the audience, they are still only going through the mechanical motions. The audience is still waiting for the performance to begin.

Now, in all systems of architecture, both function and expression have a place. Every building performs work, if it is only to keep off the rain or to remain upright against the wind. At the same time, even the simplest structure produces a visual impression upon those who use it or look at it: unconsciously or by design, it says something to the beholder and modifies, in some slight degree at least, even his bodily reactions. Functions permanently invisible, like those performed by the foundations or the heating apparatus, may remain outside the architectural picture; but every function that is visible contributes in some degree to expression. In simple monuments, like obelisks, or even in more complex structures like temples, the function of the building is subordinate to the human purpose it embodies: if such structures do not delight the eye and inform the mind, no technical audacity can save them from becoming meaningless. Indeed, ideological obsolescence is more fatal than technical obsolescence to a work of architecture. As soon as a building becomes meaningless, it disappears.

Modern architecture crystallized at the moment that people realized that the older modes of symbolism no longer spoke to modern man; and that, on the contrary, the new functions brought in by the machine had something special to say to him. Unfortunately, in the act

154

of realizing these new truths, mechanical function has tended to absorb expression, or in more fanatical minds, to do away with the need for it. As a result, the architectural imagination has, within the last twenty years, become impoverished: so much so that the recent prize-winning design for a great memorial, produced by one of the most accomplished and able of the younger architects, was simply a gigantic parabolic arch. If technics could not, by itself, tell the story of the pioneer, moving through the gateway of the continent, the story could not, in the architectural terms of our own day, be told. This failure to do justice to the symbolic and expressive functions of architecture perhaps reached its climax in the design of the United Nations Headquarters, where an office building has been treated as a monument, and where one of the three great structures has been placed so as to be lost to view by most of the approaches to the site.

By now, many architects have become aware of a self-imposed poverty: in absorbing the lessons of the machine and in learning to master new forms of construction, they have, they begin to see, neglected the valid claims of the human personality. In properly rejecting antiquated symbols, they have also rejected human needs, interests, sentiments, values, that must be given full play in every complete structure. This does not mean, as some critics have hastily asserted, that functionalism is doomed: it means rather that the time has come to integrate objective functions with subjective functions: to balance off mechanical facilities with biological needs, social commitments, and personal values. And to understand the new prospects that open before architecture, we must first do justice to functionalism and to see how it came about in our time that the mechanical part or the even more abstract spatial form was taken for the whole.

As so often happens, functionalism came into the world as a fact long before it was appraised as an idea. The fact was that for three centuries engineering had been making extraordinary advances in every department except architecture: a passion for economy, a methodical concentration upon productive work, a growing concern with practical needs, had given authority to mechanical methods, rational calculations, repetitive processes; and had opened up new resources and energies. Even before the machine began to exert its special discipline, functional needs had tended to produce strong geometric or organic forms in building: a barn, a haystack, or a silo, a castle, a bridge, a seaworthy sailing vessel — all these are functional forms whose cleanness of line and rightness of shape spring, like the shape of a sea-gull, from the work to be performed.

"In the cathedrals of the Middle Ages, economy, comfort and good acoustic properties were all cheerfully sacrificed to the magnification of glory and mystery, in a fashion designed to overwhelm the worshipper"

By and large, people do not consciously enjoy such structures until they have ceased to use them, or at least until they pause long enough to take in the meaning of what they have done. But these structures have at least the quality of all organic creations: they identify themselves and express the functions they serve. When a steam locomotive is fully developed, for example, so that all its excrescences and technological leftovers are absorbed in the final shape — streamlined as we now say — that locomotive not merely *is* more speedy than the primitive form, but it unmistakably says speed, too. These fresh mechanical interests had a vital message for modern architects, for they reopened a vista of constructive possibilities that had been closed in the Renaissance by a deliberate sacrifice of function to expression, and of expression itself, once the baroque impulse died, to mere correctness and archaeological refinement. What Durham Cathedral says, by reason of its massive stone columns and free space, could not be said with bamboo poles and thatched roofs. By the varied means modern engineering had placed at the architects' disposal, the architects' imagination should have been effectively expanded, if human purposes in other departments of

". . . that locomotive not merely is more speedy . . . but it unmistakably says speed"

". . . functional forms whose cleanness of line spring, like the shape of a sea-gull, from the work to be performed"

life had kept pace with modern man's technical aptitudes.

One of the first people to understand the implications of functionalism as a criterion of good form was the American sculptor, Horatio Greenough. In the middle of the nineteenth century, at the end of his all-too-brief life, he published a series of papers that for the first time formulated the new esthetic of the machine and widened its applications to all forms of beauty. Greenough, a student of current biology as well as of sculpture, carried further the great theorem of Lamarck: Form follows function. He saw that this generalization applies to all organic forms, even man-created ones.

Greenough recognized that the effective works of

art in his own day, the primitives of a new era, were not the derivative symbols of eclectic painting and architecture, but the strong virile forms, without any historic attachment than to their own age, of the new tools and machines and engineering structures that met the needs of modern life. The American ax, the American clock, the clipper ship — in every line of these utilities and machines necessity or function played a determining part. They were without ornament or decorative device of any kind, except perhaps for a surviving ship's figurehead: like the naked body, when harmoniously developed, they needed no further ornament or costume to achieve beauty. For what was beauty? "The promise of function."

As formulated by Greenough, that was a breathtaking, a spine-tingling thought; and in the minds of Greenough's successors, such as Louis Sullivan, who may have breathed in Greenough's ideas with his native New England air, this doctrine provided a genuine starting point for the new architecture. No building could hope to do justice to the values of our age that did not, by design, follow the lines dictated by effective function: the beautiful, as Emerson put it, must rest on the foundations of the necessary.

But while Greenough's doctrine was a salutary one, it was incomplete; for it failed to do justice to those specifically human values that are derived, not from the object and the work, but from the subject and the equality of life the architect seeks to enhance. Even mechanical function itself rests on human values: the desire for order, for security, for power; but to presume that these values are, in every instance, all-prevailing ones, which do away with the need for any other qualities, is to limit the nature of man himself to just those functions that serve the machine. One may therefore profitably contrast Greenough's doctrine with that advanced by his contemporary, John Ruskin, in The Seven Lamps of Architecture.

Contrary to popular misinterpretation, Ruskin had a very healthy respect for the utilitarian triumphs of the Victorian age: he said that a British ship-of-the-line, that early triumph of standardization and pre-fabrication, was one of the chief reasons for admiring his period. But Ruskin insisted that building was one thing and architecture was another: on his theory, a building became a work of architecture only when the bare structure was embellished with original works of sculpture and painting. In the form that Ruskin put it, this theory, which made architecture dependent upon the non-architectural arts, was glaringly false. Followed to its end, it would lead to the conclusion Geoffrey Scott reached in The Architecture of Humanism: a doctrine that would readily mask the organic anatomy of a building beneath a contradictory costume, designed by a painter, a decorator, or an "industrial designer."

But Ruskin's notion, that architecture is more than mere building, was in fact sound: it becomes acceptable as soon as one re-states it, so as to derive the specifically architectural element, not from painting and sculpture, but from the architect's treatment of the whole building as an image and a plastic form, in order to express, by his modification of pure functional needs, the meanings and values that are integrally related to the structure: underlining the relevant human purposes and values, designing an office-building so that it will make the workers in it feel more efficient and business-like, a university so that the students will be prompted to habits of study and intellectual intercourse, a church so that its communicants will feel more indrawn and exalted. To apply to all the diverse activities and needs of a community, the standards that are appropriate to a factory is clearly a case of irrelevant symbolism. Those qualities that differentiate architecture from building cannot be derived from the mechanical requirements of the structure: they spring from the character and purpose of the user, as these are interpreted and remolded by the architect.

There are doubtless moments when the architect needs the painter and the sculptor, just as he may have need for other handicrafts. But when an architect uses all the resources of his art, the building itself becomes a multi-dimensional image, a whole series of pictures that change in quality with every hour of the day, and with every change in position by the observer. So, too, it becomes a highly complex plastic form, whose interior space and openings are as significant as the mass, since in a building the possibility of movement through space provides the architect with resources that are not at the disposal of the sculptor. By his choice of materials and textures and colors, by the contrasting play of light and shade, by the advance and recession of planes, by the clarification and organization of the plan in relation to the elevation, the architect produces a highly complex symbol of human purposes and values, emotions, feelings, and sentiments.

Our age properly renounced the use of antiquated symbols in its architecture; and at that moment, many architects thought it was possible to renounce every manner of symbolism as well. But the actual effect of the contemporary effort to strip architecture down to building was to make the machine — the dynamic instrument of this change — itself an object of veneration. Feelings and emotions that had hitherto attached themselves to organisms and persons, to political institutions

"It was the desire to embrace nature that led to the introduction of the garden into the interior"

or religious ideals, were now canalized into the machine. Like the hero of an almost forgotten play by Eugene O'Neill, the modern architect made a god of the Dynamo, as if the sole meaning of life for modern man lay in his control of matter and energy, or in his further transposition of austere machine-forms into depersonalized abstractions, such as the Cubists and the later abstractionists gave form to in their paintings. As a result, symbolism, driven out the front door by the doctrine that form follows function, came in at the rear. Much of what was masked as strict functionalism or as austere rationalism during the last generation in architecture was in fact a sort of fetishism: an overvaluation of the machine — or of the abstract shadow the machine cast on the mind — as an object of love.

Now as a symbol, the machine might properly have represented the crude industrial culture of the mid-nineteenth century: an age overconfident of the benefits of mechanical progress, brutally negligent of the many inhumanities that accompanied this process. Indeed, even at its starkest and barest, the machine represented

157

"To presume that the desire for order, for security, for power do away with the need for any other qualities is to limit the nature of man"

something higher than the debased humanism of Victorian ornament, with its sordid, ill-proportioned, mechanical forms, its beery sentimentality. But we today know in 1951, as people could not know in 1851, that the machine, even in its highest developments, represents only a fragment of the human spirit: the very power that it has placed at man's disposal may, so far from ushering in an era of peace and plenty, reduce mankind to the utter barbarism of a war of radioactive extermination. Fortunately, ours is not just the age of Faraday, Clerk-Maxwell, and Einstein, of Watt, Bessemer, and Taylor: it is also the age of Darwin and Bergson and Haldane, of Freud and Geddes and Toynbee, **of Kropotkin and Howard and Schweitzer. In short, ours is an age of deep psychological exploration and heightened social responsibility.** Thanks to advances in biology, sociology. and psychology, we begin to understand the whole man; and it is high time for the architects to demonstrate that understanding in other terms than

economy, efficiency, and abstract mechanical form.

In the multi-dimensional world of modern man, subjective interests and values, emotions and feelings, play as large a part as the objective environment: the nurture of life becomes more important than the multiplication of power and standardized goods, considered as ends in themselves. The Machine can no more adequately symbolize our culture than can a Greek Temple or a Renaissance Palace. On the contrary, we know that our almost compulsive preoccupation with the rigid order of the machine is itself a symptom of weakness: of emotional insecurity, of repressed feelings, or of a general withdrawal from the demands of life. To persist in the religious cult of the machine, at this late day and date, is to betray an inability to interpret the challenges and dangers of our age. In this sense, Le Corbusier's polemical writings, beginning with his publication of Towards a New Architecture, were in no small measure reactionary influence: retrospective rather than prophetic.

Now all this is not to say that the doctrine that form follows function was a misleading one. What was false and meretricious were the narrow applications that were made of this formula. Actually, functionalism is subject to two main modifications. The first is that we must not take function solely in a mechanical sense, as applying only to the physical functions of the building. Certainly new technical facilities and mechanical functions required new forms; but so, likewise, did new social purposes and new psychological insights. There are many elements in a building, besides its physical elements, that affect the health, comfort, and pleasure of the user. When the whole personality is taken into account, expression or symbolism becomes one of the dominant concerns of architecture; and the more complex the functions to be served, the more varied and subtle will the form be. In other words — and this is the second modification — expression itself is one of the primary functions of architecture.

On hygienic grounds, for example, the architect may calculate the number of cubic feet of space necessary to provide air for a thousand people in a public hall; and with the aid of the exact science of acoustics — plus a little luck — he may design a hall which will enable every person to hear with a maximum of clarity every sound that is made for the benefit of the audience. But after the architect has made all these calculations. he has still to weigh them with other considerations that have to do with the effect of space and form on the human soul. In the cathedrals of the Middle Ages economy, comfort, and good acoustic properties were all cheerfully sacrificed to the magnification of glory and mystery, in a fashion designed to overwhelm the worshipper.

In terms of medieval culture, that was both effective symbolism and true functionalism. In the strictly graded aristocratic society of the Renaissance, in which music itself was subservient to the ostentatious parade of upper class families, seeking to impress each other and the populace, the Palladian horseshoe form of opera house, with poor acoustic properties but excellent visibility for the boxholders, likewise did justice to the functions of the building in the order of their social importance, within that culture.

In other words, every building is conditioned by culture and personal aims as well as by physical and mechanical needs. An organic functionalism, accordingly, cannot stop short with a mechanical or a physiological solution. So in the re-building of the House of Commons, Mr. Winston Churchill wisely insisted that the seating space should be considerably smaller than the actual membership, in order to preserve the closeness and intimacy of debate in the House, under normal conditions of attendance. That decision was as wise as the medieval decoration that went with it was inept and meretricious; though an original modern architect might have found a means of echoing, in works of original sculpture, the traditional ceremonies and symbols so assiduously preserved in the British Parliament, beginning with that medieval relic, the Speaker's mace.

The architecture of Frank Lloyd Wright was subjected to a considerable amount of arbitrary critical disparagement during the twenties when mechanization and Cubist depersonalization were regarded, with Le Corbusier, as the all-sufficient ingredients of contemporary form. But this disparagement was based on the very qualities that made Wright's architecture superior to the work of Le Corbusier's school. In Wright's work, the subjective and symbolic elements were as important as the mechanical requirements. From his earliest prairie houses onward, both the plan and the elevations of Wright's buildings were informed by human ideals, and by a sense of what is due to the person whose varied needs and interests must be reflected in the building. It was the idea of the organic itself, the desire to embrace nature, that led to the introduction of the garden into the interior; it was the idea of horizontality as an expression of the prairie that led Wright to emphasize horizontal lines in his early regional houses. So, too, in Wright's later work, a geometrical figure, a circle or a hexagon or a spiral, the expression of a subjective human preference, supplies the ground pattern for the whole building. In such instances, as the late Matthew Nowicki pointed out, the old formula is reversed — function follows form.

Now, when subjective expression is overplayed the

"*Every building is conditioned by culture and personal aims as well as by physical and mechanical needs*"

"*Now, when subjective expression is overplayed the results are not always happy*"

results are not always happy — any more than was the case in Renascence buildings, where the ideal of axial balance and symmetry determined both plan and elevation. But to say this is only to admit that, if mechanical functions, taken alone, do not fulfill all human needs, so subjective expressions, if divorced from practical considerations, may become wilful, capricious, defiant of common sense. Accordingly, the more sensitive the architect is to expression, the more capable he is of transforming "building" into "architecture," the greater the need for his own self-knowledge, self-control, self-discipline: above all, for subordinating his own inner wilfulness to the character and purposes of his client.

159

"Like the naked body, when harmoniously developed, they needed no further ornament or costume to achieve beauty"

module, as an essential discipline for the modern architect: the minimum ingredient for form. In such designs as that for the great amphitheater in the State Fair Grounds at Raleigh, North Carolina, now under construction, he used that typical modern form, the parabolic arch, to enclose the suspended facing ranks of the grandstand: an acrobatic feat of great audacity and beauty, appropriate to the functions it served.

But Nowicki knew that all buildings speak a language, and that this language must be understood by the people who use it. When he worked on the preliminary designs for the library and the museum that were to be erected near the State House in Raleigh, he took into account the love and affection the people of North Carolina feel toward that sober piece of provincial classicism. For the sake of meeting their sentiment half way, he was ready to utilize artificial lighting throughout the new buildings in order to create a solid masonry structure which, in its own modern way, would carry on the theme of the beloved older building. That tact, that understanding, that human sympathy stands in full contrast to Le Corbusier's constant demand for people cut to the measure of his own architecture: like old Procrustes, he would amputate the human leg or stretch the human soul to fit the form he has arbitrarily provided for it.

So, again, when Matthew Nowicki went to India to work on the design of a new capitol for the East Punjab (with Mayer and Whittlesey), he brought with him no ready-made stereotypes from the West, but absorbed, with his marvelous sensitivity and intuitive grasp, the Hindu way of life, sympathetic even to the fathomless richness and complexity that expressed itself traditionally in ornament. In the intimate plans for housing and neighborhood units, above all in one of the sketches for the Capitol itself, Nowicki translated this richness into patterns and plans that were wholly in the vernacular of modern building, yet were native to the scene and in resonance with the Hindu personality and with Hindu family life.

Rigorous in its mechanical and spatial foundations, his architecture rose above them to the plane of the social and the personal. Through his human sympathy, through his reverence for all genuine expressions of life, he was equipped as no other architect of his generation perhaps was to effect a fuller reconciliation of the organic and the mechanical, the regional and the universal, the abstract-rational and the personal. Along the path that he began to blaze, modern architecture, if it is to develop and grow, must follow, creating forms that will unite every aspect of the human organism, body and spirit.

On this latter score, Frank Lloyd Wright's work is sometimes not impeccable; for all too rarely has he been faced with a client sufficiently strong in his own right to stand up to Wright's overbearing genius, in a way that will do justice to every dimension of the problem. The architect who perhaps came closest among our contemporaries, to resolving function and expression, was the late Matthew Nowicki, he whose early death in an airplane accident in 1950 was a loss comparable to that architecture sustained when John Wellborn Root died at an equally early age. In the course of some forty intense years of life, Nowicki had passed through the various phases of modern architecture represented by Cubism, by mechanical functionalism and *Sachlichkeit*, by Le Corbusier's "International Style." Firmly rooted in our own age, he regarded the standard unit, the

What is a City?

MOST OF OUR housing and city planning has been handicapped because those who have undertaken the work have had no clear notion of the social functions of the city. They sought to derive these functions from a cursory survey of the activities and interests of the contemporary urban scene. And they did not, apparently, suspect that there might be gross deficiencies, misdirected efforts, mistaken expenditures here that would not be set straight by merely building sanitary tenements or straightening out and widening irregular streets.

The city as a purely physical fact has been subject to numerous investigations. But what is the city as a social institution? The earlier answers to these questions, in Aristotle, Plato, and the Utopian writers from Sir Thomas More to Robert Owen, have been on the whole more satisfactory than those of the more systematic sociologists: most contemporary treatises on "urban sociology" in America throw no important light upon the problem.

One of the soundest definitions of the city was that framed by John Stow, an honest observer of Elizabethan London, who said: "Men are congregated into cities and commonwealths for honesty and utility's sake, these shortly be the commodities that do come by cities, commonalties, and corporations. First, men by this nearness of conversation are withdrawn from barbarous fixity and force, to certain mildness of manners, and to humanity and justice. . . . Good behavior is yet called *urbanitas* because it is rather found in cities than elsewhere. In sum, by often hearing, men be better persuaded in religion, and for that they live in the eyes of others, they be by example the more easily trained to justice, and by shamefastness restrained from injury.

"And whereas commonwealths and kingdoms cannot have, next after God, any surer foundation than the love and good will of one man towards another, that also is closely bred and maintained in cities, where men by mutual society and companying together, do grow to alliances, commonalties, and corporations."

It is with no hope of adding much to the essential insight of this description of the urban process that I would sum up the sociological concept of the city in the following terms:

The city is a related collection of primary groups and purposive associations: the first, like family and neighborhood, are common to all communities, while the second are especially characteristic of city life. These varied groups support themselves through economic organizations that are likewise of a more or less corporate, or at least publicly regulated, character; and they are all housed in permanent structures, within a relatively limited area. The essential physical means of a city's existence are the fixed site, the durable shelter, the permanent facilities for assembly, interchange, and storage; the essential social means are the social division of labor, which serves not merely the economic life but the cultural processes. The city in its complete sense, then, is a geographic plexus, an economic organization, an institutional process, a theater of social action, and an esthetic symbol of collective unity. The city fosters art and *is* art; the city creates the theater and *is* the theater. It is in the city, the city as theater, that man's more purposive activities are focused, and work out, through conflicting and cooperating personalities, events, groups, into more significant culminations.

Without the social drama that comes into existence through the focusing and intensification of group activity there is not a single function performed in the city that could not be performed—and has not in fact been performed—in the open country. The physical organization of the city may deflate this drama or make it frustrate; or it may, through the deliberate efforts of art, politics, and education, make the drama more richly significant, as a stage-set, well-designed, intensifies and underlines the gestures of the actors and the action of the play. It is not for nothing that men have dwelt so often on the beauty or the ugliness of cities: these attributes qualify men's social activities. And if there is a deep reluctance on the part of the true city dweller to leave his cramped quarters for the physically more benign environment of a suburb—even a model garden suburb!—his instincts are usually justified: in its various and many-sided life, in its very opportunities for social disharmony and conflict, the city creates drama; the suburb lacks it.

One may describe the city, in its social aspect,

PICKWICK LANDING, a TVA town where deficient planning permitted strewing of houses along a roadway cut without relation to schools, community centers, or even to its superb natural setting.

as a special framework directed toward the creation of differentiated opportunities for a common life and a significant collective drama. As indirect forms of association, with the aid of signs and symbols and specialized organizations, supplement direct face-to-face intercourse, the personalities of the citizens themselves become many-faceted: they reflect their specialized interests, their more intensively trained aptitudes, their finer discriminations and selections: the personality no longer presents a more or less unbroken traditional face to reality as a whole. Here lies the possibility of personal disintegration; and here lies the need for reintegration through wider participation in a concrete and visible collective whole. What men cannot imagine as a vague formless society, they can live through and experience as citizens in a city. Their unified plans and buildings become a symbol of their social relatedness; and when the physical environment itself becomes disordered and incoherent, the social functions that it harbors become more difficult to express.

One further conclusion follows from this concept of the city: social facts are primary, and the physical organization of a city, its industries and its markets, its lines of communication and traffic, must be subservient to its social needs. Whereas in the development of the city during the last century we expanded the physical plant recklessly and treated the essential social nucleus, the organs of government and education and social service, as mere afterthoughts, today we must treat the social nucleus as the essential element in every valid city plan: the spotting and inter-relationship of schools, libraries, theaters, community centers, is the first task in defining the urban neighborhood and laying down the outlines of an integrated city.

In giving this sociological answer to the question: What is a City? one has likewise provided the clue to a number of important other questions. Above all, one has the criterion for a clear decision as to what is the desirable size of a city —or may a city perhaps continue to grow until a single continuous urban area might cover half the American continent, with the rest of the world tributary to this mass? From the standpoint of the purely physical organization of urban utilities—which is almost the only matter upon which metropolitan planners in the past have concentrated—this latter process might indeed go on indefinitely. But if the city is a theater of social activity, and if its needs are defined by the opportunities it offers to differentiated social groups, acting through a specific nucleus of civic institutes and associations, definite limitations on size follow from this fact.

In one of Le Corbusier's early schemes for an ideal city, he chose three million as the number to be accommodated: the number was roughly the size of the urban aggregate of Paris, but that hardly explains why it should have been taken as a norm for a more rational type of city development. If the size of an urban unit, however, is a function of its productive organization and its opportunities for active social intercourse and culture, certain definite facts emerge as to adequate ratio of population to the process to be served. Thus, at the present level of culture in America, a million people are needed to support a university. Many factors may enter which will change the size of both the university and the population base; nevertheless one can say provisionally that if a million people are needed to provide a sufficient number of students for a university, then two million people should have two universities. One can also say that, other things being equal, five million people will not provide a more effective university than one million people would. The alternative to recognizing these ratios is to keep on overcrowding and overbuilding a few existing institutions, thereby limiting, rather than expanding, their genuine educational facilities.

What is important is not an absolute figure as to population or area: although in certain aspects of life, such as the size of city that is capable of reproducing itself through natural fertility, one can already lay down such figures. What is more important is to *express size always as a function of the social relationships to be served*. There is an optimum numerical size, beyond which each further increment of inhabitants creates difficulties out of all proportion to the benefits. There is also an optimum area of

airchild Surveys, Inc.

POUGHKEEPSIE, N. Y. (above); **GREENHILLS, OHIO,** urban
neighborhood (right). "The block-by-block accretion of the
big city, along its corridor avenues, is in all important
respects a denial of the vastly improved type of urban
grouping that our fresh inventions have brought in."

Resettlement Administration

SCHOOL by Richard J. Neutra.

ROW HOUSES, Greenbelt, Md.

"Today we must treat the social nucleus as the essential element in every valid city plan: the spotting and inter-relationship of schools, libraries, theaters, community centers, is the first task in defining the urban neighborhood and laying down the outlines of an integrated city."

expansion, beyond which further urban growth tends to paralyze rather than to further important social relationships. Rapid means of transportation have given a regional area, with a radius of from forty to a hundred miles, the unity that London and Hampstead had before the coming of the underground railroad. But the activities of small children are still bounded by a walking distance of about a quarter of a mile; and for men to congregate freely and frequently in neighborhoods the maximum distance means nothing, although it may properly define the area served for a selective minority by a university, a central reference library, or a completely equipped hospital.

The area of potential urban settlement has been vastly increased by the motor car and the airplane; but the necessity for solid contiguous growth, for the purposes of intercourse, has in turn been lessened by the telephone and the radio. In the Middle Ages a distance of less than a half a mile from the city's center usually defined its utmost limits. The block-by-block accretion of the big city, along its corridor avenues, is in all important respects a denial of the vastly improved type of urban grouping that our fresh inventions have brought in. For all occasional types of intercourse, the region is the unit of social life: but the region cannot function effectively, as a well-knit unit, if the entire area is densely filled with people—since their very presence will clog its arteries of traffic and congest its social facilities.

Limitations on size, density, and area are absolutely necessary to effective social intercourse; and they are therefore the most important instruments of rational economic and civic planning. The unwillingness in the past to establish such limits has been due mainly to two facts: the as-

sumption that all upward changes in magnitude were signs of progress and automatically "good for business", and the belief that such limitations were essentially arbitrary, in that they proposed to "decrease economic opportunity"— that is, opportunity for profiting by congestion —and to halt the inevitable course of change. Both these objections are superstitious.

Limitations on height are now common in American cities; drastic limitations on density are the rule in all municipal housing estates in England: that which could not be done has *been* done. Such limitations do not obviously limit the population itself: they merely give the planner and administrator the opportunity to multiply the number of centers in which the population is housed, instead of permitting a few existing centers to aggrandize themselves on a monopolistic pattern.

These limitations are necessary to break up the functionless, hypertrophied urban masses of the past. Under this mode of planning, the planner proposes to replace the "mononucleated city", as Professor Warren Thompson has called it, with a new type of "polynucleated city", in which a cluster of communities, adequately spaced and bounded, shall do duty for the badly organized mass city. Twenty such cities, in a region whose environment and whose resources were adequately planned, would have all the benefits of a metropolis that held a million people, without its ponderous disabilities: its capital frozen into unprofitable utilities, and its land values congealed at levels that stand in the way of effective adaptation to new needs.

Mark the change that is in process today. The emerging sources of power, transport, and communication do not follow the old highway network at all. Giant power strides over the hills,

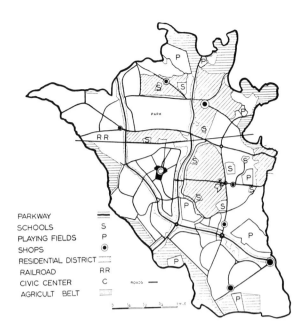

WYTHENSHAWE, MANCHESTER, ENGLAND, A TOWN FOR 100,000. A permanent agricultural belt of 1,000 acres. Scattered open spaces comprise another 1,000 acres. A total open space of 1 acre to 50 people. Space for outdoor recreation including a 100-acre golf course. The park contains 250 acres. Two parkways with an average right-of-way of 300 feet. Sites are reserved for a civic center, schools, churches, shopping, and industry. The shopping districts are placed at the juncture of four "neighborhood units."

ignoring the limitations of wheeled vehicles; the airplane, even more liberated, flies over swamps and mountains, and terminates its journey, not on an avenue, but in a field. Even the highway for fast motor transportation abandons the pattern of the horse-and-buggy era. The new highways, like those of New Jersey and Westchester, to mention only examples drawn locally, are based more or less on a system definitively formulated by Benton MacKaye in his various papers on the Townless Highway. The most complete plans form an independent highway network, isolated both from the adjacent countryside and the towns that they bypass: as free from communal encroachments as the railroad system. In such a network no single center will, like the metropolis of old, become the focal point of all regional advantages: on the contrary, the whole region becomes open for settlement.

Even without intelligent public control, the likelihood is that within the next generation this dissociation and decentralization of urban facilities will go even farther. The Townless Highway begets the Highwayless Town in which the needs of close and continuous human association on all levels will be uppermost. This is just the opposite of the earlier mechanocentric picture of Roadtown, as pictured by Edgar Chambless and the Spanish projectors of the Linear City. For

the highwayless town is based upon the notion of effective zoning of functions through initial public design, rather than by blind legal ordinances. It is a town in which the various functional parts of the structure are isolated topographically as urban islands, appropriately designed for their specific use: with no attempt to provide a uniform plan of the same general pattern for the industrial, the commercial, the domestic, and the civic parts.

The first systematic sketch of this type of town was made by Messrs. Wright and Stein in their design for Radburn in 1929; a new type of plan that was repeated on a limited scale—and apparently in complete independence—by planners in Köln and Hamburg at about the same time. Because of restrictions on design that favored a conventional type of suburban house and stale architectural forms, the implications of this new type of planning were not carried very far in Radburn. But in outline the main relationships are clear: the differentiation of foot traffic from wheeled traffic in independent systems, the insulation of residence quarters from through roads; the discontinuous street pattern; the polarization of social life in specially spotted civic nuclei, beginning in the neighborhood with the school and the playground and the swimming pool. This type of planning was carried to a logical conclusion in perhaps the most functional and most socially intelligent of all Le Corbusier's many urban plans: that for Nemours in North Africa, in 1934.

Through these convergent efforts, the principles of the polynucleated city have been well established. Such plans must result in a fuller opportunity for the primary group, with all its habits of frequent direct meeting and face-to-face intercourse: they must also result in a more complicated pattern and a more comprehensive life for the region, for this geographic area can only now, for the first time, be treated as an instantaneous whole for all the functions of social existence. Instead of trusting to the mere massing of population to produce the necessary social concentration and social drama, we must now seek these results through deliberate local nucleation and a finer regional articulation. The words are jargon; but the importance of their meaning should not be missed. To embody these new possibilities in city life, which come to us not merely through better technical organization but through acuter sociological understanding, and to dramatize the activities themselves in appropriate individual and urban structures, forms the task of the coming generation.

For Older People —
NOT SEGREGATION BUT INTEGRATION

PROBABLY AT NO PERIOD and in no culture have the old ever been so completely rejected as in our own country, during the last generation. As their numbers have increased, their position has worsened. The breakup of the three-generation family coincided here with the curtailment of living space in the individual household; and from this physical constriction has come social destitution as well. Unwanted in the cramped small home, even when they are loved, and too often unloved because they are unwanted, the aged find their lives progressively meaningless and empty, while their days ironically lengthen. The years that have been added to their portion have come, unfortunately, at the wrong end of their lives.

Now the problem of housing the aged is only one part of the larger problem of restoring old people to a position of dignity and use, giving them opportunities to form new social ties to replace those that family dispersal and death have broken, and giving them functions and duties that draw on their precious life experience and put it to new uses. "Old age hath yet his honor and his toil," as Tennyson's Ulysses put it. The first step toward framing a sound program is, I believe, to examine the human situation as a whole, not to center attention solely upon the problems of destitution, chronic diseases, and hospital care. We shall not, perhaps, be able to care for the aged, on the scale their needs and our national wealth demand, until we are ready to put into the re-building of human communities something like the zeal, the energy, the skill, the dedication we give to the monomaniac production of motor cars and super-highways.

As things are now, the process of aging seems to go through three stages. The first, which begins around the age of forty-five, but may not be final for another twenty years, brings liberation from biological repro-duction and increasing detachment from the active nurture of children within the family. For the sake of their own growth and independence, young people start at the earliest possible moment to live by themselves. Poverty or a housing shortage may prolong the two-generation family or even restore, in shaky desperation, the three generation family. But in general early marriages and early child bearing hasten the hiving off of the next generation.

Some time during this period of transition, those who have maintained a household big enough for a large family find their quarters empty but burdensome: for they are too expensive for their incomes, and even too large to keep clean, except at an extravagant cost in menial service. In cities, this leads either to a re-making of the single family house, if owned, into multiple dwellings, or to removal to a small apartment. This shrinkage of space is often accompanied by other losses, such as the breaking of neighborhood ties, the abandonment of a garden and a workshop; and that in turn brings about a further contraction of opportunities and interests. Mark the result: well before senescence has set in, even people in the upper income groups, in robust health, may find the orbit of their lives uncomfortably narrowing, in a way not adequately compensated by increased local mobility in the motor car and increased opportunities for general travel.

The second stage in senescence is that of economic retirement: withdrawal at the age of sixty-five, often enforced by benign pension provisions, from the active working life. Unfortunately our wide practice of automatic retirement often brings on a severe psychological crisis: but even if we showed greater flexibility in imposing retirement, still at some moment, early or late, this blow would fall. In addition to removing a worker from the main sphere of his life-interest and competence, it often halves his income or — as the recent Twentieth Century Fund report shows — cuts it down to a starvation level. At the same time, for those who have invested their energies too exclusively in their work, retirement tends to make their whole life seem meaningless. If at this moment, the community sharpens the crisis by weakening other social connections, too, it may psychosomatically aggravate the physical disabilities that begin to dog this period.

The final stage, that of physiological deterioration, is more variable than the cessation of reproduction or work. Whether the old are happy or bitter, active or frustrated, depends partly upon how long the period of health and vigor is in relation to that covered by the lapse of biological functions that leads to death. But also it depends partly upon how well the community's efforts are directed toward preventing minor impairments from turning, through lack of prompt and adequate care, into major disasters. In any event, senescence proper brings about a gradual slowing down of the vital processes, the deterioration of bodily functions, eyesight, hearing, locomotion, fine coordinations, memory. With this goes a loss of self-help and with that, self-confidence. In the end this loss may necessitate institutional care, in a nursing home or a hospital. Since the cost of such institutional care, if prolonged over any considerable period, taxes heavily even the upper ten per cent of our income groups, every effort must be made, not merely to lengthen the period of active health, but to restore, through neighborly cooperation and friendly oversight, the kind of voluntary care that the three-generation family once made possible.

If we carry our analysis far enough, we shall find, I think, that the three phases of old age — liberation from reproduction, economic retirement, and physiological breakdown — demand a common solution. We shall also find that no present institution, certainly no simple architectural scheme, and no mere extensions of existing services, will supply that solution.

The main point I would make is that the transition from middle aged maturity to old age is a long process; and if we meet it imaginatively at the earliest period possible, instead of waiting till the last desperate moment, we can make the transition without a jar, and in some degree turn a crisis, full of cruel decisions and bitter acceptances, into a positive and fruitful phase of life. Even more, by extending active life on the upgrade we can perhaps shorten the period, now so burdensome, when it is on the downgrade. By contrast, the worst possible attitude toward old age is to regard the aged as a segregated group, who are to be removed, at a fixed point in their life course, from the presence of their families, their neighbors, and their friends, from their familiar quarters and their familiar neighborhoods, from their normal interests and responsibilities,

to live in desolate idleness, relieved only by the presence of others in a similar plight. Let us ask rather by what means we can restore to the aged the love and respect that they once enjoyed in the three-generation family at its best.

Unfortunately for any such aim, specialization, mechanization, institutionalization, in a word, segregation, are the order of the present day: a meaningless, effortless, parasitic, push-button existence is now put forward as the beautiful promise of an advanced technology, indeed, the ultimate goal of our whole civilization. If those terms were actually final ones, I, for one, should hardly be concerned with the fate of the aged; for it should be plain that a whole society that can conjure up no better goals is already moving swiftly toward early euthanasia, or at least toward mass suicide. If we wish something better for ourselves, we must be prepared to put forward a program, at every phase of life, that challenges many of the dominant habits and customs of our society and moves boldly in a contrary direction.

At some point in conceiving a good habitat for the aged, we must of course come to an architectural solution; but we must not for a moment imagine that the architect himself, even when backed by ample financial resources, can provide the answers that are needed, or that beauty and order and convenience alone are sufficient. One of the most generous quarters for the aged I have seen is the old Fuggerei in Augsburg, built in the sixteenth century, composed of one-story row dwellings, giving privacy to each old couple, with a handsome fountain and a chapel. But this "city for the aged and poor" is set apart from the rest of the town; though it has beauty and order, it lacks animation; at best it is only a handsome ghetto. The objection against this solution was indignantly put to me by an old man in another comely quadrangle for the aged near Manchester: a modern building set in ample grounds looking inward on a spacious grassy close: also with a little chapel where the dead rested before burial. At first glance, the peace and beauty of this spot seemed "ideal" —but the inmates knew better. They now had, alas! only one occupation: remaining alive. When the bell tolled, it tolled not only for the departed: it ominously summoned those who were left. "All we do here," said my bitter informant, "is to wait for each other to die. And each time we ask ourselves: 'Who will be next?' What we want is a touch of life. I wish we were near the shops and the bus station where we could see things."

To normalize old age, we must restore the old to the community. In order to make clear what this means, let me assume that we have a free hand and can plan a whole neighborhood community, as one does in an urban re-development area in the United States or a New Town in Britain. If we establish the right relationships under such ideal conditions, we shall have a clearer view of what to aim for in situations where only a piecemeal solution is possible. We cannot have even a good half-loaf unless we know what ingredients should go into a whole loaf.

The first thing to be determined is the number of aged people to be accommodated in a neighborhood unit; and the answer to this, I submit, is that the normal age distribution in the community as a whole should be maintained. This means that there should be from five to eight people over sixty-five in every hundred people; so that in a neighborhood unit of, say, six hundred people there would be between thirty and forty old people. Any large-scale organization of habitations for the aged, which upsets this proportion, should be avoided. And this brings us to the second requirement. For both companionship and easier nursing care, the aged should not be scattered in single rooms or apartments through the whole community; but neither should they be thrown together in one large barracks labelled by the architecture, if not the signboard, Old Peoples' Home. They should rather be grouped in small units of from six to perhaps a dozen apartments. The old monastic rule, that one needs a dozen members to form a community, has had long enough trial to give one confidence in it as a rough measure: when there are less than a dozen, a single cantankerous individual may have a disruptive effect. When there are too many together, they bring on institutional regulations. As an old Navy man once pertinently remarked: There is freedom on a destroyer but not on a battleship.

But once a reasonable degree of closeness is established between small groups of the aged, there is much to be gained by giving them apartments on the lower floors of two- or three-story houses whose upper floors will be occupied by childless people in other age groups: there is likewise reason for providing a covered way or arcade, to make visiting back and forth easier in in-

clement weather, and to serve as a sheltered place for chatting and sunning at other times. This mixing of age groups within a housing unit primarily designed for the accommodation of the aged would make it possible for those past sixty-five, who found stairs difficult, or who wanted to be more accessible, to adapt themselves to their infirmities with no greater hiatus than moving downstairs.

Now it happens that the number of people over sixty-five in a community are roughly the equivalent of the number of children under six or seven; and in meeting the needs of both extremes pretty much the same conditions hold. Young children need special protection and bodily care; they must be guarded from wheeled vehicles; their difficulties in locomotion and coordination when under three make it desirable to avoid unnecessary obstacles and long flights of stairs. Even psychologically, there are parallels between the self-absorption of the young child and the tendency to withdrawal and inner concentration that mark the last phase of senescence. In a well-designed neighborhood unit, the aged should be able to go to any part of it, including the shopping area, the library, the church, the community center, without crossing a traffic artery; indeed, without if possible climbing a step. Someday, when our motor car production is designed to fill varied human needs, rather than the requirements of the assembly line, we will produce electrically-powered rolling chairs for the aged, which can go safely anywhere a pedestrian can go. That will lessen one of the serious handicaps of old age, if medical remedies for arthritis and feeble limbs remain ineffective. But until then, the ambit of the five-year-old child and the seventy-five-year old senescent is their normal walking distance. Once these conditions are fulfilled in a neighborhood unit, a larger life would begin to open before the aged.

Now we are ready to re-build, in our ideal scheme, the other facilities and activities and services that were once performed, more or less effectively, by the three-generation family. And just as the young proceed with their growth through multiplying their contact with the environment and enlarging their encounters with people other than their families, so the aged may slow down the processes of deterioration, overcoming their loneliness and their sense of not being wanted, by finding within their neighborhood a fresh field for their activities.

But before such an environment can be created, we must challenge the whole theory of segregation upon which so many American communities, not least those that call themselves "progressive," have been zoned: zoned so that one-family houses and apartment houses, or row houses and free-standing houses, cannot be built side by side; zoned so strictly for residence that in many suburban communities one cannot buy a loaf of bread or a tin of tobacco without going a mile or two by car or bus to the shops. The pernicious effect of this kind of zoning was first adequately characterized by the Committee on Community Planning of the A.I.A. as far back as 1924, and time has abundantly proved all their contentions. Under our zoning ordinances, it is impossible to give either the young or the old the kind of occupational and environmental variety that both a superblock and neighborhood unit should have.

In a mixed community, however, many opportunities for service, both voluntary and paid, would open to the aged. Gardening is an occupation that can be carried on at odd hours, and that can be adapted to the strength and staying power of the old: when a community is well planned, with sufficient amount of parked and gardened open space, it makes greater demands for collective care than it can now often afford. Certainly old people with a turn for gardening should have a little garden plot of their own, too, to look after. Similarly other opportunities for handicraft should be met by the provision of workshop facilities; making toys, repairing mechanical fixtures, binding books, painting furniture would not merely provide older people with new forms of work: it would, even more importantly, give them the human contacts that a more restricted life fails to offer. Such little shops  would have a further educational value for the younger members of the community: indeed, they might be incorporated, with a separate entrance from outside, in a modern school, with great advantage to both the old and the young, who now too often miss the precious experience of intercourse with their grandparents' generation. I know a small town where the car-

penter's shop, situated in the old residential area, is the place where school children come to get little repair jobs done; and their contact with the carpenter himself is an affectionate and rewarding one. Such a program would be far more efficacious, psychologically speaking, than merely putting the aged to work on some monotonous specialized task, producing in quantity for the market, under factory conditions.

In addition there are other services that the aged can perform only in a mixed community, beginning with their most obvious service as baby-sitters. This again, at a dollar an hour, has become a prohibitive luxury even in middle class communities; and the hazards of leaving the young to the sometimes irresponsible care, if not criminal levity, of inexperienced adolescents only underline the desirability of enlisting the old in the same fashion as they would have been used in the three-generation family. In addition, there are many experienced old women, proud of their skill at baking a cake, or even cooking a whole dinner, who would think better of themselves and their life if they might cook and bake occasionally for pay. By having such opportunities, old age pensions and annuities might be made to go a little farther, with greater happiness for both the server and the served. To cause the aged to spend all their time glued to a television set is to damn them prematurely to a second childhood. Though these passive amusements have their place in the life of the aged, especially for the crippled and bedridden, there is little reason for reducing their lives as a whole to such a soporific routine. What the aged need is activities: not just hobbies, but the normal participation in the activities of a mixed community.

No single institution, however amply financed and humanely planned, could provide anything like the range of interests that a mixed neighborhood community would do, once age ceases to be regarded as a disease, best treated in an isolation ward. Still there usually comes a time in everyone's life sooner or later when he requires specialized nursing and medical care. The skillful organization of such care is the duty of the community as a whole; but some fatal inertia has kept our hospital services in an antiquated centralized pattern, and has prevented the creation of small nursing homes, close at hand for family and neighborly visitors, who could, if the hospital were conveniently at hand, take over no small part of the otherwise prohibitively expensive nursing service.

Even before active hospitalization there is need for a public organization of visiting nurses and visiting houseworkers, such as are now provided for on a national scale in England and likewise in certain individual American cities. Here again, by drawing upon all the resources of the community, a much more favorable situation can be created than the most elaborately equipped central institution can provide. I look forward to a day when a small nursing home, for illness and for maternity cases, will be part of the normal requirement of a neighborhood: perhaps as a direct adjunct to a medical clinic and a visiting nurse service. Only when these normal functions of the family are drawn back into the circle of the neighborhood community is there any prospect of our catching up with our needs without raising to a prohibitive height the present cost of institutional care.

Now we can put together these requirements for the aged. They should, first of all, be part of a normal mixed community, whether they become members of it at twenty-five or at seventy-five. Their quarters should be undistinguishable outwardly from those of other age groups; but they should be sited, as far as possible, where there is a constant play of diverting activity, near a shopping center or a school, so that their chance of being visited, casually and effortlessly, will be increased. Frequent visits, though short, are more refreshing than formal visits, tediously prolonged, that leave desolate intervals of loneliness between them. Many people would find their own family life replenished if the grandparents, though not under their feet, were near at hand; and above all, the young would be the gainers from this; for there are special bonds of sympathy between them and their grandparents' generation, through its very detachment, which often makes them far more ready to heed their advice than that of their own parents. Who can say how much delinquency and brutalized mischief in our American towns may not be due to the very absence of a warm, loving, reciprocal intercourse between the three generations?

Through their nearness to each other, in small units, personal contacts within their own group may easily pass beyond the pleasantries of daily intercourse, the hospitalities of a cup of coffee in the afternoon or a friendly game of cards or checkers or chess at night; it would also involve visiting each other when ill and performing little services for each other. Everything that makes the aged more independent, yet more confident of the fact that their presence is welcome, increases their capacity to love and be loved; and it is only, in the end, by providing an environment in which the gifts of love may be more easily interchanged, that old age can be kept from shrinking and drying till what is left of life is only a dismal waste. But to say this is also to say that there is no easy shortcut to improved care of the aged: to do well by them, we must give a new direction to the life of the whole community. If we fail here, we shall, in prolonging life, only prolong the possibilities of alienation, futility, and misery.

The Highway and the City

The God on Wheels

When the American people, through their Congress, voted last year for a twenty-six-billion-dollar highway program, the most charitable thing to assume about this action is that they hadn't the faintest notion of what they were doing. Within the next fifteen years they will doubtless find out; but by that time it will be too late to correct all the damage to our cities and our countryside, to say nothing of the efficient organization of industry and transportation, that this ill-conceived and absurdly unbalanced program will have wrought. Yet if someone had foretold these consequences before this vast sum of money was pushed through Congress, under the specious guise of a national defense measure, it is doubtful whether our countrymen would have listened long enough to understand; or would even have been able to change their minds if they did understand. For the current American way of life is founded not just on motor transportation but on the religion of the motor car, and the sacrifices that people are prepared to make for this religion stand outside the realm of rational criticism. Perhaps the only thing that could bring Americans to their senses would be a clear demonstration of the fact that their highway program will, eventually, wipe out the very area of freedom that the private motor car promised to retain for them.

Our Motorized Mistress

As long as motor cars were few in number, he who had one was a king: he could go where he pleased and halt where he pleased; and this machine itself appeared as a compensatory device for enlarging an ego which had been shrunken by our very success in mechanization. That sense of freedom and power remains a fact today only in low-density areas, in the open country; the popularity of this method of escape has ruined the promise it once held forth. In using the car to flee from the metropolis the motorist finds that he has merely transferred congestion to the highway; and when he reaches his destination, in a distant suburb, he finds that the countryside he sought has disappeared: beyond him, thanks to the motorway, lies only another suburb, just as dull as his own. To have a minimum amount of communication and sociability in this spread out life, his wife becomes a taxi-driver by daily occupation, and the amount of money it costs to keep this whole system running leaves him with shamefully overtaxed schools, inadequate police, poorly staffed hospitals, overcrowded recreation areas, ill-supported libraries.

In short, the American has sacrificed his life as a whole to the motor car, like someone who, demented with passion, wrecks his home in order to lavish his income on a capricious mistress who promises delights he can only occasionally enjoy.

Illustrations by Alan Dunn

"The countryside (the motorist) sought has disappeared"

"The building of a highway has about the same result . . . . as the passage of a tornado."

Delusions of Progress

For most Americans, progress means accepting what is new because it is new, and discarding what is old because it is old. This may be good for a rapid turnover in business, but it is bad for continuity and stability in life. Progress, in an organic sense, should be cumulative, and though a certain amount of rubbish-clearing is always necessary, we lose part of the gain offered by a new invention if we automatically discard all the still valuable inventions that preceded it. In transportation, unfortunately, the old-fashioned linear notion of progress prevails. Now that motor cars are becoming universal, many people take for granted that pedestrian movement will disappear and that the railroad system will in time be abandoned; in fact, many of the proponents of highway building talk as if that day were already here, or if not, they have every intention of making it dawn quickly. The result is that we have actually crippled the motor car, by placing on this single means of transportation the burden for every kind of travel. Neither our cars nor our highways can take such a load. This overconcentration, moreover, is rapidly destroying our cities, without leaving anything half as good in their place.

What's Transportation For?

This is a question that highway engineers apparently never ask themselves: probably because they take for granted the belief that transportation exists for the purpose of providing suitable outlets for the motor car industry. To increase the number of cars, to enable motorists to go longer distances, to more places, at higher speeds has become an end in itself. Does this over-employment of the motor car not consume ever larger quantities of gas, oil, concrete, rubber, and steel, and so provide the very groundwork for an expanding economy? Certainly, but none of these make up the essential purpose of transportation, which is to bring people or goods to places where they are needed, and to concentrate the greatest variety of goods and people within a limited area, in order to widen the possibility of choice without making it necessary to travel. A good transportation system minimizes unnecessary transportation; and in any event, it offers a change of speed and mode to fit a diversity of human purposes.

Diffusion and concentration are the two poles of transportation: the first demands a closely articulated network of roads—ranging from a foot-path to a six-lane expressway and a transcontinental railroad system. The second demands a city. Our major highway systems are conceived, in the interests of speed, as linear organizations, that is to say as arteries. That conception would be a sound one, provided the major arteries were not over-developed to the exclusion of all the minor elements of transportation. Highway planners have yet to realize that these arteries must not be thrust into the delicate tissue of our cities; the blood they circulate must rather enter through elaborate network of minor blood vessels and capillaries. As early as 1929 Benton Mac-Kaye worked out the rationale of sound highway development, in his conception of the Townless Highway; and this had as its corollary the Highwayless Town. In the quarter century since, all the elements of MacKaye's conception have been carried out, except the last—certainly not the least.

The Highway as a Work of Art

In many ways, our highways are not merely masterpieces of engineering, but consummate works of art: a few of them, like the Taconic State Parkway in New York, stand on a par with our highest creations in other fields. Not every highway, it is true, runs through country that offers such superb opportunities to an imaginative highway builder as this does; but then not every engineer rises to his opportunities as the planners of this highway did, routing the well-separated roads along the ridgeways, following the contours, and thus, by this single stratagem, both avoiding towns and villages and opening up great views across country, enhanced by a lavish planting of flowering bushes along the borders. If this standard of comeliness and beauty were kept generally in view, highway engineers would not so often lapse into the brutal assaults against the landscape and against urban order that they actually give way to when they aim solely at speed and volume of traffic, and bulldoze and blast their way across country to shorten their route by a few miles without making the total journey any less depressing.

Perhaps our age will be known to the future historian as the age of the bulldozer and the exterminator; and in many parts of the country the building of a highway has about the same result upon vegetation and human structures as the passage of a tornado or the blast of an atom bomb. Nowhere is this bulldozing habit of mind so disastrous as in the approach to the city. Since the engineer regards his own work as more important than the other human functions it serves, he does not hesitate to lay waste to woods, streams, parks and human neighborhoods in order to carry his roads straight to their supposed destination.

The Need for a Transportation System

The fatal mistake we have been making is to sacrifice every other form of transportation to the private motor car—and to offer as the only long-distance alternative the airplane. But the fact is that each type of transportation has its special use; and a good transportation policy must seek to improve each type and make the most of it. This cannot be achieved by aiming at high speed or continuous flow alone. If you wish casual opportunities for meeting your neighbors, and for profiting by chance contacts with

"We have forgotten how much more efficient and how much more flexible the footwalker is"

"Provided that a miniscule size town car takes the place of the long-tailed dinosaurs that now lumber about our metropolitan swamps"

acquaintances and colleagues, a stroll at two miles an hour in a relatively concentrated area, free from vehicles, will alone meet your need. But if you wish to rush a surgeon to a patient a thousand miles away, the fastest motorway is too slow. And again, if you wish to be sure to keep a lecture engagement in winter, railroad transportation offers surer speed and better insurance against being held up than the airplane. There is no one ideal mode or speed: human purpose should govern the choice of the means of transportation. That is why we need a better transportation *system*, not just more highways. The projectors of our national highway program plainly had little interest in transportation. In their fanatical zeal to expand our highways, the very allocation of funds indicates that they are ready to liquidate all other forms of land and water transportation.

The Traffic Pyramids

In order to overcome the fatal stagnation of traffic in and around our cities, our highway engineers have come up with a remedy that actually expands the evil it is meant to overcome. They create new expressways to serve cities that are already overcrowded within, thus tempting people who had been using public transportation to reach the urban centers to use these new private facilities. Almost before the first day's tolls on these expressways have been counted, the new roads themselves are overcrowded. So a clamor arises to create other similar arteries and to provide more parking garages in the center of our metropolises; and the generous provision of these facilities expands the cycle of congestion, without any promise of relief until that terminal point when all the business and industry that originally gave rise to the congestion move out of the city, to escape strangulation, leaving a waste of expressways and garages behind them. This is pyramid building with a vengeance: a tomb of concrete roads and ramps covering the dead corpse of a city.

But before our cities reach this terminal point, they will suffer, as they now do, from a continued erosion of their social facilities: an erosion that might have been avoided if engineers had understood MacKaye's point that a motorway, properly planned, is another form of railroad for private use. Unfortunately, highway engineers, if one is to judge by their usual performance, lack both historic insight and social memory: accordingly, they have been repeating, with the audacity of confident ignorance, all the mistakes in urban planning committed by their predecessors who designed our railroads. The wide swathes of land devoted to cloverleaves and expressways, to parking lots and parking garages, in the very heart of the city, butcher up precious urban space in exactly the same way that freight yards and marshalling yards did when the railroads dumped their passengers and freight inside the city. These new arteries choke off the natural routes of circulation and limit the use of abutting properties, while at the points where they disgorge their traffic, they create inevitable clots of congestion, which effectively cancel out such speed as they achieve in approaching these bottlenecks.

Today the highway engineers have no excuse for invading the city with their regional and transcontinental trunk systems: the change from the major artery to the local artery can now be achieved without breaking the bulk of goods or replacing the vehicle: that is precisely the advantage of the motor car. Arterial roads, ideally speaking, should engirdle the metropolitan area and define where its greenbelt begins; and since American cities are still too impoverished and too improvident to acquire greenbelts, they should be planned to go through the zone where relatively high-density building gives way to low-density building. On this perimeter, through traffic will by-pass the city, while cars that are headed for the center will drop off at the point closest to their destination. Since I don't know a city whose highways have been planned on this basis, let me give as an exact parallel the new semi-circular railroad line, with its suburban stations, that by-passes Amsterdam. That is good railroad planning, and it would be good highway planning, too, as the Dutch architect H. Th. Wijdeveld long ago pointed out. It is on relatively cheap land, on the edge of the city, that we should be building parking areas and garages: with free parking privileges, to tempt the commuter to leave his car and finish his daily journey on the public transportation system. The public officials who have been planning our highway system on just the opposite principle are likewise planning to make the central areas of our cities unworkable and uninhabitable. Route 128 in Boston is a belated effort to provide such a circular feeder highway; but its purpose is cancelled by current plans for arterial roads gouging into the center of the city.

Down and Up with the Elevated

Just as highway engineers know too little about city planning to correct the mistakes made in introducing the early railroad systems into our cities, so, too, they have curiously forgotten our experience with the elevated railroad—and unfortunately most municipal authorities have been equally forgetful. In the middle of the nineteenth century the elevated seemed the most facile and up-to-date method of introducing a new kind of rapid transportation system into the city; and in America, New York led the way in creating four such lines on Manhattan Island alone. The noise of the trains and the overshadowing of the structure lowered the value of the abutting properties even for commercial purposes; and the supporting columns constituted a dangerous obstacle to surface transportation. So unsatisfactory was elevated transportation even in cities like Berlin, where the structures were, in contrast to New York, Phila-

delphia, and Chicago, rather handsome works of engineering, that by popular consent subway building replaced elevated railroad building in all big cities, even though no one could pretend that riding in a tunnel was nearly as pleasant to the rider as was travel in the open air. The destruction of the old elevated railroads in New York was, ironically, hailed as a triumph of progress precisely at the moment that a new series of elevated highways were being built, to repeat on a more colossal scale the same errors.

Highway Robbery

Like the railroad, again, the motorway has repeatedly taken possession of the most valuable recreation space the city possesses, not merely by thieving land once dedicated to park uses, but by cutting off easy access to the waterfront parks, and lowering their value for refreshment and repose by introducing the roar of traffic and the bad odor of exhausts, though both noise and carbon monoxide are inimical to health. Witness the shocking spoilage of the Charles River basin parks in Boston, the arterial blocking off of the Lake Front in Chicago (after the removal of the original usurpers, the railroads), the barbarous sacrifice of large areas of Fairmount Park in Philadelphia, the proposed defacement of the San Francisco waterfront. One may match all these social crimes with a hundred other examples of barefaced highway robbery in every other metropolitan area. Even when the people who submit to these annexations and spoliations are dimly aware of what they are losing, they submit without more than a murmur of protest. What they do not understand is that they are trading a permanent good for a very temporary advantage, since until we subordinate highway expansion to the more permanent requirements of regional planning, the flood of motor traffic will clog new channels. What they further fail to realize is that the vast sums of money that go into such enterprises drain necessary public monies from other functions of the city, and make it socially if not financially bankrupt.

The Cart Before the Horse

Neither the highway engineer nor the urban planner can, beyond a certain point, plan his facilities to accommodate an expanding population. On the overall problem of population pressure, regional and national policies must be developed for throwing open, within our country, new regions of settlement, if this pressure, which appeared so suddenly, does not in fact abate just as unexpectedly and just as suddenly. But there can be no sound planning anywhere until we understand the necessity for erecting norms, or ideal limits, for density of population. Most of our congested metropolises need a lower density of population, with more parks and open spaces, if they are

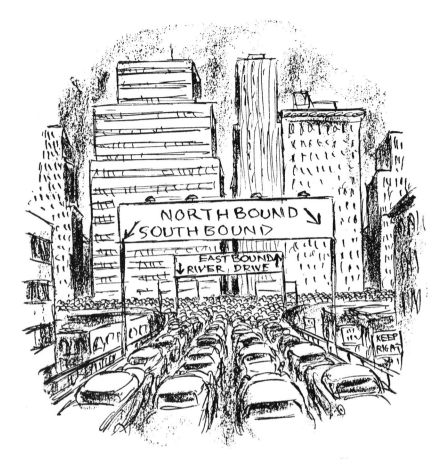

"At the point where (these new expressways) disgorge their traffic they create inevitable clots of congestion"

"Mass transportation by rail . . . . has been permitted to languish"

to be attractive enough physically to retain even a portion of their population for day-and-night living; but most of our suburban and exurban communities must replan large areas at perhaps double their present densities in order to have the social, educational, recreational, and industrial facilities they need closer at hand. Both suburb and metropolis need a regional form of government, working in private organizations as well as public forms, to reapportion their resources and facilities, so as to benefit the whole area.

To say this is to say that both metropolitan congestion and suburban scattering are obsolete. This means that good planning must work to produce a radically new pattern for urban growth. On this matter, public policy in the United States is both contradictory and self-defeating. Instead of lowering central area densities, most urban renewal schemes, not least those aimed at housing the groups that must be subsidized, either maintain old levels of congestion, or create higher levels than existed in the slums they replaced. But the Home Loan agencies, on the other hand, have been subsidizing the wasteful, ill-planned, single-family house, on cheap land, ever remoter from the center of our cities; a policy that has done as much to promote the suburban drift as the ubiquitous motor car. In order to cement these errors in the most solid way possible, our highway policy maximizes congestion at the center and expands the area of suburban dispersion—what one might call the metropolitan "fall-out." The three public agencies concerned have no official connections with each other: but the total result of their efforts proves, once again, that chaos does not have to be planned.

Tiny Tims on Wheels

Motor car manufacturers look forward confidently to the time when every family will have two, if not three, cars. I would not deny them that hope, though I remember that it was first voiced in 1929, just before the fatal crash of our economic system, too enamored of high profits even to save itself by temporarily lowering prices. But if they don't want the motor car to paralyze urban life, they must abandon their fantastic commitment to the indecently tumescent chariots they have been putting on the market. For long-distance travel, the big car of course has many advantages; but for town use, let us insist upon a car that fits the city's needs: it is absurd to make over the city to fit the swollen imaginations of Detroit. The Isetta and the Gogomobil have already pointed the way; but what we need is an even smaller vehicle, powered by electricity, delivered by a powerful storage cell, yet to be invented. Maneuverability and parkability are the prime urban virtues in cars; and the simplest way to achieve this is by designing smaller cars. These virtues are lacking in all but one of our current American models. But why should our cities be destroyed just so that De-troit's follies should remain unchallenged and unchanged?

The Place of the Pedestrian

If we want to make the most of our New Highway program, we must keep most of the proposed expressways in abeyance until we have done two other things. We must re-plan the inner city for pedestrian circulation, and we must rebuild and extend our public forms of mass transportation. In our entrancement with the motor car, we have forgotten how much more efficient and how much more flexible the footwalker is. Before there was any public transportation in London, something like 50,000 people an hour used to pass over London Bridge on their way to work: a single artery. Mass public transportation can bring from forty to sixty thousand people per hour, along a single route, whereas our best expressways, using far more space, cannot move more than four to six thousand cars, and even if the average occupancy were more than one and a half passengers, as at present, this is obviously the most costly and inefficient means of handling the peak hours of traffic. As for the pedestrian, one could move a hundred thousand people, by the existing streets, from, say, downtown Boston to the Common, in something like half an hour, and find plenty of room for them to stand. But how many weary hours would it take to move them in cars over these same streets? And what would one do with the cars after they had reached the Common? Or where, for that matter, could one assemble these cars in the first place? For open spaces, long distances and low densities, the car is now essential; for urban space, short distances and high densities, the pedestrian.

Every urban transportation plan should, accordingly, put the pedestrian at the center of all its proposals, if only to facilitate wheeled traffic. But to bring the pedestrian back into the picture, one must treat him with the respect and honor we now accord only to the automobile: we should provide him with pleasant walks, insulated from traffic, to take him to his destination, once he enters a business precinct or residential quarter. Every city should heed the example of Rotterdam in creating the Lijnbaan, or of Coventry in creating its new shopping area. It is nonsense to say that this cannot be done in America, because no one wants to walk. Where walking is exciting and visually stimulating, whether it is in a Detroit shopping center or along Fifth Avenue, Americans are perfectly ready to walk. The legs will come into their own again, as the ideal means of neighborhood transportation, once some provision is made for their exercise, as Philadelphia is now doing, both in its Independence Hall area, and in Penn Center. But if we are to make walking attractive, we must not only provide trees and wide pavements and benches, beds of flowers and outdoor cafes, as they do in Rotterdam: we must also scrap the monotonous uniformities of American zoning practice, which turns vast areas, too spread out for pedestrian movement, into single-district zones, for commerce, industry, or residential purposes. (As a result, only the mixed zones are architecturally interesting today despite their disorder.)

Why should anyone have to take a car and drive a couple of miles to get a package of cigarettes or a loaf of bread, as one must often do in a suburb? Why, on the other hand, should a growing minority of people not be able again to walk to work, by living in the interior of the city, or, for that matter, be able to walk home from the theater or the concert hall? Where urban facilities are compact, walking still delights the American: does he not travel many thousands of miles just to enjoy this privilege in the historic urban cores of Europe? And do not people now travel for miles, of an evening, from the outskirts of Pittsburgh, just for the pleasure of a stroll in Mellon Square? Nothing would do more to give life back to our blighted urban cores than to re-instate the pedestrian, in malls and pleasances designed to make circulation a delight. And what an opportunity for architecture!

The Case for Mass Transportation

While federal funds and subsidies pour without stint into highway improvements, the two most important modes of transportation for cities—the railroad for long distances and mass transportation, and subway for shorter journeys—are permitted to languish and even to disappear. This is very much like what has happened to our postal system. While the time needed to deliver a letter across the continent has been reduced, the time needed for local delivery has been multiplied. What used to take two hours now sometimes takes two days. As a whole our postal system has been degraded to a level that would have been regarded as intolerable even thirty years ago. In both cases, an efficient system has been sacrificed to a new industry, motor cars, telephones, airplanes; whereas, if the integrity of the system itself had been respected, each of these new inventions could have added enormously to the efficiency of the existing network.

If we could overcome the irrational drives that are now at work, promoting shortsighted decisions, the rational case for re-building the mass transportation system in our cities would be overwhelming. The current objection to mass transportation comes chiefly from the fact that it has been allowed to decay: this lapse itself reflects the general blight of the central areas. In order to maintain profits, or in many cases to reduce deficits, rates have been raised, services have decreased, and equipment has become obsolete, without being replaced and improved. Yet mass transportation, with far less acreage in roadbeds and rights of way, can deliver at least ten times more people per hour than the private motor car. This means that if such means were allowed to lapse

in our metropolitan centers—as the inter-urban electric trolley system, that beautiful and efficient network, was allowed to disappear in the nineteen twenties—we should require probably five to ten times the existing number of arterial highways to bring the present number of commuters into the city, and at least ten times the existing parking space to accommodate them.

This reduces a one-dimensional transportation system, by motor car alone, to a calamitous absurdity, as far as urban development goes, even if the number of vehicles and the population count were not increasing year by year. Now it happens that the population of the core of our big cities has remained stable in recent years: in many cases, the decline which set in as early as 1910 in New York seems to have ceased. This means that it is now possible to set an upper limit for the daily inflow of workers, and to work out a permanent mass transportation system that will get them in and out again as pleasantly and efficiently as possible. In time, if urban renewal projects become sufficient in number to permit the design of a system of minor urban throughways, at ground level, that will by-pass the neighborhood, even circulation by motor car may play a valuable part in the total scheme—provided, of course, that minuscule size town cars take the place of the long-tailed dinosaurs that now lumber about our metropolitan swamps. But the notion that the private motor car can be substituted for mass transportation should be put forward only by those who desire to see the city itself disappear, and with it the complex, many-sided civilization that the city makes possible.

Brakes and Accelerations

There is no purely engineering solution to the problems of transportation in our age: nothing like a stable solution is possible without giving due weight to all the necessary elements in transportation—private motor cars, railroads, airplanes and helicopters, mass transportation services by trolley and bus, even ferryboats, and finally, not least, the pedestrian. To achieve the necessary over-all pattern, not merely must there be effective city and regional planning, before new routes or services are planned; we also need eventually—and the sooner the better—an adequate system of federated metropolitan government. Until these necessary tools of control have been created, most of our planning will be empirical and blundering; and the more we do, on our present premises, the more disastrous will be the results. What is needed is more thinking on the lines that Robert Mitchell, Edmund Bacon, and Wilfred Owens have been following, and less action, until this thinking has been embodied in a new conception of the needs and possibilities of contemporary urban life. We cannot have an efficient form for our transportation system until we can envisage a better permanent structure for our cities.

THE CASE AGAINST "MODERN ARCHITECTURE"

A famous critic charges that modern architecture, once
too occupied with machine esthetics, now is disintegrating
into a multitude of sects and mannerisms; he offers
a principle of order, with three sources of enrichment

". . . special courses must now be offered . . . to provide
architects with sufficient historical knowledge to maintain
and restore ancient monuments . . ."

Drawings by Alan Dunn

Three quarters of a century ago, the tides of modern architecture were rising, as the great technical resources that engineers like Telford, Paxton, and Brunel had introduced were applied, at last, to other forms of building. This was the period when Jenney, Sullivan, and their colleagues developed steel frame construction and found a form for the skyscraper, when Eiffel produced his tower and Freyssinet his Hall of Machines, and when the new spirit that Richardson had brought to the design of traditional domestic buildings in stone and wood was spreading everywhere, from the houses of Ashbee, Voysey and Parker in England to the far shores of California, where at the turn of the century Maybeck had begun work.

For reasons that no one has successfully uncovered, this wave spent itself during the decade before the First World War: except in the design of purely utilitarian structures, there was a return to the pseudo-historic and outwardly traditional, at least in the decorative facing of buildings: skyscrapers with Gothic pinnacles vied with those that were crowned with Greek temples of love; and the splendid train hall of the Grand Central station, now effaced by a loud smear of advertisement, was betrayed earlier by its imitative Renaissance façade. When modern architecture came back in the Twenties, first in France with Le Corbusier and Lurçat, and in Germany with Mendelsohn and Gropius, it was forced to refight the battle that had already seemed won in 1890.

Within the last thirty years, modern architecture has swept around the world. The victory of the modern movement over its traditional enemies has been so complete that special courses must now be offered, outside the usual architectural school curriculum, to provide architects with sufficient historic knowledge to maintain and restore ancient monuments preserved for their historic value. Yet many ominous signs have appeared, during the last fifteen years, that indicate that the victorious forces do not know how to make full use of the victory; that contradictions and conflicts have developed among various groups of architects sufficient already to have broken up the once united front of the C.I.A.M.; that, indeed, the differences that have developed within the ranks of the modern architects are quite as serious as those that divided the pioneers of modern architecture from the traditionalists who sought to continue the old forms and the eclectics who sought to mask the new ones.

The order and the consensus that modern architecture seemed ready to establish in the Thirties is still far to seek: indeed, some of the most brilliant exponents, like the late Eero Saarinen, boasted a theory of form that denied the need for continuity and made of each separate project an essay in abstract design, without any affiliation to the work of other architects in our period or to the architect's own designs, before or after. As in the advertising copy of our period, the successful modern architects have been saying, in effect: "And now! a new taste sensation." Or, "You, too, can be *years ahead* with the latest model."

This situation has given hope and comfort to minds that are so radically committed to past forms that they would solve the problems that modern architecture faces by merely erasing the history of the last century and going back to the classic shells of antiquity, particularly Roman antiquity. This is the last hope of Henry Reed; too empty and vulnerable to merit more than a passing smile. But though Mr. Reed's remedies are absurd, the situation in modern architecture is in fact profoundly unsatisfactory: almost as chaotic and irrational as the political situation of the modern world, in which the heads of state solemnly threaten each other to solve their problems, if the other side does not yield, by mutilating the human race and wiping out civilization.

The very fact that one can make such a comparison points to certain underlying errors about the nature of technical and social progress that crept into modern architecture almost from the moment that the conception of new forms, which reflected the needs and ideals of our period, became articulate in the writings of a few architectural critics and thinkers, like Adolf Loos and, much later, Le Corbusier. The moment has come to examine these conceptions and to reformulate the ideas and ideals that have, up to this moment, governed the development of the whole movement. We shall perhaps find, when we do so, a need for restoring some of the values that were too ruthlessly discarded in the development of modern form.

"And now! A new taste sensation"

1. THE BASIS
OF MODERN FORM

Beneath the belief in modern architecture lay certain preconceptions about the nature of modern civilization; and these preconceptions have proved so inadequate that it is time to give them a thorough overhauling.

Perhaps the most central of these beliefs was the belief in mechanical progress. Concealed within this notion was the assumption that human improvement would come about more rapidly, indeed almost automatically, through devoting all our energies to the expansion of scientific knowledge and to technological inventions; that traditional knowledge and experience, traditional forms and values, acted as a brake upon such expansion and invention, and that since the order embodied by the machine was the highest type of order, no brakes of any kind were desirable. Whereas all organic evolution is cumulative and purposeful, in that the past is still present in the future, and the future, as potentiality, is already present in the past, mechanical progress existed in a one-dimensional time, the present. Under the idea of mechanical progress only the present counted, and continual change was needed in order to prevent the present from becoming *passé,* and thus unfashionable. Progress was accordingly measured by novelty, constant change and mechanical difference, not by continuity and human improvement.

In every department, the nineteenth century ruthlessly swept away old ideas, old traditions and institutions, and not least old buildings, confident that nothing would be lost that the machine could not replace or improve. Have we forgotten that the central shrine of our Independence and our Constitution, Independence Hall, was almost sold off to the highest bidder in the early part of that century? But this anti-traditionalism imposed a penalty upon modern architecture; and that is, it was deprived by its own assumptions of either recognizing its essential continuity with the past or of building upon its own tradition. In wiping out the past, unfortunately, the cult of the machine surreptitiously destroyed its own future—and left only an under-dimensioned present, scheduled like any specualative building investment, for quick replacement.

Beneath this belief in mechanical progress as an end in itself was still another conviction: that one of the important functions of architecture was to express its civilization. This conviction was a sound one; and indeed, even without conviction, that condition whether openly recognized or unconsciously fulfilled is unavoidable. But those of us who insisted upon the value of this expression were perhaps unprepared for what it would reveal about "modern times." We used the word modern as a "praise-word," in Robert Frost's vocabulary; and we overlooked the possibility that modern technics, which had given us instant communication, would also provide us with instantaneous mass extermination: or the fact that in its hospitals and medical services and sanitary precautions it would reduce diseases and allay pain; but it has also polluted our food, befouled the air with smog, and produced new tensions and new diseases and new anxieties, as crippling as those that have been banished. Modern psychology has introduced man to the depths of his own nature, in all its immense variety and creative potentiality; but it has also produced the bureaucratic personality, sterilized, regimented, overcontrolled, ultimately hostile to every other form of life than its own: cut off from human resources and human roots.

Since modern architecture has begun to express modern civilization, without the hypocrisy and concealment that the eclectic architects used to practice, it is not perhaps surprising that the unpleasant features of our civilization should be as conspicuous as its finest and most admirable achievements. We have been living in a fool's paradise, so far as we took for granted that mechanical progress would solve all the problems of human existence, by introducing man into the brave new, simplified, automatic world of the machine. If we look at our buildings today, with open eyes, we shall find that even in handling the great positive forces of our time, with admirable constructive facility, the greater number of them have neglected even the scientific data they need for a good solution. There is hardly a single great innovation in building this last thirty years—total air conditioning, all-day fluorescent lighting, the all-glass wall—that pays any respect to either the meteorological, the biological or the psychological knowledge already available, for this knowledge calls for radical alterations in their use. And still less do these innovations heed human activities or personal desires.

In so far as modern architecture has succeeded in expressing modern life, it has done better in calling attention to its lapses, its rigidities, its failures, than in bringing out, with the aid of the architect's creative imagination, its immense latent potentialities. The modern architect has yet to come to grips with the multi-dimensional realities of the actual world. He has made himself at home with mechanical processes, which favor rapid commercial exploitation, and with anonymous repetitive bureaucratic forms, like the high-rise apartment or office building, which lend themselves with mathematical simplicity to financial manipulation. But he has no philosophy that does justice to organic functions or human purposes, and that attempts to build a more comprehensive order in which the machine, instead of dominating our life and demanding ever heavier sacrifices in the present fashion, will become a supple instrument for humane design, to be used, modified, or on occasion rejected at will.

2. FROM THE MACHINE TO THE PACKAGE

Despite the shallowness of the theory of mechanical progress, the first erections of modern architecture, beginning with the Crystal Palace in 1851, rested on a firm foundation: the perception that the technology of the nineteenth century had immensely enriched the vocabulary of modern form and facilitated modes of construction that could hardly have been dreamed of in more ponderous materials, while it made possible plans of a far more organic nature than the heavy shells that constituted buildings in the past.

In their pride over these new possibilities, the engineers who turned these processes over to the architect naturally over-emphasized this contribution; and when Louis Sullivan proclaimed that form followed function, his successors falsely put the emphasis on mechanical form and mechanical function. Both are in fact essential to the constitution of modern architecture; but neither by itself—nor both together—is sufficient. Frank Lloyd Wright understood this from the beginning, and insisted, quite properly, that he was something more than a "functionalist," though in the last phase of his great career, as in the Johnson laboratory and the Guggenheim museum, he succumbed to the fascination of an elegant mechanical solution, treated as an end in itself.

In the new beginning that dates from Le Corbusier's *Vers une Architecture*, the machine occupied a central place: its austerity, its economy, its geometric cleanness were proclaimed almost the sole virtues of the new architecture. Thus the kitchen became a laboratory, and the bathroom took on the qualities of a surgical operating room; while the other parts of the house, for a decade or so, achieved excellence almost to the degree that they, too, were white, cleanable, empty of human content. This was in fact a useful period of cleansing and clarification. A few critics, notably Henry-Russell Hitchcock, recognized that this was the primitive state in the evolution of an historic style; and that, at a later date, certain elements, like ornament, that had been discarded in this new effort at integrity, might return again—though in fact they had never been abandoned by Wright.

Unfortunately, this interpretation of the new mechanical possibilities was in itself dominated by a superficial esthetic, which sought to make the new buildings *look* as if they respected the machine, no matter what the materials or methods of construction; and it was this superficial esthetic, openly proclaiming its indifference to actual mechanical and

". . . it is not perhaps surprising that the unpleasant features of our civilization should be as conspicuous as its finest and most admirable achievements"

biological functions or human purposes that was formally put forward, by Philip Johnson and his associate Hitchcock, as The International Style, though it was Alfred Barr who coined the dubious name. From this, only a short step took the architect, with Mies van der Rohe to guide him, from the Machine to the Package. Mies van der Rohe used the facilities offered by steel and glass to create elegant monuments of nothingness. They had the dry style of machine forms without the contents. His own chaste taste gave these hollow glass shells a crytalline purity of form: but they existed alone in the Platonic world of his imagination and had no relation to site, climate, insulation, function or internal activity; indeed, they completely turned their backs upon these realities just as the rigidly arranged chairs of his living rooms openly disregarded the necessary intimacies and informalities of conversation. This was the apotheosis of the compulsive, bureaucratic spirit. Its emptiness and hollowness were more expressive than van der Rohe's admirers realized.

Here perhaps was the turning point in the development of modern architecture. The principle of functionalism, stated even in its crudest terms, was sound as far as it went; and if modern architecture was to develop further, that principle needed to be applied to every aspect of architecture. It was necessary to develop functional analysis to its limits, not merely embracing the physical elements of building, but the internal services; not merely the external structure, but the plan, and the relation of the building to its site; and the site itself to the rest of the urban or rural environment. And even this is only a beginning, because human purposes modify all these functional characteristics; so that the so-called open plan for the dwelling house turns out to be far from acceptable as a universal solution, once one takes account of the need for privacy, solitude, withdrawal, or of the differences between the extroverted, the introverted, and the integrated personality. As one adds biological and social functions, and personal desires and needs, to those of the purely physical requirements of structure, one must get, as a resultant design, a much more complex and subtle result, than if one centered attention upon only one set of conditions.

How far modern architecture has withdrawn from the effort to achieve such organic richness one learns from recent architectural exhibitions, which have shown modern buildings as spatialized abstractions, in utter isolation. Some of the most famous architects of our time defiantly throw away their best opportunities: thus more than one new business building has been placed in the middle of a large country estate, with all the advantages of a lovely landscape, only to turn its back completely to its surroundings, defiling the approach with an acre of parking lot, whilst the building itself, air-conditioned and curtained in Venetian blinds, mocks its open site, its possible exposure to sunlight and fresh air, by turning inward upon a closed court. The result is the characterless package, which has become the main hallmark of fashionable architecture for the last decade.

Is Le Corbusier's Unity House at Marseille an exception to this rule? Far from it. Its powerful concrete façade, with variations produced by the ill-conceived and almost abandoned market area, esthetically distinguishes it from the less expensive and less sculptural façades of similar buildings; but for all that, it is a mere package, because the plan of the individual apartments is cramped and tortured to fit the arbitrary allotment of space, in a fashion that is as archaic as that of a New York brownstone front that has been built over the back yard and is full of narrow, dark rooms, without exposure. The genius of Le Corbusier here consisted in making a mere package look like a real building; and the feebleness of current architectural criticism is recorded in the chorus of praise that this extravagant piece of stage decoration still calls forth.

3. THE PACKAGE
AND THE FASHION PLATE

Meanwhile, the advance of technology has presented the architect with a vast array of new metallic alloys and new plastics, with new structural materials like prestressed concrete, with new large-scale elements useful for modular designs, and with new mechanical devices that add to the total cost of the structure, as well as the upkeep. On the assumption that mechanical progress is itself more important than human purposes, the architect has felt, it would seem, almost a moral obligation to use all these materials and methods, if only to maintain his status as a creative designer. In this respect, the architect finds himself in almost the same unfortunate position as the physician, overwhelmed by the enormous number of new antibiotics and other drugs that are thrust on the market by the great pharmaceutical organizations, and often unable to follow through one remedy before a new one is thrust on him.

But the advances of technology, which have opened those possibilities for the new forms that Eric Mendelsohn so brilliantly anticipated in his imaginative sketches back in the Twenties, have also revealed the possibility of two new architectural perversions. One of them is the utilization of sensational methods of construction merely to produce equally sensational forms, which have no purpose other than that of demonstrating the esthetic audacity of the designer. The external shell of the new opera house at Sydney reveals this order of design; so, for that matter, does the too-often quoted Guggenheim museum in New York, and even more Wright's new municipal building in Marin County; and all over the country today, one finds new churches whose very form of construction reveals nothing except a desire to compete on equal esthetic terms with the supermarket and the hot dog emporium. This is not functional and purposeful creativity: it is the creativity of the kaleidoscope, so far the most successful of all inventions for imitating creativity by juggling mechanical forms.

When a child is bored or an adult is ill, the esthetics of the kaleidoscope is enchanting; and I do not underestimate its fascination. Nor would I deny that, related to our emergent needs, many new forms must and will appear in modern architecture, which will reveal meanings and values, intuitions about the nature of the cosmos or the condition of man, that are not present in any earlier architectural system. But creativity, in order to be assimilated, requires an underlying basis of order; and what is more, the most original form needs to be repeated, with modifications, if its full value is to be absorbed by the user and the spectator. The desire for architectural originality through a succession of kaleidoscopic changes, made possible by modern technological agents, when the inner purpose and contents are ruled out of the equation, inevitably degrades the creative process. Such technical facility, such esthetic audacity, poured forth on a large scale, promises only to enlarge the domain of chaos. Already the architectural magazines show projects, and even buildings, that look as if they were ingeniously cut out of paper and twisted together, shapes full of fantasy and capable of giving childish pleasure—provided they are not carried out in more solid constructions.

One may explain this excessive virtuosity, with which modern architecture is now threatened, by two conditions. This is plainly, on one hand, a revolt against the excessive regimentation that has gone on in every part of our lives: that regimentation whose symbol is the vast repetitive inanity of the high-rise slab. And on the other hand, it is due to the fact that genuine creativity, which takes into account all the possibilities of structure, the nature of an institution's function and purposes, the values that the client draws from the community and in turn must give back to the community, is a slow process. Because such knowledge and such facility cannot be improvised in a few weeks, the creative architect must build from structure to structure on his own experience, and absorb that of other architects, past and present. It is far easier to create a sensational shell, with the constructive facilities now available, than to fulfill all the functions of architecture. An engineer of genius, like Nervi, has shown the way toward more solid achievement; but even he has succeeded best when the inner content of the building was as simple as tiers of spectators

". . . human purposes modify all these functional characteristics"

watching sport, or an exhibition or market hall whose contents could be adequately enclosed by a mere shell.

But there is an alternative to kaleidoscopic creativity that would be equally disastrous to architecture and to the human spirit, though the threat comes from the opposite point of our machine economy. Instead of an endless succession of superficial new forms, dazzling Christmas packages that have no relation to contents, we are threatened by another form of technologic facility, whose present favored form is the geodesic dome. Under this potential technical triumph, buildings as such would disappear, except perhaps as improvised rooms within a mechanically controlled environment, dedicated to producing uniform temperature, lighting, and ultimately, with the aid of drugs, surgery and genetic intervention, uniform human beings. Whether above ground or below ground, this development would bring to an end, in a world of colorless uniformity, the long history of man's building: he would return to the cave from which he originally emerged, none the richer or wiser for his experience. I will not examine this particular possibility in detail, except to note that many minds are now busily engaged in preparing for this grand act of suicide. So committed indeed are many architects in our day to the automatism of the machine, that they fall under a compulsion to follow the process to its limit, even though that final stage is a colorless and dehumanized existence, just one breath more alive than the world that might emerge from a nuclear catastrophe.

4. POLYTECHNICS
AND MULTI-FUNCTIONALISM

If modern architecture is not to continue its disintegration into a multitude of sects and mannerisms —international stylists, empiricists, brutalists, neo-romantics, and what not—it must rest on some principle of order; and that order must ally architecture to an equally coherent theory of human development. The notion of mechanical progress alone will not do, because it leaves out the one element that would give significance to this progress, man himself; or rather, because it makes the human personality a mere tool of the processes that should in fact serve it.

Man himself is an organism whose existence is dependent upon his maintaining the delicate balance that exists between all the forces of nature, physical and organic, from sunlight and air and the soil, the bacteria, the molds, and growing plants right up to the complex interaction of thousands of species. Despite the great advances in technology, man controls only a small part of these processes: for neither destruction nor mechanical substitution is in fact a mode of control. From this complex biological inheritance man extracts and perfects those portions that serve his own purposes. Organic order is based on variety, complexity, and balance; and this order provides continuity through change, stability through adaptation, harmony through finding a place for conflict, chance, and limited disorder, in ever more complex transformations. This organic interdependence was recognized and expressed in every historic culture, particularly in its cosmic and religious conceptions, with their genuinely sacred buildings, and though these buildings have outlived their technologies they still speak to the human soul.

Greenough's original analysis of form, on a basis of the biological and physiological nature of organisms, did justice to both process and function, but overlooked their transformation through a still higher and more complex category, that of human purpose. Man is not just an actor and a fabricator: he is an interpreter and a transformer. On the higher levels of existence, form determines function, no less than function form. At this point the continued development of the whole man takes precedence over the continued development of his instruments and his machines; and the only kind of order that can ensure this is one that provides a many-sided environment capable of sustaining the greatest variety of human interests and human purposes. An environment or a structure that has been reduced to the level of the machine, correct, undeviating, repetitious, monotonous, is hostile to organic reality and to human purpose: even when it performs, with a certain efficiency, a positive function, such as providing shelter, it remains a negative symbol, or at best a neutral one.

There are three sources for this larger order: nature is one, the cumulative processes of history and historic culture are another; and the human psyche is the third. To turn one's back upon these sources, in the name of mechanical progress, for the sake of purely quantitative production, mechanical efficiency, bureaucratic order, is to sterilize both architecture and the life that it should sustain and elevate. An age that worships the machine and seeks only those goods that the machine provides, in ever larger amounts, at ever rising profits, actually has lost contact with reality; and in the next moment or the next generation may translate its general denial of life into one last savage gesture of nuclear extermination. Within the context of organic order and human purpose, our whole technology has still potentially a large part to play; but much of the riches of modern technics will remain unusable until organic functions and human purposes, rather than the mechanical process, dominate.

An organic approach will handle, with equal dexterity, but with greater freedom of choice, every kind of function: it will not automatically reject daylight in favor of a facile mechanical substitute, or fresh air, renovated by vegetation, for a purely mechanical system of modifying the air. But neither will it turn banks into frivolous glass-enclosed pleasure palaces, office building entrances into cathedrals, or churches into airport hangers. On the contrary, purpose and function will provide an organic criterion of form at every stage of the design process; and in the end this will produce, not merely an esthetic variety and exuberance that are now almost unknown, but even mechanical economies that have been flouted by our compulsive overcommitment to the machine.

There are two movements now visible that indicate a beginning in the right direction, which will lead, not away from functionalism, but toward a multi-functional approach to every architectural problem.

One of these movements, visible in the architectural schools today, is the students' demand for architectural and town planning history. The desire behind this is not for forms to imitate, but for experience and feeling to assimilate, for spiritual nourishment beyond that which is offered by the immediate environment or a brief present moment. This is a healthy reaction against the notion that the experience of a single generation, or a single decade in a generation, is sufficient to provide the knowledge and insight man needs to create a human environment of sufficient richness and depth.

The other movement became visible last summer in the meeting of the younger architects who have broken away from the Old Masters of the C.I.A.M. In their attempt to redefine the province of architecture today they expressed many differences with the generation of Le Corbusier and Gropius, as well as personal and characterological differences within their own ranks; but at the end they were united, in a large degree, on one final conclusion: that architecture was more than the art of building: it was rather the art of transforming man's entire habitat. This concept had already struck root in California, when the school of architecture at Berkeley was reconstituted and renamed as the School of Environmental Design.

If human development does not become sterile and frustrated through an excessive effort to conquer nature without drawing upon all the resources of history and culture to rehumanize man, the architecture of the future will again be a true polytechnics, utilizing all the resources of technics, from the human hand to the latest automatic device. It will be closer in spirit and form to the earlier work of Frank Lloyd Wright, and even more perhaps to Bernard Maybeck, than to the masters of the C.I.A.M.; and it will go beyond them, because it will draw upon the richer human resources now worldwide in cultural scope, which are happily available for collective as well as individual expression.

"The desire for architectural originality through a succession of kaleidoscopic changes . . . inevitably degrades the creative purpose"

The great historic quarrels between the classicists and the romanticists, between the conservatives and the innovators, have been fruitless, because both parties in the past ignored the common foundations that set their problem: the technical innovations brought by the machine, the new arts of engineering and hygiene, and the new patterns of social life. Each party sought to establish a common goal without accepting a common point of departure: they divided over little details like columns and acanthus leaves, at the very time that the whole ground of traditional architecture was being swept from under them. This does not say that the symbolic interests they showed, their concern over "ornament" or "style" were meaningless: it would be more accurate to say that they were ill-timed. The problem of style was insoluble until the new architecture had made a beginning. Whether a formalized classic capital is superior to a naturalistic Gothic capital or to a free modern one is a meretricious question once modern methods of construction have made the stone column itself an anachronism.

Looking back over the 19th century, one finds little to choose between the work of the classicists, the medievalists, and the eclectics or the originals; or, rather, the best that can be said for the latter is that they were as much alive to the problem of form, the technical problem, as they were to that of symbolic expression. Hence an eclectic architect like John Root, deliberately modeling his Monadnock Building after an Egyptian pylon, remained close enough to his materials and functions to create a strong and fresh work of the imagination, and did not let himself be prevented by stylistic considerations from creating those well-conceived bays which were necessary to bring sufficient light past the thick masonry walls. The same was true of Louis Sullivan. He prided himself on his original ornament, those snowflakes and lacy flowers that his teeming hand so easily turned out; but one of his greatest steps forward was in the Schlesinger and Meyer Building in Chicago, where the unbroken horizontal window, later to become the happy cliché of modernism, was first achieved in a business building; and where the surviving ornament was plainly indifferent.

Now that the fundamental technical problems of building have become a little more clear to us, we are perhaps at last ready to approach those ultimate questions of expression which were unfortunately put first during the battle of the styles. Let us consider the two fundamental stylistic movements of the last 30 years: both of them were modern, both of them were anti-traditional; but they differed in every other particular. Using one of the battle-cries of the early 1900's, one may call the first the school of the wavy line, the second the school of the cube.

The Wavy Line versus The Cube

By Lewis Mumford
from Architecture *December 1930*

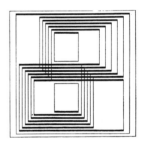

Thirty-three years ago Lewis Mumford looked back upon the preceding thirty years and concluded that L'Art Nouveau and Cubism were the significant artistic movements of that period. Looking forward he predicted that the spirit of these styles would be a strong influence upon the architecture to come. From the vantage point of today the contemplation of our immediate architectural past affirms Mumford's prophecy and suggests its continuing relevance for the future.

August Endell: Atelier Elvira. Munich. 1897
Courtesy Museum of Modern Art

". . . but [L'Art Nouveau] was capable of sinking to such depths of absurdity as a balustrade falling in a metallic cascade, and breaking at the bottom of the stairway into a spray of electroliers."

TWA Flight Center

Van de Velde: Tropon. c. 1899.
Poster, Adolph Studly photo

II

The romantic architects, under Ruskin's lead, had popularized the notion that the living flower or animal or fruit was preferable, in art, to any abstract form or stylization. Ruskin himself was not altogether of one mind about this; for, after "Modern Painters," he recommended abstract forms and colored tiles as the one possible fruitful form of modern ornament; but the belief in nature remained with his followers, and toward the end of the century it received a fresh sanction in the work of a new school of architects and decorators, under the talented Dutch architect, Van de Velde, and under the industrial leadership of the firm of Bing in Paris.

This school established the dogma of the living form as the source of ornament and design, and the wavy line as its characteristic expression: "nature never geometrizes." The fixed, the static, the hard line, the unbroken surface, the right angle, the geometrical emphasis of structure, all these were anathema to it. Not merely must decoration use flowers and leaves, vines and tendrils, human figures and

[L'Art Nouveau designers] "also sought freedom in the sense of being unconditioned by their material, and in making the symbolic exuberance of their imagination dominate the problem of form."

Pankok: Smoking room,
International Exposition, Paris. 1900

Saarinen Associates: TWA Flight Center, Idlewild, New York International Airport, N.Y. 1962. © Ezra Stoller Assoc's. photos

Grasset: Typographic ornament. 1898

TWA Flight Center

Van de Velde: Angels' Guard. 1893

Flight Center

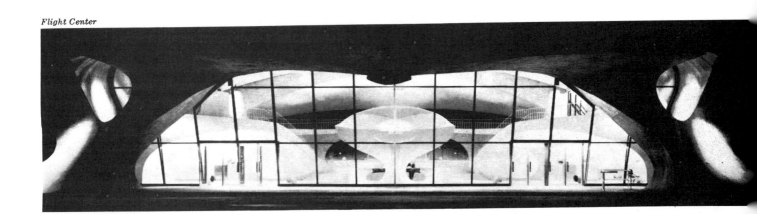

Skidmore, Owings & Merrill: Warehouse and Vinegar
Plant, H. J. Heinz Co. Pittsburgh, Pennsylvania.
1950-52 © Ezra Stoller Assoc's. photo

Nervi: Canopy Support. Fiumicino Intercontinental Airport Project, Rome. 1957

"Beneath the appearance of things the Cubist sought for structure . . . the esse
tial of art was no longer to represent or interpret living nature, but to embody t
mathematics of spatial order . . . this respect for the object, this interest in
mechanical components . . . leads to an interest in new materials, new metho
of construction, new processes, as such . . . concrete and steel and fabricate
wall compositions suggest new forms."

Paul Rudolph: Endo Laboratories, Long Island, N. Y.
Under construction. David Attie photo

Mies van der Rohe and Philip Johnson:
The Seagram Building, New York City. 1958.
©Ezra Stoller Assoc's. photo

"Most of the best [Cubist] sculptors now take delight in the refractoriness of the material . . ."

Philip Johnson: Glass House. New Canaan, Conn. 1949.
©Ezra Stoller Assoc's. photo

Skidmore, Owings & Merrill: Office building, Connecticut General Life Insurance
Company, Bloomfield, Conn. 1954-57. © Ezra Stoller Assoc's. photo

A 1930 Mumford prophecy: "Once the background is stripped clean of every piece
of meaningless ornament, the foreground again becomes prominent; and in this
foreground one may reinstate once more the living form . . . valuing the living
line, we will find it rather in flowers, pictures, sculptures, . . . and in a relevant
relation to these elements our austere mechanical forms will come finally to life."

House in Czechoslovakia. c. 1930

"The [Cubist] building not only becomes rationally simple, which is all to the good; it becomes irrationally simplified too, by reason of considerations which have nothing whatever to do with functional requirements. . . ."

Louis Kahn: Richards Medical Research Laboratories, University of Pennsylvania, Philadelphia, Pa. 1960. Joseph Molitor photo

Mumford predicted that the functionalist concept would expand: "Once the creative effort of the new architecture becomes centered in our life as a whole, not alone in its mechanical performances, its dogmas will be modified, and its merely empty restrictions will be removed."

swirling draperies, in preference to any other emblems; but the building itself, the chairs and desks and tables, must exhibit these flowing lines. Even in the new type of suburban city planning, partly through a misreading of Camillo Sitte, the accidental contour lines of nature became a law, and the palpable fact, which every one may read in the snow, that one naturally chooses the easiest and not necessarily the shortest distance between two points, led to an exaggerated respect for useless deviations.

Through continued experiment, this movement finally reached such well-considered expressions in architecture as Van de Velde's theater for the Werkbund Exhibition in Cologne in 1914; but it was capable of sinking to such depths of absurdity as a balustrade falling in a metallic cascade, and breaking at the bottom of the stairway into a spray of electroliers. In its application to the other decorative arts, the wavy line would even disregard the objective form of a china plate, which is determined by the physical properties of clay and the potter's wheel; no form remained as it was, if there was any possibility of torturing it into a leaf, a flower or an abstract swirl.

L'Art Nouveau enthusiasts not merely demanded freedom from the conventions of the past, freedom to express the conditions and interests of their own times; this, indeed, was a necessary condition of experiment. They also sought freedom in the sense of being unconditioned by their material, and in making the symbolic exuberance of their imagination dominate the problem of form. In this their point of view was no different from that of the revivalists, except that the latter chose to apply dead patterns to the new problems and conditions: the design and the ornament, instead of being developed in continuous interrelation with the new forms, was deliberately imported. Aside from an occasional subway kiosk—the best being those of the Paris Metro—L'Art Nouveau had very little relation to the typical problems of the new age: in architecture it confined itself largely to the monumental and the luxurious, to problems where a rigorous facing of actual conditions was not essential. Its pinnacle in the crafts was the jewelry of Lalique; and it had by good fortune the independent support of a sculptor of genius, Auguste Rodin; but outside these departments its work lacked logic and conviction—and even Rodin's best pupils departed from his fluid and impressionistic use of marble.

This movement had almost spent itself before the war; and it had called forth its antithesis, Cubism. A new set of dogmas came into existence. Beneath the appearance of things the Cubist sought for structure; and Cezanne's chance remark, that everything in nature was either an egg or a cube, was narrowed into the observation that only cubes were significant. In the graphic arts, the static and geometric aspect of things preoccupied the artist; and before the war had come in Europe this influence had made itself felt among the younger architects, like the Dutchmen of De Stijl group. The essential of art was no longer to represent or interpret living nature, but to embody the mathematics of spatial order, to reduce the living object to its mechanical components. Duchamps-Villon converts a horse into a mechanical model; Brancusi takes the trunk of a tree with two branches, and prides himself upon creating, by the smallest possible transformation of the material, the torso of a young man. Most of the best sculptors now take delight in the refractoriness of the material; they use the chisel on stone and the buffer on bronze, to bring out the grain or the surface of their medium, as well as the character of the object they are representing or symbolizing.

This respect for the object, this interest in its mechanical components, carries over into architecture; it leads to an interest in new materials, new methods of construction, new processes, as such; and, being indifferent to traditional requirements, it is as much at home in the design of a factory as traditional architecture felt in the erection of a church. Concrete and steel and fabricated wall compositions suggest new forms: the cantilever takes the place of the post, and makes possible the unbroken expanse of horizontal window. This movement in architecture, which was a necessary answer to that complete deliquescence of forms brought in by L'Art Nouveau—as Cezanne was a necessary answer to the dissolution of the impressionists like Monet— this abstract symbolism of the cube sought to justify itself also on more rational grounds; it professed to be in harmony with modern industrial conditions and to express the Machine Age. By a curious transposition, the cube was made the equivalent of the machine; and the machine took on a symbolic function. The gas tank, the factory, the grain silo became the embodiment of our current mechanical and financial ideal. Instead of making a schoolhouse look like a medieval college, the architect now sought to make it look like a factory; the symbolism changed, but the inherent form was still far to seek.

If L'Art Nouveau was marked by a meaningless stylistic exuberance, the Neue Sachlichkeit, as it is called in Germany, or the work of the New Pioneers, as Mr. H. R. Hitchcock has called it in America, is marked at first by an equally meaningless sense of restriction. There is first of all a limitation of materials to concrete and stucco; there is further, during the early experiments, a limitation as to color— only "industrial" colors, white, gray, black, may be used—and there is finally an abolition of any form of ornamental enrichment, even that derived directly from the material itself. The building not only becomes rationally simple, which is all to the good; it becomes irrationally simplified too, by reason of considerations which have nothing whatever to do with functional requirements: questions such as the amount of sunlight necessary for a particular kind of room or choices like that between a flat and a gabled roof are solved by dogma, not by a reference to realities. This sort of architecture has a powerful symbolic effect, as any thoroughly logical design must have in a world filled with slipshod compromises and ineffectual reminiscences; but to an alert mind it conveys two contrasting meanings: one is the cool excellence of many of our mechanical utilities; the other is the meagerness of a system of life and thought that is entirely bounded by them.

Both L'Art Nouveau and Cubism sought in their applications to architecture to interpret modern life. One emphasized its plasticity and fluidity, the other its rigor and restraint; one prided itself upon its variations, the other upon its curt acceptance of monotony; one sought to be unique and the other to be completely standardized. An adequate symbolism, a really comprehensive interpretation of modern life, must, I think, get beyond the dogmas of both schools and yet retain the element of truth that gave each of them a career. From those who have sought to embody the strict mechanical requirements of modern building, we achieve that fundamental respect for function which leads to such humanly desirable qualities as sunlight, cleanliness, efficiency, space, absence of servile labor, hygiene, play, order, composure. These are precious gifts. Once the background is stripped clean of every piece of meaningless ornament, the foreground again becomes prominent; and in this foreground one may reinstate once more the living form. We will not ask the wall-paper to dance or the furniture to swoon; such agility has nothing to do with their proper functions: valuing the living line, we will find it rather in flowers, pictures, sculptures, above all in people, and in a relevant relation to these elements our austere mechanical forms will come finally to life. From the very economies and rigors of the new architecture we will obtain the leisure and the extra means necessary to cultivate the landscape and to proceed with the fine arts. Once the creative effort of the new architecture becomes centered in our life as a whole, not alone in its mechanical performances, its dogmas will be modified, and its merely empty restrictions will be removed. This is already happening in Europe; and in the work of Mr. Frank Lloyd Wright, who began 30 years ago at the point where the Europeans found themselves in 1914, it has already prophetically happened in America.

A NEW REGIONAL PLAN TO ARREST MEGALOPOLIS

An appraisal by LEWIS MUMFORD
of New York State's new development program.
The noted author and critic considers it a
milestone in public policy, but
warns of weaknesses that need repair

Under the title, "Change: Challenge: Response," New York State has come out with a basic plan and policy for the future development of its cities, agricultural areas, and recreation and forest reserves, over a period of the next 60 years. The publication of this report should clear the air of the largely meaningless noises that have grown in volume during the last decade on the subject of metropolitan planning and urban renewal: noises that reach a pitch of confused emptiness in the term "megalopolis," treated as if it were a new kind of city, instead of the urbanoid mish-mash that it actually is.

Nothing of similar consequence to the arts of improving the environment has been published since the announcement of the Tennessee Valley Authority. While the computers are busily turning out more sophisticated traffic counts, population predictions and mobility estimates, proving that nothing can be done except to "go with" and accelerate the forces that are already in motion, the Office of Regional Development has introduced a hitherto unused factor not embraced by computers or by computer-directed intelligences: the human imagination.

"...this report challenges the false premises

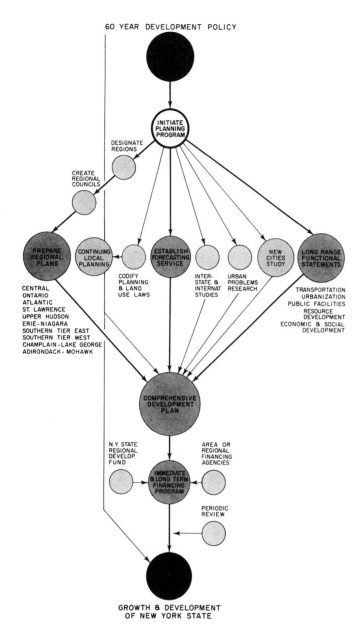

60 YEAR DEVELOPMENT POLICY

INITIATE PLANNING PROGRAM

DESIGNATE REGIONS

CREATE REGIONAL COUNCILS

PREPARE REGIONAL PLANS

CONTINUING LOCAL PLANNING

ESTABLISH FORECASTING SERVICE

NEW CITIES STUDY

LONG RANGE FUNCTIONAL STATEMENTS

CENTRAL
ONTARIO
ATLANTIC
ST. LAWRENCE
UPPER HUDSON
ERIE-NIAGARA
SOUTHERN TIER EAST
SOUTHERN TIER WEST
CHAMPLAIN-LAKE GEORGE
ADIRONDACK-MOHAWK

CODIFY PLANNING & LAND USE LAWS

INTER-STATE & INTERNAT. STUDIES

URBAN PROBLEMS RESEARCH

TRANSPORTATION
URBANIZATION
PUBLIC FACILITIES
RESOURCE DEVELOPMENT
ECONOMIC & SOCIAL DEVELOPMENT

COMPREHENSIVE DEVELOPMENT PLAN

N.Y. STATE REGIONAL DEVELOP. FUND

AREA OR REGIONAL FINANCING AGENCIES

IMMEDIATE & LONG TERM FINANCING PROGRAM

PERIODIC REVIEW

GROWTH & DEVELOPMENT OF NEW YORK STATE

*"For the present planners
emphasize that any large coordinated
effort at planning . . . rests on bringing together
. . . a multitude of municipal, county, state
and even Federal agencies, and in
persuading individual property owners
and private corporations to work
within the general pattern."*

1. *The New Departure*

The special quality of this report appears in the very first section, which shows the present situation of New York State in the perspective of the whole world community and of the great changes in population growth, technology and urbanization which underlie all plans for improvement. The very existence of New York and its great port depended, as the planners of the Erie Canal first saw, upon forces and movements that have never been entirely under local control.

Planners who lack this perspective remain as bewildered as Mr. Robert Moses over the fact that his traffic remedies have increased the conditions they sought to alleviate. They are baffled by the insight of Benton MacKaye, who in "The New Exploration" observed that in order to overcome the traffic congestion of Times Square it might be necessary to re-route the shipment of wheat through the Atlantic ports. So, too, the Federal Housing Administration's mistaken loan policy, which favored suburban builders, has done as much as Detroit to turn our cities into gaping parking lots.

The quality of imaginative insight lifts much of this planning report—but alas! not all—from the level of the dismally probable to that of the hopefully possible. Instead of accepting wholly the current tendency to allow short-sighted highway engineers, motor car manufacturers, and realty developers to create conditions that no public authority is able to remedy except by beginning all over again, they show, rather, the necessity for a policy of land planning and urban development on a regional scale, carried out under the authority of the state executive. They seek to control disorderly metropolitan growth in already congested areas by spreading urban and industrial development over the entire state.

In getting down to regional bedrock, this report re-establishes the vital contribution made by the first "Report on a Plan for the State of New York," issued by the New York State Housing and Regional Planning Commission in 1926. The new proposals do not merely build upon the work that was so well done almost 40 years ago, but go further in the direction of regional integration. In certain basic assumptions, it is true, the new report has accepted without challenge the belief that intensified mechanization and ever-accelerating locomotion will remain the one constant in an otherwise changing world. In overlooking the human reactions to this

194

process, already visible, they unnecessarily weaken both their historic analyses and their constructive proposals.

But even in its present form, this portfolio is an important public document. Let no one be put off by its deplorable Madison Avenue "presentation" in seven colors of type and four of paper: a format that might make one unfairly suspect that a piddling idea has been inflated into a staggering sales prospectus to lure an unwary investor or flatter the ego of some corporation executive. If, however, the essential ideas that are embodied in this report are understood and carried into action, they should have a widespread effect upon the whole pattern of urbanization. And if some of its serious weaknesses are corrected, it might serve as a model program for urban and regional development everywhere.

2. *The Regional Setting*

What gives this new development policy special authority is the fact that it reunites two aspects of planning that should never have been separated, even in the mind: cities and their regional matrix. As the geographer, Mark Jefferson, observed long ago, city and country are one thing, not two things; and if one is more fundamental than the other, it is the natural environment, not the man-made overlayer.

The biggest metropolis cannot expand beyond the limits of its water supply; and even when it wipes out the valuable reserves of countryside close at hand, instead of zealously preserving them, its inhabitants are still dependent for recreation and change of scene on some more distant area. Unfortunately, the more distant the area, the less open to daily common use, the more tedious to reach by motor car, the more costly to get to by plane, and the more empty it will ultimately be of recreation value, since crowds of people from other areas will likewise be drawn to it—thus turning the most striking natural landscape into a kind of recreation slum, like Yosemite in midsummer.

By recognizing that the conservation of the countryside is an essential part of any sound policy of urbanization, this report challenges the false premises of Jean Gottmann's statistical nonentity, "Megalopolis," with his picture of cities dissolving into an interminable mass of low-grade, increasingly undifferentiated, urban tissue, stretching from Maine to Georgia, and from Buffalo to Chicago. No

city, however big, can hold its own against this mode of dissolution and disintegration, and no policy of highway building or urban renewal will prove otherwise than destructive until a regional framework can be established which will give form to all our diversified economic and cultural activities.

The outlining of this new framework is the first step toward a balanced urban development. The framers of this New York State report have taken this decisive step. What the clotted metropolis did in the past, the region will have to do in the future.

But in still another respect, the report breaks fresh ground; or rather, it comes back to the classic report of 1926, which in turn was based on an earlier analysis of the present planning situation, published in May 1925 as the Regional Planning number of the Survey Graphic. For the present planners emphasize that any large coordinated effort at planning lies beyond the scope of municipal action in any one city, however large: it rests on bringing together in a working partnership a multitude of municipal, county, state and even Federal agencies, and in persuading individual property owners and private corporations to work within the general pattern. Unfortunately the regrouping of urban units within the regional setting cannot take place automatically through the unregulated operation of private interests—for it must halt or reverse many present tendencies that work against a sound urban development.

Not a little of the large-scale planning and construction being done today, by highway departments, municipalities and housing agencies, comes to nothing, or worse than nothing, for lack of any agreed social purposes: many radical changes are made, such as that which is now turning Long Island, New York City's last nearby seashore recreation area, into a mere expressway bypass, merely to provide fat jobs and profits to construction companies and speculative builders, while many essentials of conservation are neglected just because they contribute nothing to the insensate dynamism of our affluent society.

Too often our most active planning agencies, for lack of any clearly defined social ends, cancel each other out. Thus, in New York City one municipal department has been commissioned to reduce the amount of air pollution. Meanwhile, the traffic commissioner and the Port of New York Authority, abetted by the State Highway Department, have been zealously working to bring an ever greater number of motor vehicles into the city. But not

"... many essentials of conservation are nothing to the insensate dynamism

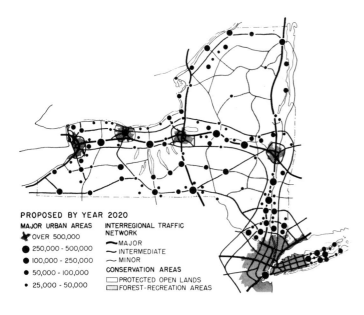

PROPOSED BY YEAR 2020
MAJOR URBAN AREAS
🐾 OVER 500,000
● 250,000 - 500,000
● 100,000 - 250,000
● 50,000 - 100,000
• 25,000 - 50,000

INTERREGIONAL TRAFFIC NETWORK
⌒ MAJOR
⌒ INTERMEDIATE
⌒ MINOR
CONSERVATION AREAS
▢ PROTECTED OPEN LANDS
▢ FOREST-RECREATION AREAS

"Too often our most active planning agencies, for lack of any clearly defined social ends, cancel each other out. Thus, in New York City one municipal department has been commissioned to reduce the amount of air pollution. Meanwhile, the traffic commissioner and the Port of New York Authority, abetted by the State Highway Department, have been zealously working to bring an even greater number of motor vehicles into the city. But not merely are the poisonous exhausts from motor cars a major cause of air pollution, but the amounts of nitric oxide and lethal carbon monoxide in New York's air have doubled during the last year. This in turn defeats the municipal drive to abate cancer and heart disease, since the medical evidence that directly connects cigarette smoking with these diseases applies likewise to the concentration of dangerous motor exhausts."

merely are the poisonous exhausts from motor cars a major cause of air pollution, but the amounts of nitric oxide and lethal carbon monoxide in New York's air have doubled during the last year. This in turn defeats the municipal drive to abate cancer and heart disease, since the medical evidence that directly connects cigarette smoking with these diseases applies likewise to the concentration of dangerous motor exhausts.

Up to now planners, with only a few exceptions, have assumed that cities, or at least big metropolises, could be treated as if they were self-contained units. If they lacked the space needed to improve conditions in the existing municipal area, then the remedy was to widen the periphery and take in such independent towns, suburbs or swathes of open land as were accessible. Metropolitan government has been put forward as if it were a cure-all for our present confusion: but the city of Philadelphia has had metropolitan government for more than a century without showing the least benefit from it.

The process of metropolitan extension and aggrandizement has gone on steadily in New York, London, Paris, Rome and Tokyo without producing anything except congestion, blight and urban decay; and the fact that the same processes are now at work in some 41 other metropolitan areas in the United States does not improve the prospects for urban living or architecture: quite the contrary. This situation was analyzed clearly for the first time in the 1926 "Report on a Plan for the State of New York" already referred to; and to understand what the new development policy has added to that report, one may profitably take a look at that classic original document, and the background thinking that made it possible.

3. The Background of Regional Planning

The extraordinarily rapid growth of both New York State and New York City during the 19th century increased the magnitude of their problems and the enormity of their mistakes. But likewise, it brought about an early series of efforts to correct them. Thus New York City introduced the first pure water supply from distant sources in the Croton system, 1842; mass transportation, first by elevated railway, 1869; improved tenement house designs (Al-

196

neglected just because they contribute of our affluent society"

fred T. White), 1877; housing by neighborhood communities, Forest Hills, 1909; and public housing for the lower income groups, 1927.

Some of these remedies, like mass transportation and public housing, turned sour, because their effect was to add to the already formidable congestion; other efforts, like Forest Hills, did not catch on, for what was meant originally to be an experiment in workers' housing proved so expensive that the new housing estate was turned into a superior suburb for the well-to-do. But in the early 1920's a fresh start was made, in two radically different directions, by two different groups, both using the term "regional" in an entirely different context.

The first group was that created to produce a "Regional Plan for New York." This organization was under the directorship of an experienced planner, Thomas Adams, backed by the financial resources of the Russell Sage Foundation. With a freedom no single municipal agency possessed, this group focused attention upon the metropolitan area of New York, an area then covered by a circle with a 40-mile radius. With little difficulty, their economists showed that, since this was a highly concentrated market, the intensive urbanization of the entire area was inevitable: indeed, the more people here, the bigger the market and the greater the commercial prosperity. On those terms, there was no reason to look beyond the metropolitan area for a solution of New York's problems.

The other group, the Regional Planning Association of America, challenged both the premises and the conclusions of the Russell Sage group. This association was founded in 1923; it consisted of a handful of architects, planners, economists, "geotects" and writers who believe that the new forces that were already visible—giant power, the telephone, the radio, the motor car—had made metropolitan congestion obsolete, and necessitated a large-scale regional coordination of the institutions that were almost automatically producing the wrong type of urban development in the wrong place for the wrong purpose.

One of the members of this little group, Clarence Stein, persuaded Governor Alfred E. Smith to create the New York State Housing and Regional Planning Commission; and another member, Henry Wright (senior) became its planning consultant. In 1926 this commission brought out its final report on the regional development of New York State, past, present, and possible.

This report shifted the focus of interest and political authority from a single metropolis to the whole state, with its highly diversified regional components. Viewing the state as a whole, it traced the early development of the state through two periods, the first that of water power, canals and highroads, with a fine balance of industry and population, the second, that of the railroad and the steam engine, with an over-concentration of population in the principal port terminuses, Buffalo and New York.

Instead of carrying metropolitan concentration further, Wright showed that if new technical facilities were utilized, and old human values were respected, a better development of the whole state would be possible, with a diffusion of power and the building of many new urban centers that would form part of a larger regional complex. This would not merely restore the balance between town and country, but make it possible for the whole population everywhere to have the advantages of genuine city life, without the dreary drill of long subway rides, crowded tenement quarters, insufficient play space and a constant expenditure of municipal funds upon repairing conditions that would, in a better-ordered environment, never have come into existence.

This was the first time any public body had taken a broad historic and geographic view of urban development. In its method of approach, it broke with all one-sided specialist attempts to deal only with piecemeal problems and patchwork solutions. Instead of wiping out urban variety by taking for granted that a single model, Megalopolis, would take its place, Henry Wright's contribution was to demonstrate that a multi-centered approach would not only give fresh life to every part of the state but would relieve the population pressures upon the Empire City itself and so, for the first time, give it opportunity to catch up with its human arrears.

Despite its apparent failure and its long neglect, this report remains the basic American document in regional planning; and nothing that covers a smaller area of life deserves to be called regional planning. Though the many planning and housing agencies created under President Franklin D. Roosevelt failed to understand the new approach made by Wright, Stein and their colleagues, the ideas behind

"...if new technical facilities were utilized, a better development of the

The report recommends the division of New York State into 10 great regions

it were too sound to be indefinitely buried. If Wright's report now comes back, through the Office of Regional Development, with renewed authority, it is perhaps because the purely metropolitan or anti-regional approach of all the specialized planning agencies has done nothing to counteract the cataclysmic economic forces that are now producing something close to total urban chaos, in which purposeless violence and bare-faced criminality and meaningless "happenings" contradict all the professed boasts of an advancing civilization. Art and architecture have both begun to tell the same story, embracing accident and chance, belittling purposeful order and humane design. Behind the smooth bureaucratic and technological facade, chaos continues to widen, for only machines can prosper in the environment we are now mechanically creating.

4. The New Regional Front

The analysis on which the new development policy is based begins, in effect, at the point where the report of 1926 left off. Henry Wright had shown that the valleys of the Hudson and the Mohawk were necessarily the backbone of any surface transportation system; but the zone of settlement was not confined to the strip immediately served by the railroad, since now the motor car, the telephone, the radio and the electric grid gave equal advantages to a much wider zone, where a network of new communities, and revivified older towns, would have, if properly organized, all the advantages of a metropolitan community without the disadvantages of congestion. The building of new towns to attract industries and population was the first means of coping with metropolitan overgrowth.

The new report points out that three patterns of growth can now be detected. First: the expansion of the hitherto minor metropolitan areas of Rochester, Syracuse, Utica, Rome and the tri-city complex of Schenectady, Albany and Troy. The second process, largely a result of highway development, is the inter-linking not only of the cities but of the major valley areas, which opens up an even larger area of settlement. This in turn leads to a possible further expansion of both smaller communities and remoter areas of the state, in order to take care of the current increase of population.

"In the last half century, we have had enough experience with advisory commissions in city planning to learn how little influence they exercise. If regional development is to fare better the state will have to set up competent regional authorities, with powers of planning, capital investment and corporate action similar to these exercised by, say, the Port of New York Authority . . ."

and old human values were respected, whole state would be possible..."

To handle these three kinds of change, the report has made a major advance by dividing the state into ten great regions, each with its own metropolitan center. In de-limiting these areas, the planners have given weight to both geographic and historic realities, adroitly retaining the existing counties and combining them in such a fashion as to balance environmental resources and make fuller use both of natural opportunities and the existing pattern of urban settlements. There was a beginning of such regional differentiation back in the 1920's, when the Niagara Frontier Council, the Capital District Regional Planning Association and the Central Hudson Association were formed; but now the planners propose to make these regional divisions part of the political structure of the state.

By this one stroke the Office of Regional Development has clarified and given concrete expression to the term "regional city"; it shows that it is actually a congeries of cities, big and small, including hamlets, villages, and townships, and that in this new pattern the maintenance of open spaces and rural resources is as important as the presence of economic and cultural opportunity. Unfortunately, though the writers have grasped the main factors in regional development, they are still under the spell of metropolitan expansion, with its tendency to establish centralized control. As a result, among the 15 proposals they make for carrying out a regional policy, they fail to emphasize the three that are essential to any sufficient transformation: Regional Councils, Land Control and New Towns. On these three matters, the nearly 40 years that separate the first and the second reports seem to have taught the policy-makers all too little.

5. Planning versus Inertia

Let me speak more specifically about these weaknesses, for unless they are remedied this report will be so much elegantly printed waste paper.

In the last half century, we have had enough experience with advisory commissions in city planning to learn how little influence they exercise. If regional development is to fare better, the state will have to set up competent regional authorities, with powers of planning, capital investment and corporate action similar to those exercised by, say, the Port of New York Authority: perhaps regional legislatures will be necessary to see that such authorities do not get out of hand. Advisory regional councils are certainly not enough.

All the report's proposals for rehabilitating the existing metropolitan areas and planning new cities rest upon control of the land. To propose only a "codification and classification" of existing laws on land use control, as the report does, is to evade the issue: for if the existing laws were sufficient, land planning and land utilization would be done by the state and regional governments for the benefit of the whole community. New Jersey's admirable "Green Acre" program to acquire 300,000 acres for conservation and outdoor recreation is already handicapped not only by speculative land-grabbing and price-raising but by local authorities seeking to retain taxable properties.

There is no use talking about the preservation of recreation areas and other open spaces when the mere announcement of such a purpose is sufficient to push up speculative land values beyond the reach of the state's budget. What we need are regional authorities with the power to put an embargo on uses of land that do not conform to public policy. Even in heavily settled areas like the Ruhr district of West Germany, such an embargo has proved effective. Since 1920, the authorities there have been able to keep that highly congested area from clotting into a single industrial mass: they have not merely kept 40 per cent of the area in forests and farms, but have even added to the open area.

Finally, the changeover from metropolitan congestion to regional distribution cannot be achieved without building new towns—balanced communities, not residential suburbs—on a large scale. This was the policy put forward by Clarence Stein and his associates in the early 1920's and embodied in Wright's sketches for the further development of the state. But at that time, only two new towns of limited size had yet been built on Ebenezer Howard's principles in England. Forty years ago, the present report's suggestion of "a major study of the 'new cities' concept" would have been in order; but now that 20 towns are already being built in England under government auspices, and private developers have undertaken others recently in California and Virginia, the sort of study advocated should have been an integral part of the present report. The

"...the mistake...of this report...is the tendency to treat the technological forces and institutional practices now in operation...as if...immortal..."

next "basic step to action" is not to study the concept but to begin, experimentally, to build the towns.

Strangely, the graphic emphasis of this report falls on what should *not* be done, treated as if it were something that could not possibly be avoided. The report accordingly wastes four huge pages to show the kind of urban development that its writers weakly believe is going to continue: the monotonous mass housing of the suburbs and the equally monotonous and even more inhumane mass housing in high-rise apartments, done under the comic name of urban renewal. Instead of saying at this point, "This is what we must prevent," the report says confidently that 500,000 more people will be housed in the same dismal way. This is a betrayal of the basic regional concept. In the whole elaborate presentation, indeed, there is not a single picture of a well-planned town, or even of part of such a town. What the pictures unfortunately show could be summed up in Patrick Geddes's savage phrase: "More and more of worse and worse."

In a report whose main outlines are so sound, such weaknesses and contradictions as I have touched on cannot be treated lightly; for this report is nothing if it is not an educational document, and half the value of it is destroyed because the writers did not realize that the dominant tendencies in present-day urban development do not need encouragement, and that the main use of such a fresh conspectus is to point out the many desirable alternatives that actually exist. One of the best uses of statistical predictions is to call attention to undesirable consequences that may, with further thinking and planning, be avoided.

6. The Need for Feedback

Behind the specific failures of this report stands a more central one which is all too common in most predictive statistical analyses: it treats statistical predictions as if they were commands. The report takes for granted, on the basis of the recent curve of population growth, that the number of people in New York State will rise from 16 million in 1960 to some 30 million in 2020: this then becomes auto-

matically a directive to prepare for such an expansion. To regard such statistics as final is only an excuse for succumbing to the inevitable, instead of taking action to produce what is humanely desirable.

Actually, there are many unpredictable factors, from nuclear extermination to birth control, that may nullify this prediction: not the least important factor would be an intelligent reaction, by any large part of the population, to the prediction itself, if once its consequences were spelled out. The report, instead of cheerfully preparing for the expected 30 million, might at least have pointed out that such a population could not be accommodated without a drastic shortage of recreation space and general elbow room. Thus a more realistic canvass of the possibilities of life under such conditions might lead once more to the practice of family limitation that prevailed before 1940. Even while the report was being prepared, in fact, the number of births per thousand in New York State dipped from 25.3 in 1957 to 21.7 in 1963. Given another 10 years, the population graph might be as different from the present one as those made in 1940 turned out to be.

Because it pays too much attention to statistical trends and probabilities, and not enough to fresh ideas and possibilities, except in the way of new mechanical inventions, this report lacks some of the virtues of the 1926 report. But the mistake that the framers of this report make is one that is common to a whole generation: it is the tendency to treat the technological forces and institutional practices now in operation as if they were immortal. When they plan on this assumption, they tend to make their most unwelcome predictions come true. But where they depart from this practice, as in the proposal for setting urban and rural growth within 10 newly constituted regions, the Office of Regional Development opens up a new prospect for controlling the forces that are defeating and strangling sound urban development. For this reason, the report should have the widest possible circulation and promote the most extensive critical discussion. I know no other proposed innovation in public policy since the T.V.A. that more deserves earnest attention, not merely in New York, but in every other state of the Union: indeed all over the world.

TREND IS NOT DESTINY

The title of this very special review of Albert Mayer's new book "The Urgent Future" by the leading urban scholar, author and critic reflects his conviction of the critical importance to effective planning for the urban future of that repeated admonition of Mayer. The book, developed from a series of articles "Architecture for Total Community" published in ARCHITECTURAL RECORD in 1964-65, is seen by Mumford—and by the editors—as a major contribution of synthesis and evaluation to the literature of city planning.

During the last thirty years there has been a Vesuvian eruption of books about cities —their nature, their forms, their planning, their deterioration and renewal, their probable future: in fact, more books about the city have been published in the United States alone during this brief period than in the whole previous century.

The results of all this scholarly activity are ironic. The study of urbanism, instead of being a neglected wasteland, has now produced such a heavy crop of information and knowledge that no one has been able to gather in more than a small part of it, still less assimilate it and apply it to the improvement of cities.

In spite of the amount of attention that has been given to the whole process of urbanization, a large number of the people who have been writing about the future of the city do not have the faintest notion of what they are about: or to put it more politely, what they call *the* city is only a particular *sector* of the city, or some limited aspect of its growth interpreted in terms of selected economic, social, or architectural processes. As a result, they miss the two most important features of the historic city: the fact that it brings together *within a definable and limited area* the largest possible variety of human functions and facilities; and that cities, despite their wide range of size, from two thousand in ancient Mesopotamia or Greece to three or four hundred thousand in Renaissance Italy, always, like any other organism or organic association, exhibit serious lapses in functional efficiency and in cooperative human responses when they pass beyond these limits of growth.

Fortunately, during the past half-dozen years, a handful of important books on city and regional planning have appeared, which should help us to understand the dimensions of our problem and to take the measures necessary to control and direct into new channels the forces that are at work, while establishing more comprehensive and more humane goals than those which now beckon us. Among these books I would place Tunnard and Pushkarev's *Man-Made America;* Osborn and Whittick's *The New Towns;* Colin Buchanan's *Traffic in Towns;* and Edmund Bacon's *Design of Cities.* All these books are concerned

---

The Urgent Future, by Albert Mayer. New York: McGraw-Hill Book Company, 1967. 184 pages; illustrated. $16.95.

with the city as an organic entity, at once a container and a magnet, a concentrated field for direct human cooperation, expression, communication, and stimulation. This habitat is far too complex, far too subtle in its qualitative aspects, to be handled solely by the abstract formulas, mathematical or sociological: direct observation and personal experience are essential.

These books have much to give to the professional planner and administrator and the architect: but they are too specialized to reach the public that these professions serve. And since active and intimate participation by the community itself is one of the chief requirements for urban and regional improvement on the scale that is now needed, the various positive contributions of these books and other related treatises, such as *The Urban Condition*, edited by Dr. Leonard Duhl, need to be brought together and focused upon the immediate situation. That difficult feat of selection and unification is one of the many merits of Albert Mayer's new work.

Mayer is peculiarly fitted to perform this act of synthesis. His own concern with the city developed slowly out of a private interest, as a builder of individual New York apartment houses, making miniscule innovations under the municipal and financial conditions that limit success in this field. In his awakening to the inadequacy of such piecemeal improvement and to the need for a more social approach, Mayer's development has been parallel to that of the general public. Mayer is one of the few current writers about the city who, as practicing architect and urban planner, with a basic training in engineering, has had an intimate contact with every variety of planning problem. But it was only after 1930, as he himself confesses, that his sense of public responsibility turned from private philanthropies to the public offices of housing and city design.

Since the Second World War, which brought Mayer into contact both with wide areas in his own country as consultant on war housing, and likewise with Africa and India, his scope and authority have widened. Nehru brought him to India to look freshly at Indian villages and plan their development: a commission he was intelligent enough to turn into an experiment for improving agricultural practices. Before that, he had worked with Henry Wright and Henry Churchill on the design of Greenbrook, one of the projected Greenbelt communities of the second Roosevelt administration; and in 1950 he was, in association with the brilliant and still-lamented Matthew Nowicki, the first planner of Chandigarh, thus giving to LeCorbusier, who replaced him, his first initiation into the principles of the Radburn plan. Since then, with Clarence Stein as consultant, Mayer became the designer of the new aluminum town, Kitimat, in British Columbia; and he is now designing Maumelle, a New Town of 60,000 people, in Alabama.

Mayer's long seasoning, his wide experience, his generous eagerness to learn from others and develop further their good ideas give his book still another distinction. Though alert to both technological improvement and fresh human developments, he is too well-grounded to be caught by the latest slogans or Twiggy models: nor does he reject vital ideas because, like the Garden City concept, they were formulated half-a-century ago. *The Urgent Future* is such a book as only a man ripe in years, yet still full of energy and youthful hope, could write, with no dogmas that need protection, no vanity that calls for petting, no ego that demands inflation. Mayer's face on the jacket, concentrated, deeply lined, grave, shows that his hopes and his enthusiasms have not been purchased lightly. His does not seek credit for fake "originality" by giving old ideas a new name: rather he appreciates how much excellent work has already been done, both in theory and in many actual planning experiments; and he builds on these valid precedents in projecting the large tasks that now loom before us.

The guiding idea of this book Mayer lays down at the beginning: Trend Is Not Destiny. And this idea itself is almost as

"Mayer happily sees that our present difficulties are also opportunities;
for at last, perhaps, they have jarred a whole people
sufficiently to make action on a heroic scale possible"

important as his discriminating appraisals of past accomplishments in public housing and planning, or his critical exposure of the failures in national policy, as well as in private enterprise, that have already brought our cities so close to ruin. Ever since Patrick Geddes introduced the notion of "survey before planning," the need for adequate information, both historical and statistical, has become obvious to even the most routine administrators: but unfortunately those who confine themselves to the statistical method have forgotten the lesson of history: the future is never a mechanical extension of the past. Those who assume that a curve extrapolated from past observations must be followed into the future are in effect worshipping the past as if its achievements were immortal and its errors incorrigible.

Public authorities and private corporations that project new plans solely on the basis of existing trends merely follow the line of least resistance: they surrender in advance, on the assumption that opposition is futile, and that whether you have reason to like the result or not, you had better "go along with it." This is not merely bad planning philosophy: it is bad biology. Even the lowest organisms are able to survive only because they are organized for prompt feedback, which enables them to correct mistakes that would endanger their survival or curb their further development. Instead of waiting for the future to happen, an organism's whole system is planned, from birth to death, to achieve a future consonant with its own nature; and if this is not forthcoming, the organism escapes, retreats, shrivels, or dies. The advantage of knowing current trends, when they happen to be adverse to human development, is to be able to introduce new factors that will modify, halt, or reverse any particular threatening trend.

Mayer's repeated admonition, "Trend is not destiny," should be on the walls of every planning office. If it were taken seriously, most of the silly chatter about Megalopolis as the "new form of the city"—actually the formlessness of the

non-city—would abruptly cease. Dr. Costantine Doxiadis' inflation of Megalopolis into "Ecumenopolis," a planet-covering urbanoid mass with a terminal population of 36 billion people, fortunately carries the notion that the megalopolitan "trend is destiny" to its final pitch of absurdity. If Doxiadis had any familiarity with previous population statistics, he would have realized how shaky his own picture of present population growth actually is; for during the 1930's most competent statisticians indicated that the population of all Western countries except The Netherlands was approaching stability, and might even diminish after 1980. Till 1950 indeed many population experts refused to believe that the postwar population explosion, which reversed this trend, would continue.

Had Doxiadis understood Mayer's admonition he would have realized that even if his statistical data seemed momentarily correct, they would not indicate the necessity for embracing "Ecumenopolis", however grim the prospect, as manifest destiny: they would rather call for massive efforts to control the birth-rate, by many new measures besides those already being tried. If this course were not successful, the desirable pattern of population would not be that of further congestion in continuous conurbations: rather food needs would demand the widest scattering in agricultural villages, with every possible square foot of land devoted to intensive cultivation.

To Mayer's original statement, then, one may accordingly add two corollaries: "The probable is not necessarily inevitable: so don't panic and blindly submit to probability." And the second is: "The possible is not impossible." Therefore plan boldly and imaginatively, in terms of future potentialities, not just past necessities; and never accept any probabilities as final until you have examined possible alternatives and have made sure that better choices are not—in the long run if not immediately—available. If Mayer's book did nothing else than to demolish the notion that past statistical trends provide the only safe grounds for future projections, it would be doing a salutary job toward reorganizing current practices in urbanization.

I shall not attempt to summarize Mayer's critical exposition of this crisis. By now everyone has become aware of it through the breakdowns and disorganizations and impoverishments that have become commonplaces in the routines of our "great" and "affluent" American cities—the blocked traffic, the poisoned air, the polluted waters, the unbalanced budgets, the shortage of positive urban benefits, the endless daily frustrations, the crimes, delinquencies, riots: in short, the creeping human paralysis that accompanies the big city's showy dynamism.

But Mayer happily sees that our present difficulties are also opportunities; for at last, perhaps, they have jarred a whole people sufficiently to make action on a heroic scale possible: action, Mayer hopes, sufficient to reverse the massive trend that, with glacier-grinding relentlessness and river-flowing swiftness has been wiping out the city as a recognizable human habitat. If this awakening does not lead to action, then the end is in sight: hence Mayer's sense of urgency.

"This study," Mayer emphasizes, "is an *action* book, a book to lay the factual basis for conclusions and decisions *and* to lead to those overwhelming moral impulses which alone can infuse into conclusions and decisions the necessary conviction for sustained dynamic action." While Mayer's work does not, like so much current foundation-supported research, postpone all thought of action in favor of stepping up the urban research industry, neither is it, like current programs for model cities and strictly middle-class "New Towns", an effort to avoid dealing with economic realities by plastering glamorous Madison Avenue words over a program which sedulously avoids challenging the motives and aims that now govern urban building.

Mayer is not blind to the fact that the famous public housing and urban renewal act of 1949, which was supposed to eliminate metropolitan slums and rehouse their inhabitants decently, actually ejected the slum dwellers from their miserable quarters without rehousing more than a small proportion of them, while it placed the state's special power of eminent domain at the disposal of real-estate operators, and enabled them to build luxury apartments on the vacated and cleared properties at a juicy profit, with the aid of a special government subsidy originally meant to make public housing possible at lower than slum densities.

In short, "urban renewal," up to now, has been mainly a deadfall to trap the helpless and the exploited, and a windfall for the private promoter and builder: a kind of inverted socialism for the benefit of millionaires. This indicates that our present plans for urban renewal, if they lack the "overwhelming moral impulse" that Albert Mayer attaches to them and seeks to call forth, may likewise be undermined and subverted.

In his critical analysis of current trends and programs, Mayer puts a diagnostic finger on every suspect factor—upon our current national and state highway programs, with their short-sighted emphasis on the cost-benefit appraisal, which makes even more unbalanced the present clots and flows of population; upon futile traffic gimmicks which ensure further traffic jams: upon architectural giantism as an end in itself, as a status symbol, with the tendency of all expanding metropolitan institutions—the hospitals, the universities, the museums, no less than big industrial corporations—to monstrous concentration on a single site: upon the practice of the speculative private enterpriser, with the connivance in the past of the FHA, to convert farm land into random suburban parcels, emptying out the central city and spoiling accessible recreation spaces, while replacing valuable market gardens and orchards with dreary acres of asphalt and concrete.

On all these matters Mayer's criticism is helpful because it is also discriminating. While he rejects single-factor an-

"... the current American belief that such new cities ... can be built without heavy government aid is an illusion ..."

alysis and one-shot remedies, he realizes, out of his own practical experience, how difficult it is for the busy planner or administrator to make a holistic approach to what seems, at the moment, a piecemeal problem, capable of a piecemeal solution.

But Mayer does not lose sight of the basic condition for effective city and regional planning: the fact that the land "is going to have to be considered and regulated like a public utility and that the policy on land in certain locations will have to go even further, to embrace large-scale purchases and continuing ownership by the government." This—in diametric contrast to the legalized malfeasance of public funds that took place under the Urban Renewal Act—is the indispensable basis for any adequate program for urban building and regional development, whether under private or public enterprise, as Ebenezer Howard recognized in his original specifications for the Garden City. And if I have any serious criticism to make of Mayer's presentation of the Urgent Future, it is his failure to underline this essential condition as frequently as he has underlined his thesis that trend is not destiny.

Without his detailed appraisal of both the real accomplishments and the arresting defects of the housing and planning that has been done during the last generation, Mayer's program for action would lack both its clearly defined goals and the concrete proposals he makes for achieving them. Because his emphasis is on action, this work is not merely an able treatise on contemporary city planning, but a vital contribution to the politics of regional development.

The crux of Mayer's work is a series of interrelated proposals for mastering those present trends which are inimical to good urban development, and for opening up a new period of constructive city building. This involves four closely linked measures.

First: the building of new cities of moderate size, on a large scale, as an imperative preliminary to any loosening up of metropolitan congestion and effecting

a genuine urban renewal. Here the brilliant success of the New Towns policy in England, signalized a few years ago by a canny attempt at a financial "take-over" of the oldest of the new towns, Letchworth, serves as a standard both of desirability and practicability, as do parallel developments in Sweden. But the current American belief that such new cities, sufficiently diversified to hold a mixed population with mixed incomes, with jobs near at hand, can be built without heavy government aid, is an illusion: since the most successful of such private enterprises, the Levittowns, are only monotonous suburban housing enclaves, not diversified cities.

Along with this process of urban colonization on a regional scale Mayer proposes the immediate decentralization of overexpanded and over-localized institutions within the metropolis. This has been going on in a spotty, spontaneous way since the 1930's, beginning with the decentralization of the big department stores and banks. But it has still to be planned on a larger scale, and deliberately coordinated by the municipality, in order to abate the counter-tendency to over-centralization and giantism. The multiplying of the number of in-city centers, each with its own complex of factories, offices, shops, and residential developments, would do more to permanently break the traffic paralysis of the big city than all the billions so far recklessly poured into expressways, double-decked streets, subways, and parking garages. This kind of internal decentralization of the big city was suggested in my lengthy criticism of the Plan of London County in 1945; and I am happy to find that Mayer makes it an essential feature of his program.

The second step is the re-structuring of the whole metropolitan area, by breaking away from the notion that planning must follow the trends that lead to the random spread of Megalopolis. Mayer points out that in Holland planners observed that the ring of cities from Rotterdam to Haarlem and Amsterdam was coalescing into a Randstad: a single urban smudge. Instead of backing this movement further, the planners decided to counteract it by deliberately steering industries and population into other parts of the country, thereby maintaining open spaces between the cities, and establishing a green matrix for agriculture at the center of the Randstad.

The third step demands the creation of adequate organs for federated metropolitan government. This is not a simple task, as Mayer realizes, because it involves not only giving power to a new type of centralized public authority, but also rebuilding local units, from the smallest neighborhood cell upward, so that the citizens will be organized for direct participation and active responsibility. The more complex urban society becomes, the less can it be run by administrative experts, with one-way communication and remote control, and the more necessary it is to have constant two-way inter-communication and local action, to offset the ruthlessness and insolence of public officials, too often unwilling to share power or authority with those they supposedly serve.

Admittedly such local action has so far chalked up mostly petty, preventive gains: now it saves a valuable tree, now it keeps a playground from being turned into a car-park, or again it saves a bigger area like Washington Square from violation and misuse. But if the boasted leisure of our technologically oriented society is worth anything, it is for spending time on local political efforts, as the Athenian democracy did in its heyday. Without legally instituted popular participation—such as has been proposed for the decentralization of New York City's school system—the moral urgency and vigilant local initiative that Mayer's urban program requires will be lacking.

The fourth step, finally, is the establishment of a regional scale, to take the place of the metropolitan scale and therewith the restructuring of both old and new regions so as to effect a better balance between human needs and regional resources. Mayer recognizes that though the advantages of the metropolis are indisputable, they do not demand an indefinite increase in size, or an indefinite expansion in area. He sees that, on the contrary, a moderate-size city of 500,-000 people, like Zurich, a humane and beautiful center, has—if it does not keep on expanding!—most of the advantages of metropolitan culture without the disabilities of overcrowding and overspread, which would seriously lessen these advantages. Mayer recognizes further that there are other incipient galaxies of American cities, like the Raleigh-Durham-Chapel Hill group, that might, with adroit organization and planning, turn into regional cities, with all the combined advantages of a larger metropolitan population, with ample financial and cultural resources, without the costly disabilities of congestion and giantism. And finally, Mayer points out, there are old areas like Appalachia, with now derelict industries, but possessing many positive geographic advantages, which might be rehabilitated, not by inconsecutive piecemeal improvements, still less by random highway building, as now projected, but by full-scale regional plans that would conserve the land and utilize its resources, interweave industries in a new population pattern, and multiply the cultural and social opportunities for both the existing population and a larger one.

There is no part of this program that is entirely new, no part that has not in some degree been tested. Mayer's special contribution has been to assemble the best planning thought of the last half century, to evaluate current experience and diagnose current weaknesses, to bring forward alternatives, and to show what is still lacking if we are to overcome urban disintegration. Finally he demonstrates, by well-chosen illustrations and diagrams, how attractive our urban and regional environment could become, if we engaged collectively to make use of the resources now at our disposal. Whether this book will actually have the impact it deserves to have will depend, in part, upon how many Albert Mayers are available and how deeply they can be aroused and committed to cooperative political and economic effort on the largest scale.

THE HUMAN PROSPECT
AND ARCHITECTURE

"The Package"

In dealing with the state of modern man, I wish to push beyond the conditions that have developed during the last half century; for the wars, plagues, brutalities, exterminations that have reduced life to a subhuman level are symptoms rather than causes. The great fact that underlies our whole life is that mankind is confronted today with a situation that is unique in history: some of man's oldest dreams have actually come true—the dream of flight; the dream of instantaneous communication; the dream of action at a distance—what we now call remote control—and ultimately the dream of limitless power and limitless wealth.

As dreams, expressed in religious myths, all these achievements go back to the very beginnings of civilization, in the late Stone Age and the Bronze Age, some five to seven thousand years ago. With the first achievement of power, order, and scientific knowledge in the great river cultures of Babylonia and Egypt came the desire to expand these physical functions without limit, at whatever cost to life. Provisionally, these civilizations endowed their gods with the powers their monarchs did not yet command. Owing to the lack of technical means, the increase of physical power and material abundance served only an infinitesimal minority: the rest of the population remained weak and poor and ignorant. They participated only vicariously in the aristocratic way of life. Lacking the bare necessities of food and shelter, the mass of men thought only of material abundance. So even now we fail to understand the biological irrationality of the enchanting Bronze Age dream of idle leisure and effortless wealth and unbridled power, achieved as if by magic.

Today the powers that once belonged only to absolute monarchs or primordial gods have become universal: they are a collective possession and by their very nature cannot be monopolized by a group, a class or a nation. More than that: functions and power that gods once possessed only in human fantasy are now exercised by ordinary men—bureaucrats, soldiers, civil servants, engineers—people who are not conspicuously endowed with any equivalent magnitude of love and virtue.

This is in fact the period of the Common Man.

* An address to architectural students in Rome

The Common Man, though without historical insight, without special moral discipline, or sufficiently unified and comprehensive powers of thought has, by an almost automatic process, been endowed with the functions and attributes of the primitive gods. Possibly only those who have made a study of Babylonian or Egyptian theology will fully realize all the terrible possibilities implied in this situation. But the point I wish to make is that though many, perhaps most, of our contemporaries are justly proud of their powers of organization and their organization of power, they are mythically and ideologically still living in the extremely primitive and brutal world of the early Bronze Age. Their mentality is singularly like that of an early Pharaoh. Their conception of modern civilization is not merely limited: it is ideologically antiquated—indeed as deeply archaic as the belief in the divinity of kings.

Only the ignorant or the extremely innocent could mistake this transformation of modern man into a being endowed with godlike attributes for an altogether desirable achievement, for the history of the last forty years, as well as more ancient records of organized violence and bestiality, shows that we have imprudently given power and authority to the demonic elements in man as well as the divine. Actually, the result of all our brilliant achievements in science, technics, economic administration and organization are contradictory and paradoxical. In many departments there have been striking gains not merely in energy and vitality but in a higher sense of justice and human decency. An economy of abundance promises to everyone some of the leisure and largesse that before this only the aristocracies knew. Who would deny that these are great positive values?

But modern man has lost the automatic discipline of poverty and scarcity; and as is well known in every biological process, too much "may be as fatal to life's prosperity" as too little. It is not merely during economic crises that we face "starvation in the midst of plenty." Already we have more power than we can use wisely and more scientific and technical knowledge than we can intelligently assimilate and put to good use.

What is the result? We now have external power

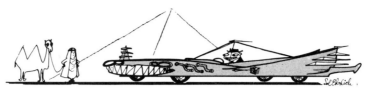

"The Pyramid"

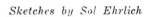
Sketches by Sol Ehrlich

on a scale that exceeds our wildest dreams: but that is counterbalanced by an inner feeling of extreme impotence, nausea, frustration, and despair. Never before in the most dismal phases of man's development has there been such a universal sense of anxiety, such a sense of the emptiness and futility of life, of a general lack of meaning and purposefulness. What the artists today are revealing in their endless symbols of disintegration, the common man, who still is healthy enough to enjoy his physical liberation, will become aware of tomorrow.

It is not a little strange that the artist of today, instead of exulting in all the possible manifestations of our godlike powers, can exhibit his creativeness only in destructive, violent, and infantile forms, without intellectual content or moral values, indeed too often demonstrating a positive love for corruption and evil, as my countryman, Tennessee Williams, recently was honest enough to admit in an interview with himself? Not a little of our modern art shows a kind of perverse vigor, as if it drew directly upon primordial sources in the Id. But this should not conceal the fact that its meaning lies in its meaninglessness, its content in its lack of contents—something not to be confused with abstraction—its only value is a denial of the possibility of values. If modern science and technology spring from the ideals of the Bronze Age, a large part of subjective modern art seems to go back even farther to a period before images or words were yet formed, when human feelings were inchoate and incommunicable.

For a long time our surface health and energy reinforced our ignorance and concealed the symptoms I have been trying here to bring to light. In the arts of construction and fabrication one must look behind the outward form to detect the inner weaknesses: for if a building consciously expressed disintegration it would not stand up; and if a motor car expressed disintegration it would not go. But even in modern architecture the symptoms are disturbing. Unhappily, when one examines modern building or urbanism with a critical eye, unmoved by current fashionplates and advertisements, one finds the same contrast between the outward form and the inward disruption. Take architecture for illustration. The dominant architecture of our day can be grouped under three heads: the Package, the Pyramid, and the Procrustean bed.

The Package may be defined as an external envelope, a covering of glass and steel or concrete, whose form bears no functional or purposeful relation to the object or the activities it encloses. The sole purpose of the package is to dazzle the spectator and to advertise and sell the product. By definition, such a shell is most effective when it is most empty. For the daily functions of family life, in the extremes of hot and cold weather, an all-glass apartment house, the perfect package, would turn into a place of torture. This neglect of the human contents is a typical vice of our time.

Perhaps it is no accident that the Pyramid, one of the most ancient of architectural perversions, is being revived in our time, though the new forms disguise its nature. Pyramid-building, whether it takes the form of a "skyscraper-a-mile-high" or a cantilevered foundation almost as expensive to construct as the building it supports, demands a sacrifice of important human needs to empty pomp and vanity. Thus, according to this definition, our new American motor cars are pure examples of pyramid-building: and so, in even greater measure are our atomic and hydrogen bombs, for they are part of the modern cult of death and might become the tombs, not of a few pharaohs but of the entire human race.

Finally, the third point of physical over-concentration and therefore organic disintegration is the Procrustean bed. Our admirable and useful mechanical aids become merely procrustean when one mechanical function, or one form of mechanical organization, dominates every other activity and represses man's own proper functions. There are many more ways than the Greek innkeeper knew to saw off human legs or stretch the human frame to fit an arbitrary iron bed. The danger does not come from the use of the machine but from the displacement of man as a responsible agent, who must control and direct its results for human purposes. Once we begin to fit people to the needs of the machine there is no limit to the physical and mental deformation that may be practiced. In a purposeless world, mechanization inevitably takes command.

Many of our contemporaries still think that the problems of our age can be solved by further applications of science and technics: but this view shows a failure to understand the limitations of these disciplines, until they become a part of a much larger and deeper conception of life and human development. We deceive ourselves if we think that by producing more elegant packages, more pretentious pyramids, and more automatic machines with built-in electronic brains, we are meeting the demands of modern life or expressing the ideals of modern culture.

Actually, most of our favorite modern activities belong by direct inheritance to the Bronze Age, and they express the childish limitations of Bronze Age minds. We are in fact using the most elaborate and refined techniques of mathematical and physical science to fulfill an archaic scheme of existence. This scheme leaves completely out of account the historic perspectives of the last five thousand years, the cumulative moral insights of the prophetic religions, and our ever-deepening understanding of the nature of life itself, which transcends all our ideological abstractions. Bronze Age man had alienated himself from the world of life by over-emphasizing the role of organization and external control. That is why he and his present-day descendants still dare to cherish such a contradictory and childish concept as limitless power, limitless wealth, or the limitless expansion of the machine in every direction, without having any inner principle of control or without any purpose or goal—power for power's sake, motion for motion's sake, speed for speed's sake, and finally in our day total destruction and extermination for no rational purpose whatever.

Unlike the world of atoms and stars, biological activities are self-directing and goal seeking. In man these tendencies rise into consciousness as ideals, projects, and plans. Once these activities relating to a possible future are neglected or repressed, life itself loses its meaning for man. The higher man's development the greater his need to re-think his past, reconstruct his present and forecast his future. To love and to create are necessities of human growth.

The needs of life, then, are much more subtle and complex than the needs of machines, and for this reason a good mechanical solution to a human problem can be only a part of an adequate organic solution which meets the needs of life in all its dimensions. In the case of an infant, we have experimental evidence to show that unless a baby is loved and fondled it will not be adequately nourished, no matter how much food we give it. By the same token, visual and aural order may be as necessary for health as hygiene and sanitation. The architecture, the engineering, the politics or the medicine, that

does not recognize the primacy of life, belongs to the barbarous Bronze Age, not to our own time and still less to the future. The world of machines corresponds to the system of reflexes and automatic processes in the body. When we are properly oriented to life and reality, the higher functions of man, those concerned with meaning, value, and form, will dominate and transform all our instrumental and practical activities, so that no part of our daily life will still be empty or insignificant. Until we recognize the role of these higher functions, the vast powers man now commands will only give scope to destructive impulses and acts, through which the forces of life seek to recapture the autonomy and freedom that have been denied them.

Man now commands the forces of nature as never before; he has achieved a godlike power to understand and direct them. But all this scientific intelligence and technical facility will prove vain unless we understand that we must create a new race of Galileos and Giambattista Vicos who will help us to realize to the full our human potentialities and enlarge all our specifically human capacities to feel, to imagine, to love and to create. Unless all our works are works of love—and I mean love in every sense, from the erotic to the divine—they are not yet in the realm of the human.

Within the dimensions of this talk I can go no further. In a little book called "The Transformations of Man"* I have given a more adequate presentation of these ideas. In that book I have tried to picture a further stage in man's development that would carry forward and unify every aspect of historic experience, and transcend the limitations that have brought every past civilization to an end. But fortunately in the very act of giving this lecture I have illustrated my most fundamental point. For I have spoken to you, not as a writer, not as a philosopher or a scholar, not as a critic of architecture or a professor of city planning, not as one having professional authority or a specialist's competence. On the contrary, I have addressed you as a man, as one who of right exercises all the biological and spiritual functions of man, and who therefore regards all other forms of authority as secondary and supernumerary. In short, I have dared to be human and I have appealed to you primarily as simple men and women. In all humility, I invite you to follow this example, in your thought, in your work, in your social and family relations. Yes: dare to be fully and wholly human: dare to put wisdom above knowledge and love above power, the imperfect but living whole above the perfect but lifeless part. It is not easy to be human; but those who have the courage not to surrender their humanity, tomorrow, under a less murky sky, may catch once more a glimpse of the divine.

* World Perspectives Series. 1956.

"The Procrustean Bed"

INDEX